MASS EFFECT

EFFECT™

HOMEWORLDS

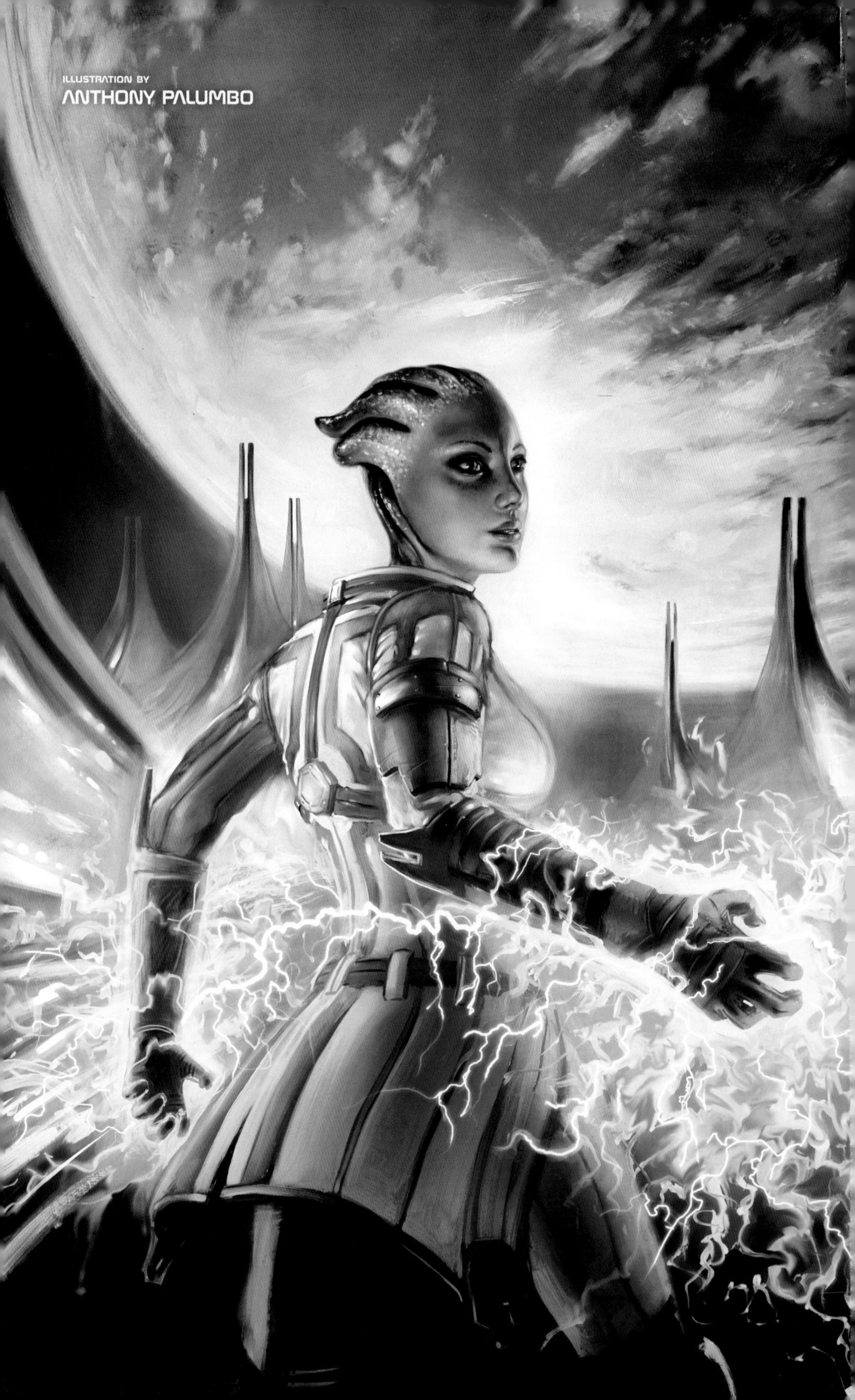
ILLUSTRATION BY
ANTHONY PALUMBO

MASS EFFECT™
HOMEWORLDS

STORY
MAC WALTERS
PATRICK WEEKES
JOHN DOMBROW
SYLVIA FEKETEKUTY

SCRIPT
MAC WALTERS
JEREMY BARLOW

ART
EDUARDO FRANCISCO
CHRIS STAGGS
MARC DEERING
GARRY BROWN
OMAR FRANCIA

COLORS
MICHAEL ATIYEH

LETTERING
MICHAEL HEISLER

DARK HORSE BOOKS

PUBLISHER
MIKE RICHARDSON

ASSISTANT EDITORS
BRENDAN WRIGHT AND SHANTEL LAROCQUE

EDITOR
DAVE MARSHALL

DESIGNER
JUSTIN COUCH

MASS EFFECT: HOMEWORLDS

This volume collects issues one through four of the Dark Horse comic-book series
Mass Effect: Homeworlds.

Special thanks to BioWare, including:
Derek Watts, Art Director • Casey Hudson, Executive Producer • Aaryn Flynn, Studio GM, BioWare
Edmonton • Ray Muzyka and Greg Zeschuk, BioWare Co-Founders

Published by Dark Horse Books
A division of Dark Horse Comics, Inc.
10956 SE Main Street | Milwaukie, OR 97222

DarkHorse.com | MassEffect.com

Walters, Mac.
Mass effect : homeworlds / story, Mac Walters, Patrick Weekes, John Dombrow, Sylvia Feketekuty ;
script, Mac Walters, Jeremy Barlow ; art, Eduardo Francisco, Chris Staggs with Marc Deering, Garry
Brown, Omar Francia ; color, Michael Atiyeh ; lettering, Michael Heisler.
pages cm
ISBN 978-1-59582-955-9 (pbk.) -- ISBN 978-1-61655-066-0 (hardcover)
1. Graphic novels. I. Weekes, Patrick. II. Dombrow, John. III. Feketekuty, Sylvia. IV. Title. V. Title: Homeworlds.
PN6727.W277M346 2012
741.5'973--dc23
2012027993

First standard edition: November 2012
ISBN 978-1-59582-955-9

Custom hardcover edition: November 2012
ISBN 978-1-61655-066-0

1 3 5 7 9 10 8 6 4 2
Printed at Midas Printing International, Ltd., Huizhou, China

MIKE RICHARDSON President and Publisher • NEIL HANKERSON Executive Vice President • TOM WEDDLE Chief Financial Officer • RANDY STRADLEY Vice President of Publishing • MICHAEL MARTENS Vice President of Book Trade Sales • ANITA NELSON Vice President of Business Affairs • DAVID SCROGGY Vice President of Product Development • DALE LAFOUNTAIN Vice President of Information Technology • DARLENE VOGEL Senior Director of Print, Design, and Production • KEN LIZZI General Counsel • MATT PARKINSON Vice President of Marketing • DAVEY ESTRADA Editorial Director • SCOTT ALLIE Senior Managing Editor • CHRIS WARNER Senior Books Editor • DIANA SCHUTZ Executive Editor • CARY GRAZZINI Director of Print and Development • LIA RIBACCHI Art Director • CARA NIECE Director of Scheduling

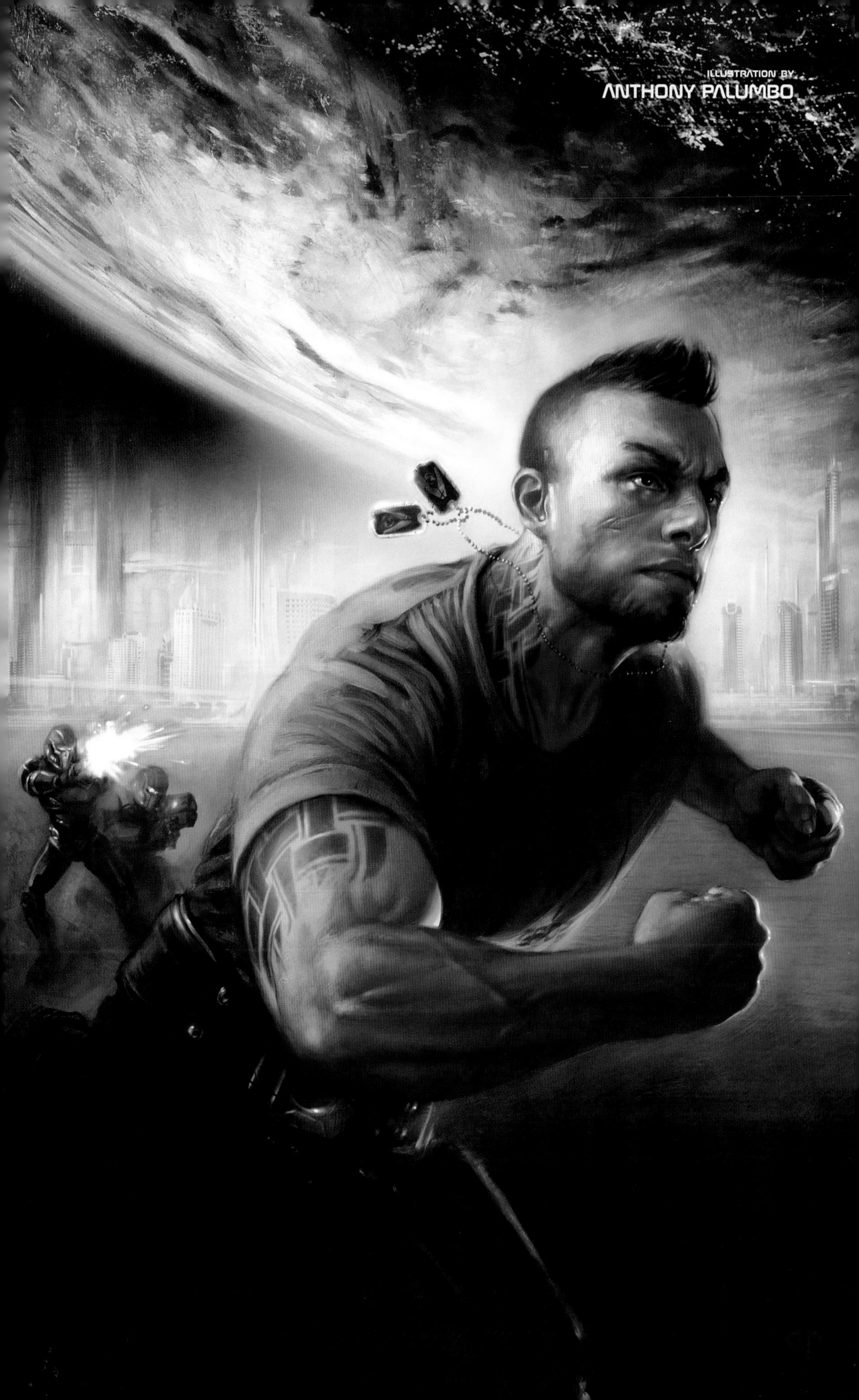
ILLUSTRATION BY
ANTHONY PALUMBO

SCRIPT
MAC WALTERS

ART
EDUARDO FRANCISCO

COLORS
MICHAEL ATIYEH

LETTERING
MICHAEL HEISLER

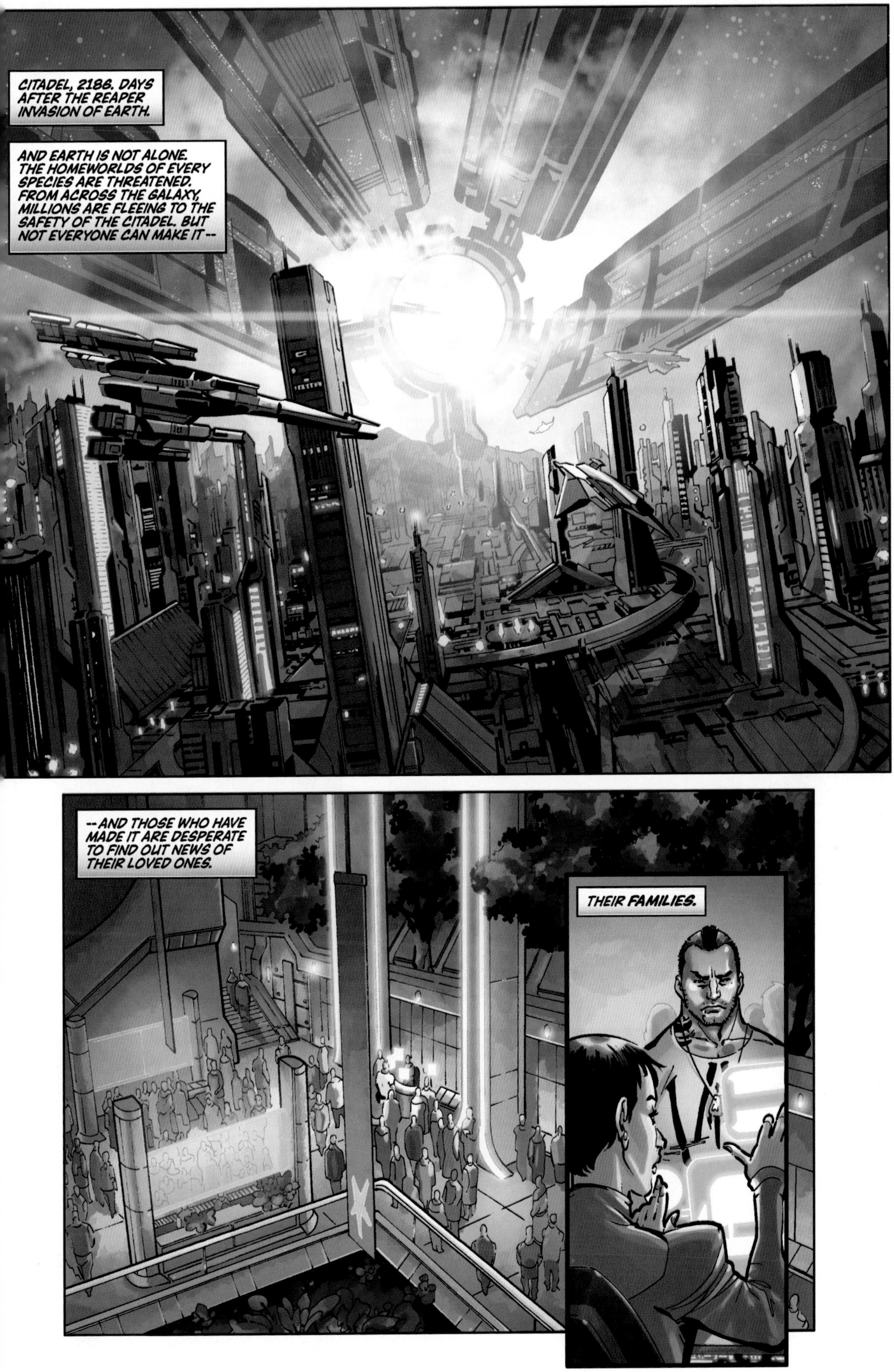
CITADEL, 2186. DAYS AFTER THE REAPER INVASION OF EARTH.
AND EARTH IS NOT ALONE. THE HOMEWORLDS OF EVERY SPECIES ARE THREATENED. FROM ACROSS THE GALAXY, MILLIONS ARE FLEEING TO THE SAFETY OF THE CITADEL. BUT NOT EVERYONE CAN MAKE IT --
-- AND THOSE WHO HAVE MADE IT ARE DESPERATE TO FIND OUT NEWS OF THEIR LOVED ONES.
THEIR FAMILIES.

SORRY, MR. VEGA. THERE'S NOTHING.

NEITHER OF THEM?

NOTHING FOR EMILIO VEGA OR JOSH SANDERS. SORRY.

YOUR REQUEST WILL REMAIN ACTIVE. IF WE FIND ANYTHING, WE'LL POST IT ON THE TERMINALS.

PLEASE PROVIDE IDENTIFICATION FOR VERIFICATION.

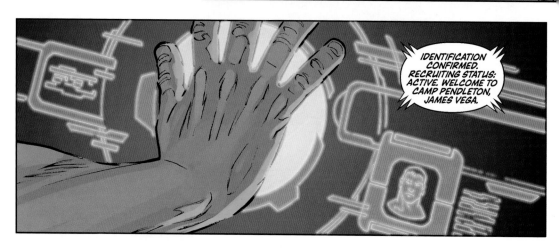

IDENTIFICATION CONFIRMED. RECRUITING STATUS: ACTIVE. WELCOME TO CAMP PENDLETON, JAMES VEGA.

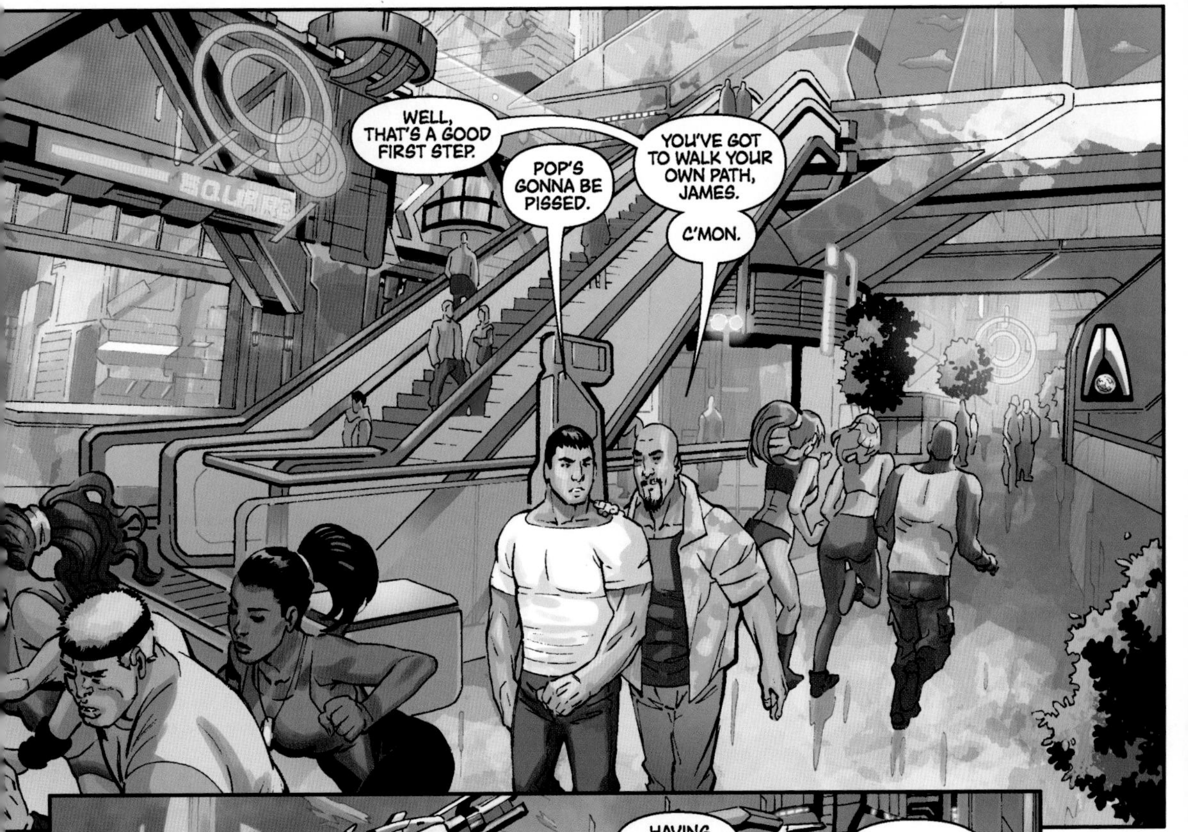
WELL, THAT'S A GOOD FIRST STEP.
POP'S GONNA BE PISSED.
YOU'VE GOT TO WALK YOUR OWN PATH, JAMES.
C'MON.

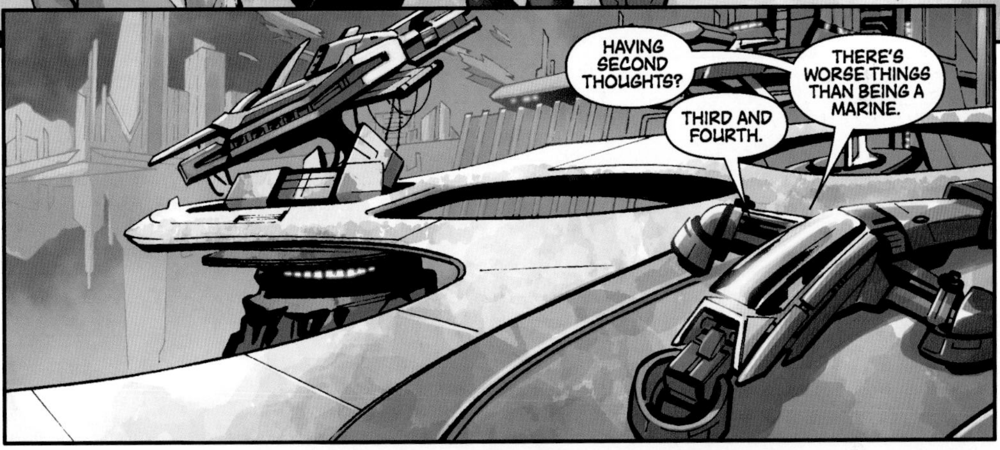
HAVING SECOND THOUGHTS?
THIRD AND FOURTH.
THERE'S WORSE THINGS THAN BEING A MARINE.

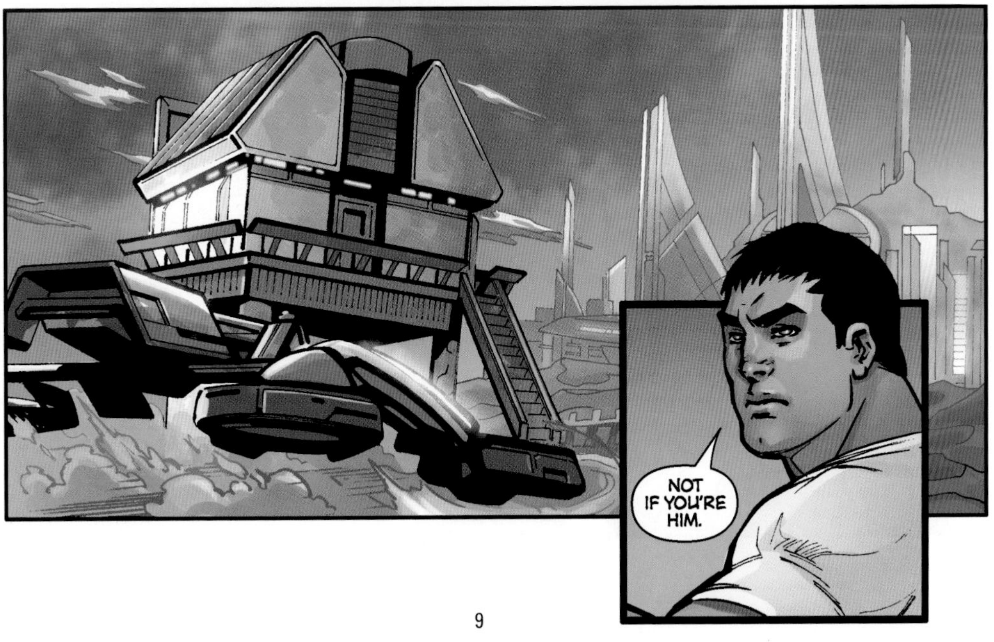
NOT IF YOU'RE HIM.

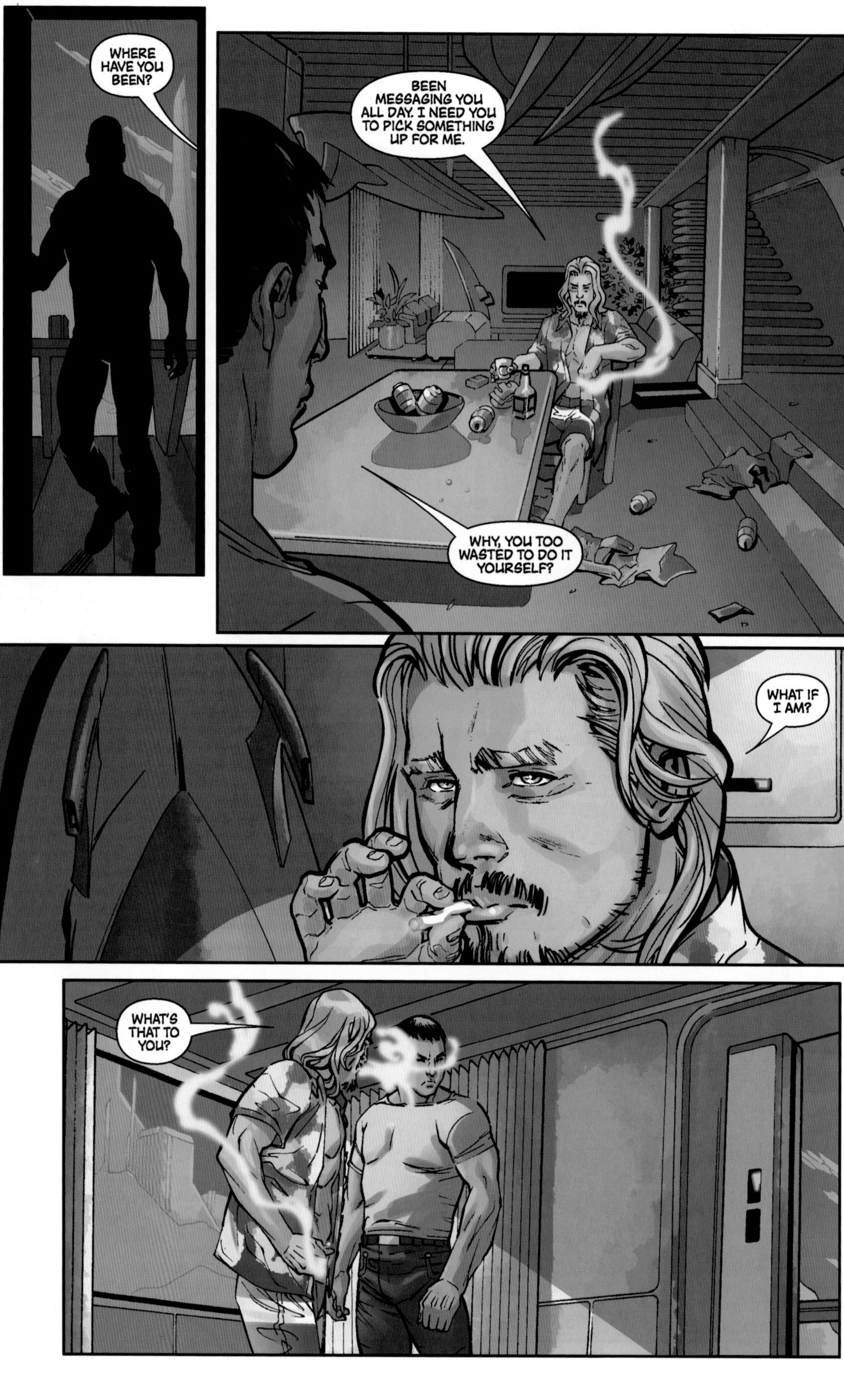
WHERE HAVE YOU BEEN?
BEEN MESSAGING YOU ALL DAY. I NEED YOU TO PICK SOMETHING UP FOR ME.
WHY, YOU TOO WASTED TO DO IT YOURSELF?
WHAT IF I AM?
WHAT'S THAT TO YOU?

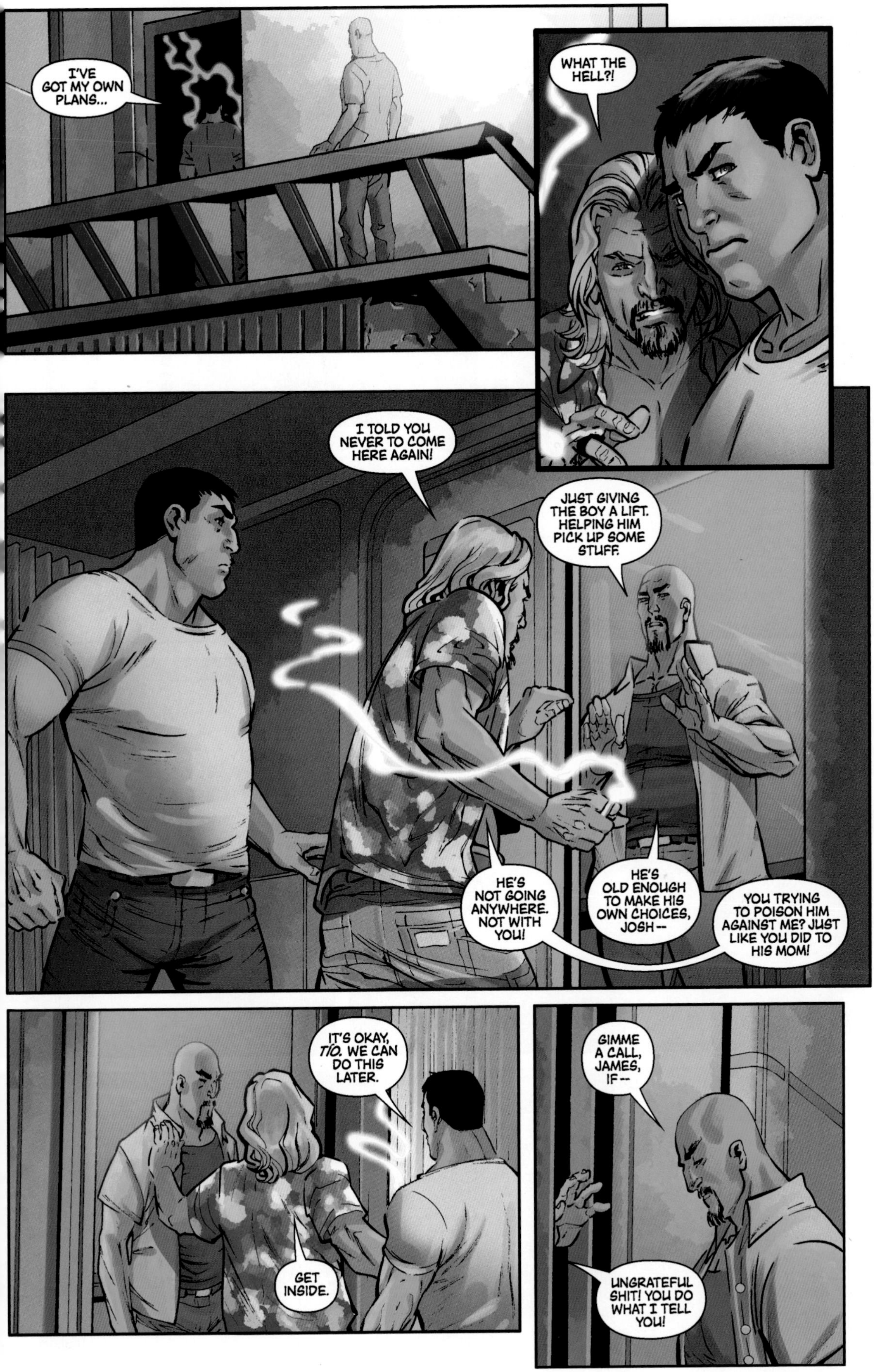
I'VE GOT MY OWN PLANS...
WHAT THE HELL?!
I TOLD YOU NEVER TO COME HERE AGAIN!
JUST GIVING THE BOY A LIFT. HELPING HIM PICK UP SOME STUFF.
HE'S NOT GOING ANYWHERE. NOT WITH YOU!
HE'S OLD ENOUGH TO MAKE HIS OWN CHOICES, JOSH --
YOU TRYING TO POISON HIM AGAINST ME? JUST LIKE YOU DID TO HIS MOM!
IT'S OKAY, *TÍO*. WE CAN DO THIS LATER.
GET INSIDE.
GIMME A CALL, JAMES, IF --
UNGRATEFUL SHIT! YOU DO WHAT I TELL YOU!

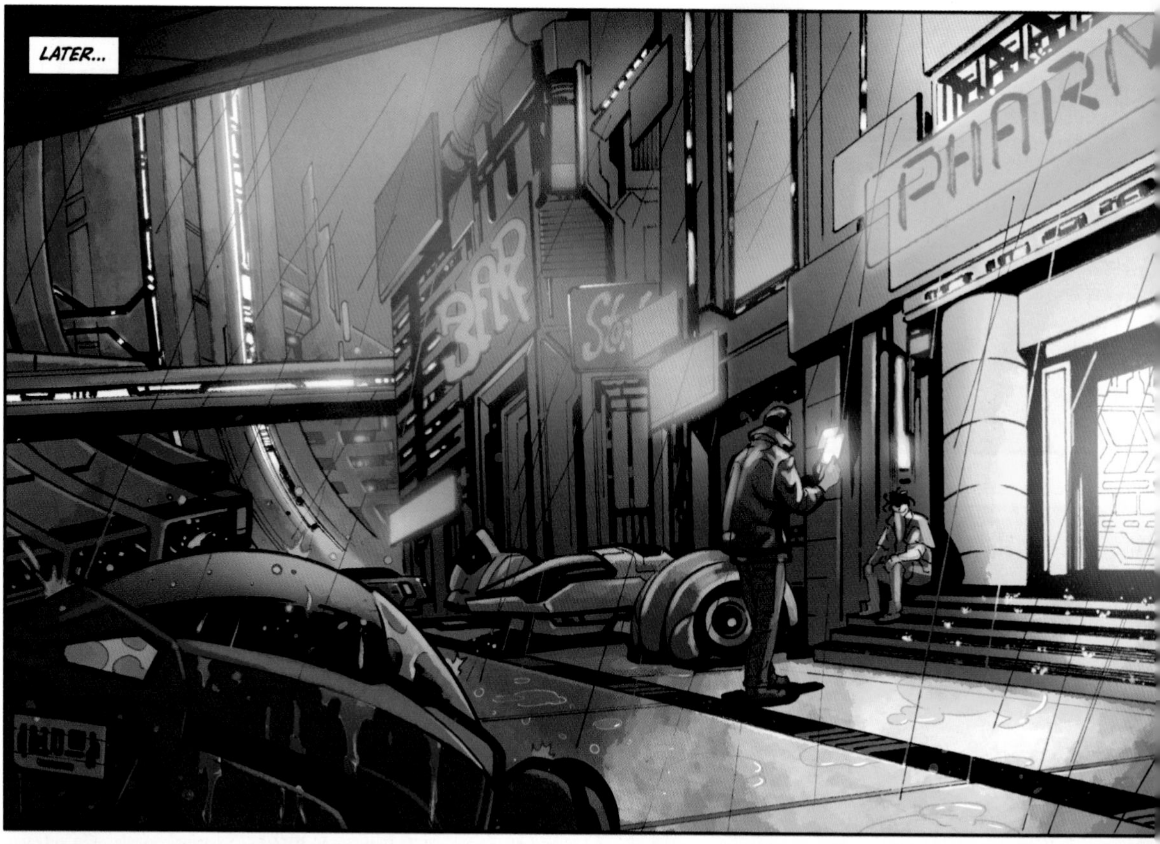
LATER...

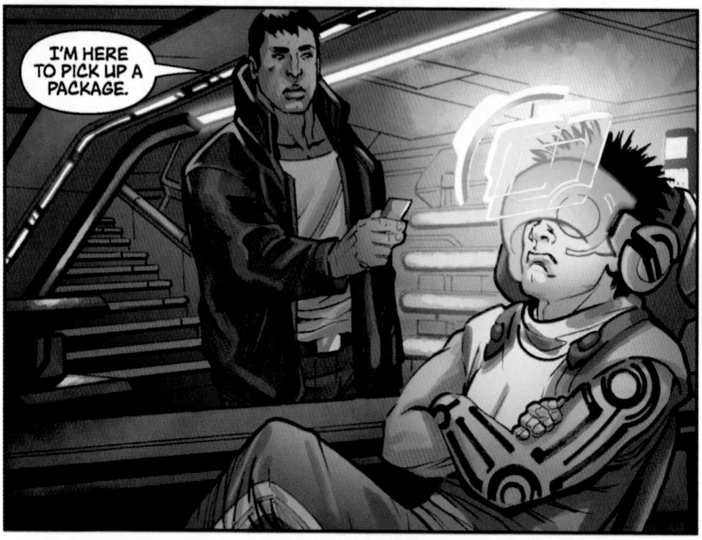
I'M HERE TO PICK UP A PACKAGE.

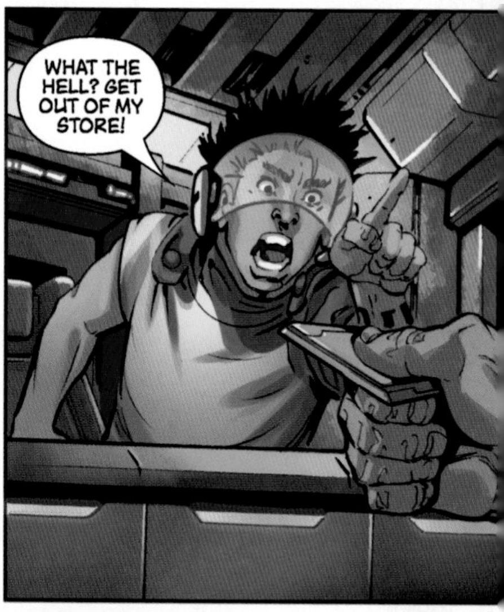
WHAT THE HELL? GET OUT OF MY STORE!

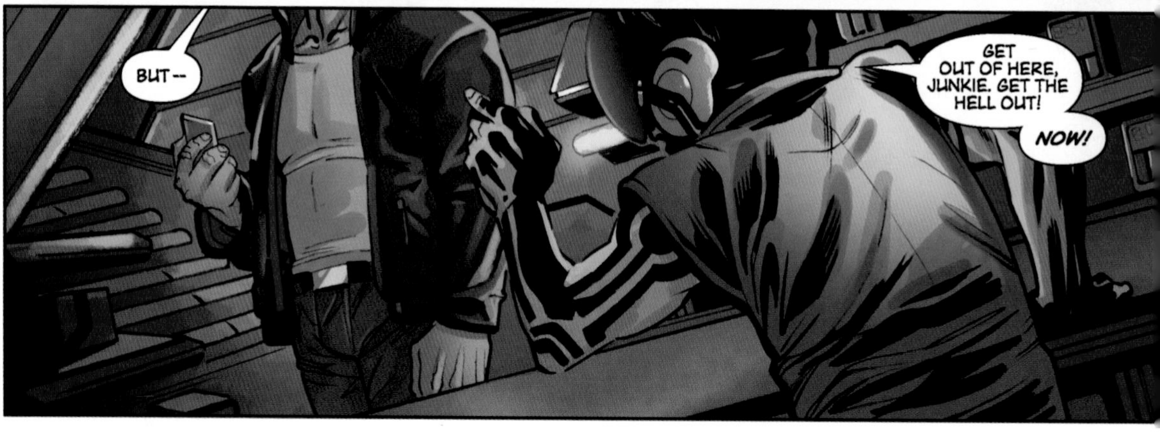
BUT --
GET OUT OF HERE, JUNKIE. GET THE HELL OUT!
NOW!

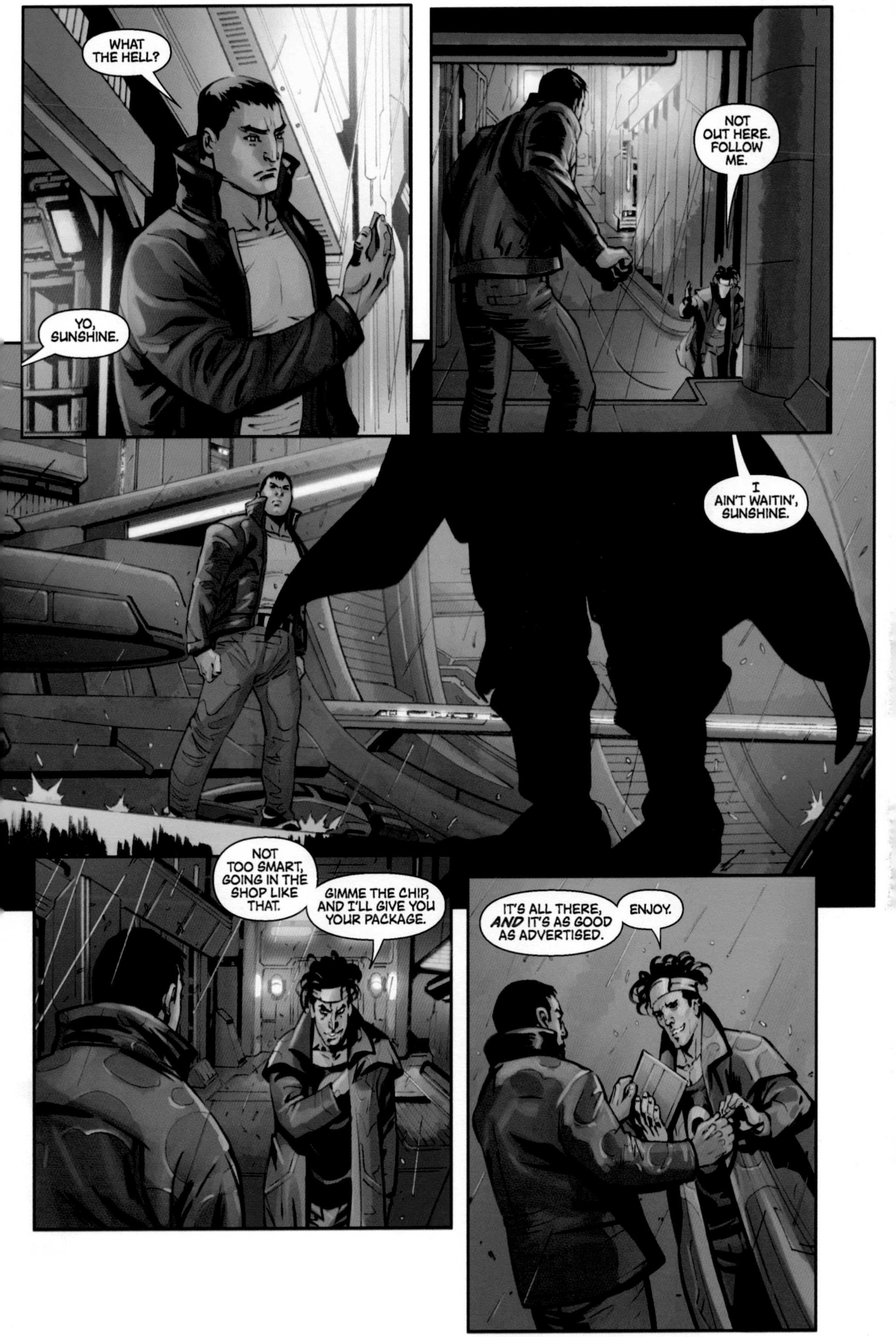
WHAT THE HELL?
YO, SUNSHINE.
NOT OUT HERE. FOLLOW ME.
I AIN'T WAITIN', SUNSHINE.
NOT TOO SMART, GOING IN THE SHOP LIKE THAT.
GIMME THE CHIP, AND I'LL GIVE YOU YOUR PACKAGE.
IT'S ALL THERE, AND IT'S AS GOOD AS ADVERTISED.
ENJOY.

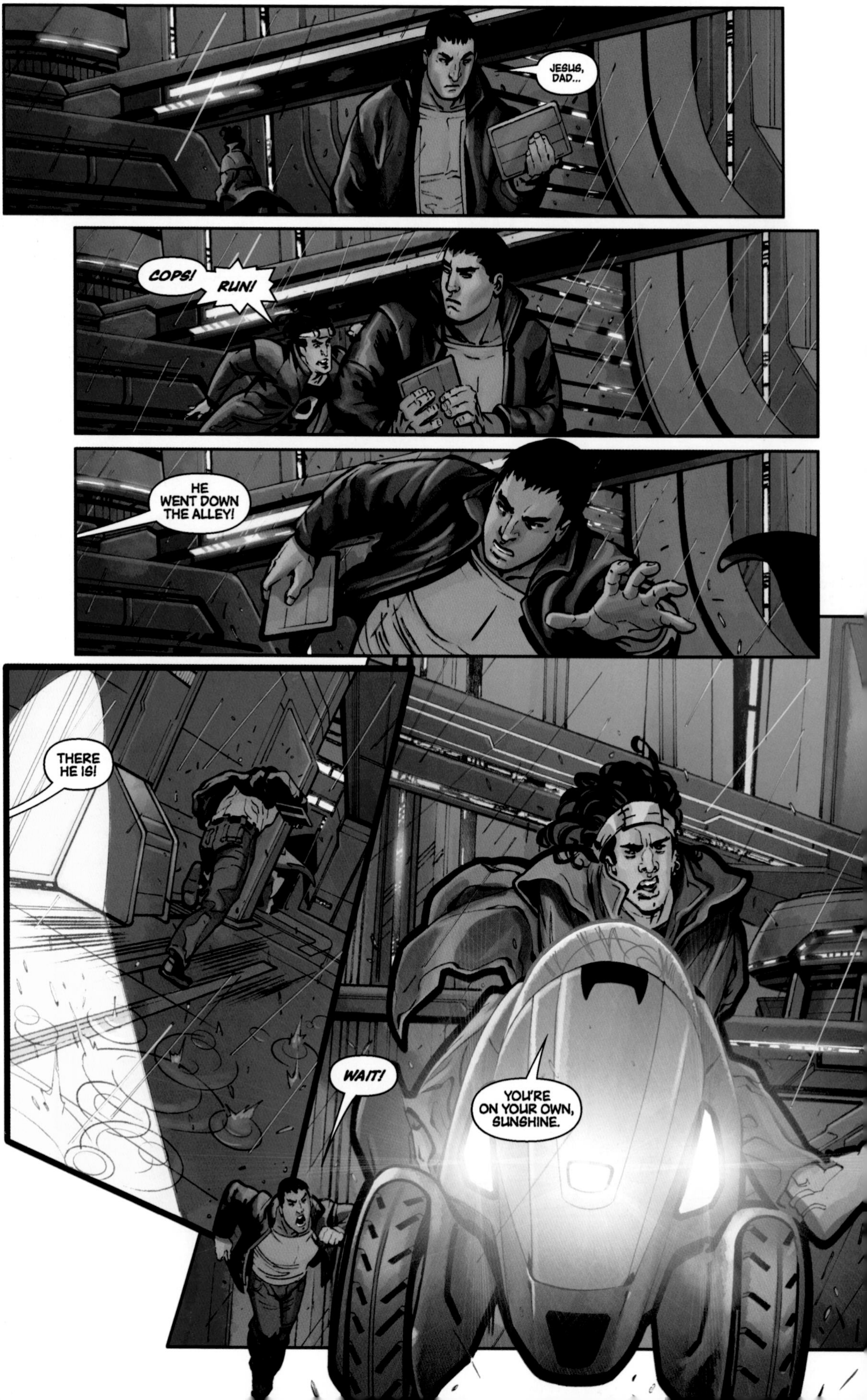
JESUS, DAD...
COPS!
RUN!
HE WENT DOWN THE ALLEY!
THERE HE IS!
WAIT!
YOU'RE ON YOUR OWN, SUNSHINE.

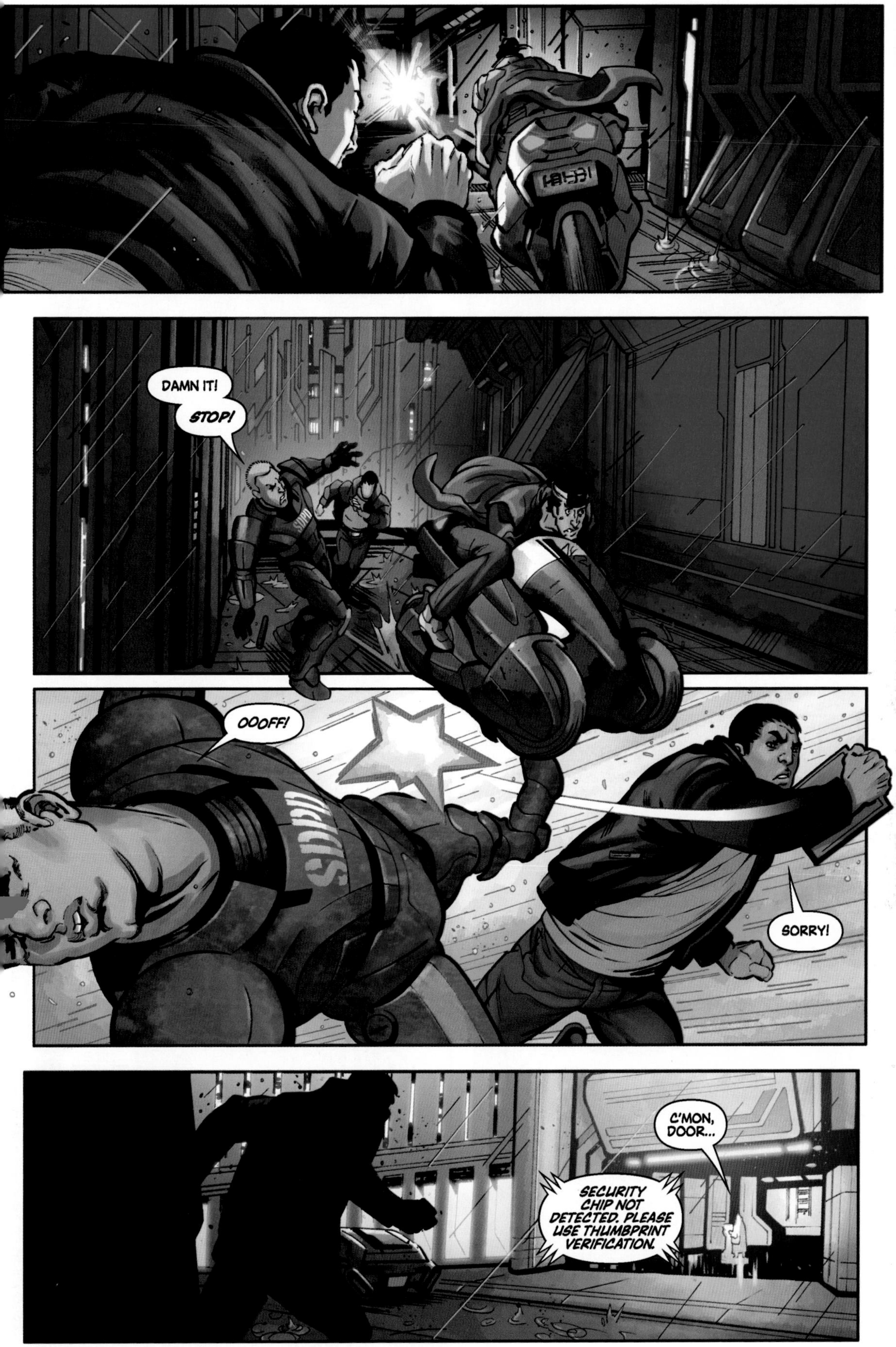
DAMN IT!
STOP!
OOOFF!
SORRY!
C'MON, DOOR...
SECURITY CHIP NOT DETECTED. PLEASE USE THUMBPRINT VERIFICATION.

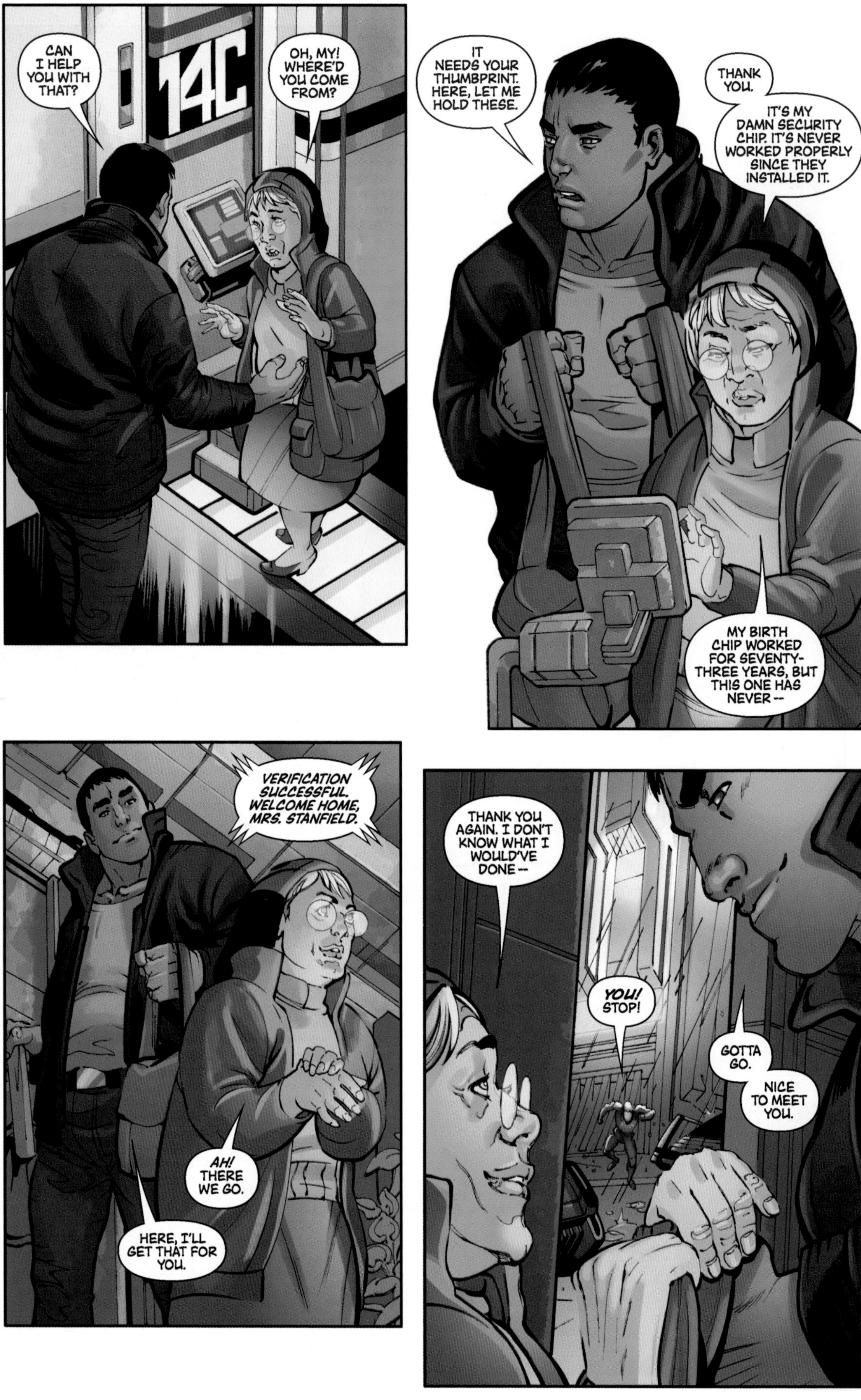
CAN I HELP YOU WITH THAT?
OH, MY! WHERE'D YOU COME FROM?
IT NEEDS YOUR THUMBPRINT. HERE, LET ME HOLD THESE.
THANK YOU.
IT'S MY DAMN SECURITY CHIP. IT'S NEVER WORKED PROPERLY SINCE THEY INSTALLED IT.
MY BIRTH CHIP WORKED FOR SEVENTY-THREE YEARS, BUT THIS ONE HAS NEVER --
VERIFICATION SUCCESSFUL. WELCOME HOME, MRS. STANFIELD.
AH! THERE WE GO.
HERE, I'LL GET THAT FOR YOU.
THANK YOU AGAIN. I DON'T KNOW WHAT I WOULD'VE DONE --
YOU! STOP!
GOTTA GO.
NICE TO MEET YOU.

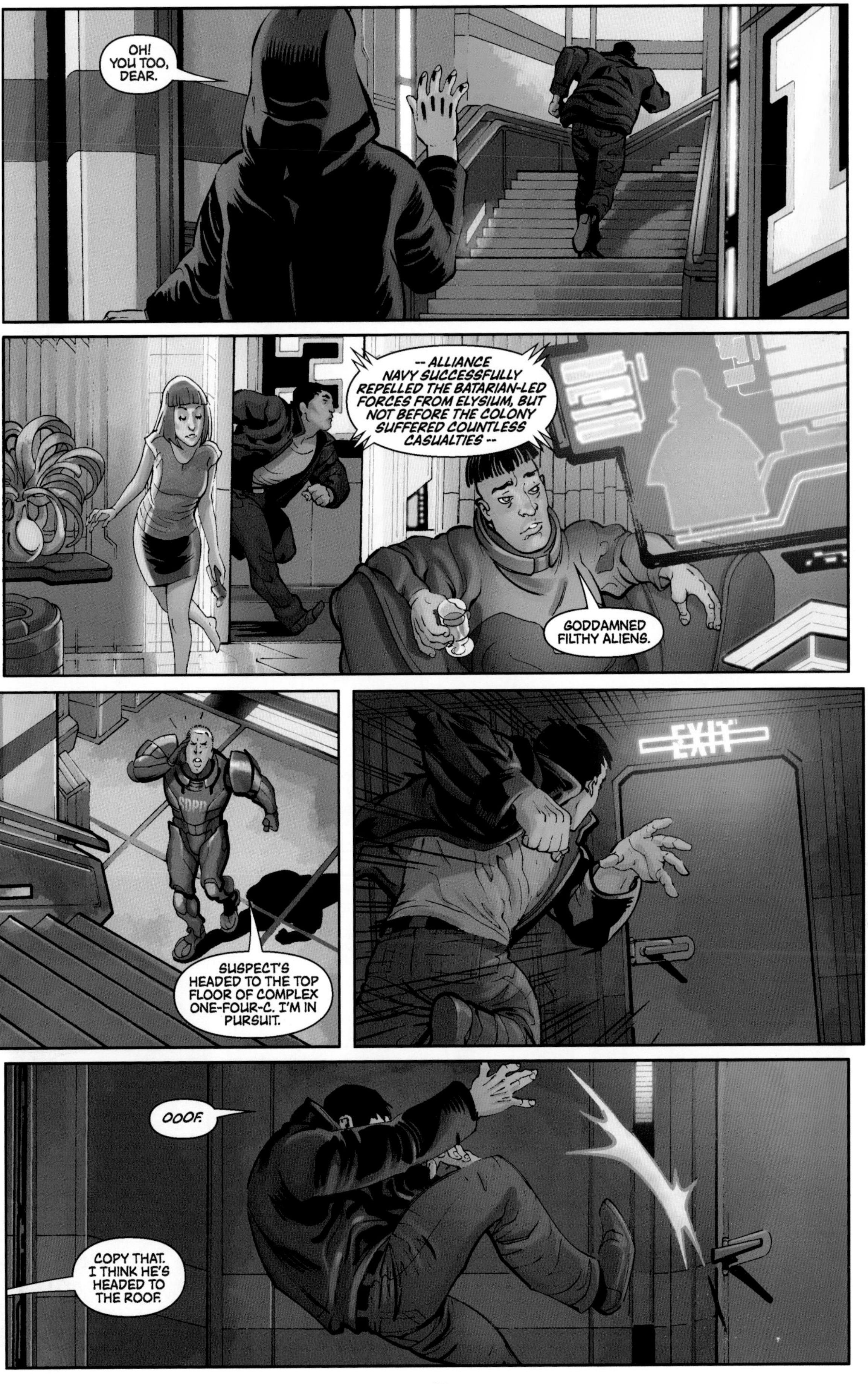
OH! YOU TOO, DEAR.
-- ALLIANCE NAVY SUCCESSFULLY REPELLED THE BATARIAN-LED FORCES FROM ELYSIUM, BUT NOT BEFORE THE COLONY SUFFERED COUNTLESS CASUALTIES --
GODDAMNED FILTHY ALIENS.
SUSPECT'S HEADED TO THE TOP FLOOR OF COMPLEX ONE-FOUR-C. I'M IN PURSUIT.
EXIT
OOOF.
COPY THAT. I THINK HE'S HEADED TO THE ROOF.

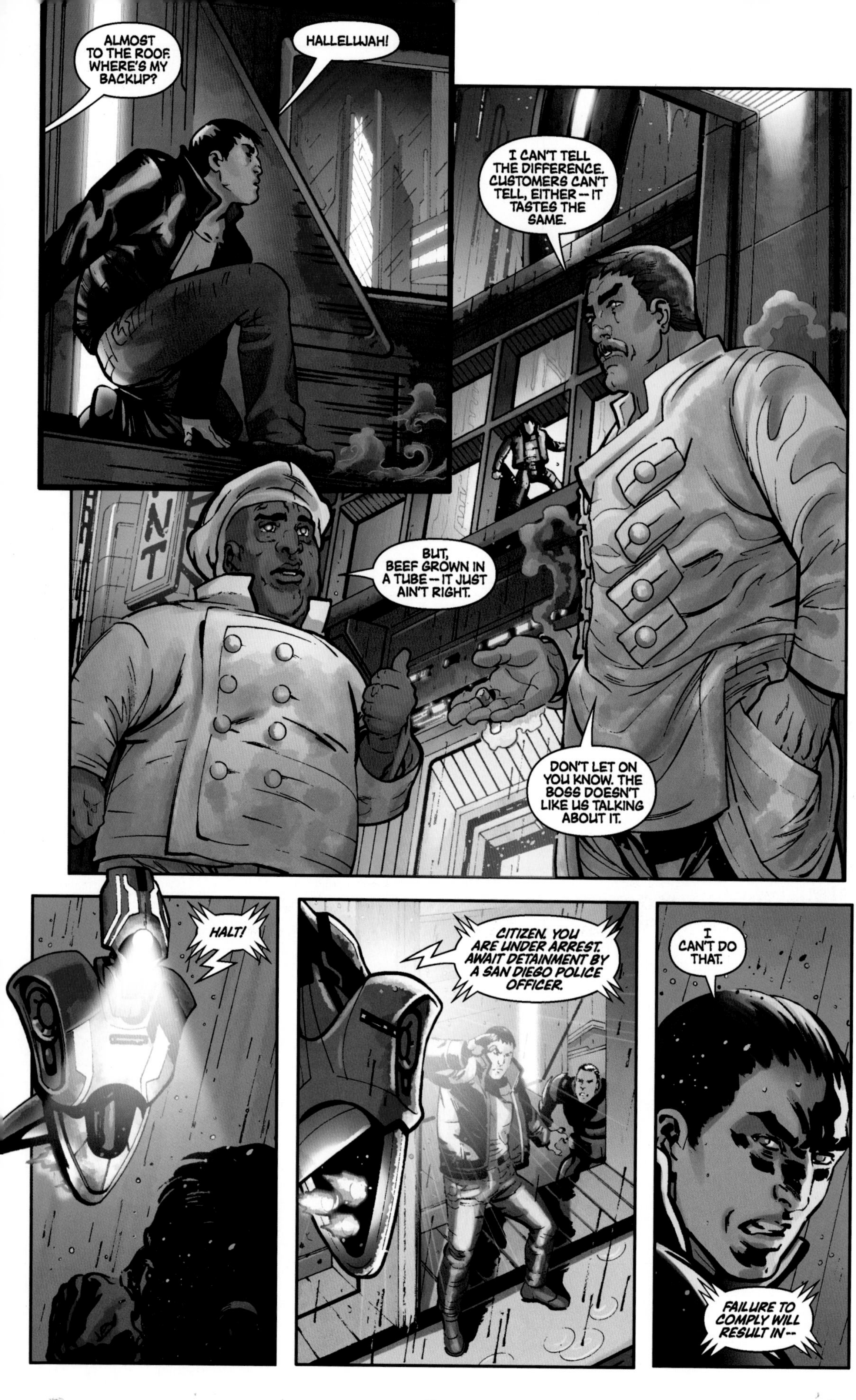
ALMOST TO THE ROOF. WHERE'S MY BACKUP?
HALLELUJAH!
I CAN'T TELL THE DIFFERENCE. CUSTOMERS CAN'T TELL, EITHER -- IT TASTES THE SAME.
BUT, BEEF GROWN IN A TUBE -- IT JUST AIN'T RIGHT.
DON'T LET ON YOU KNOW. THE BOSS DOESN'T LIKE US TALKING ABOUT IT.
HALT!
CITIZEN. YOU ARE UNDER ARREST. AWAIT DETAINMENT BY A SAN DIEGO POLICE OFFICER.
I CAN'T DO THAT.
FAILURE TO COMPLY WILL RESULT IN --

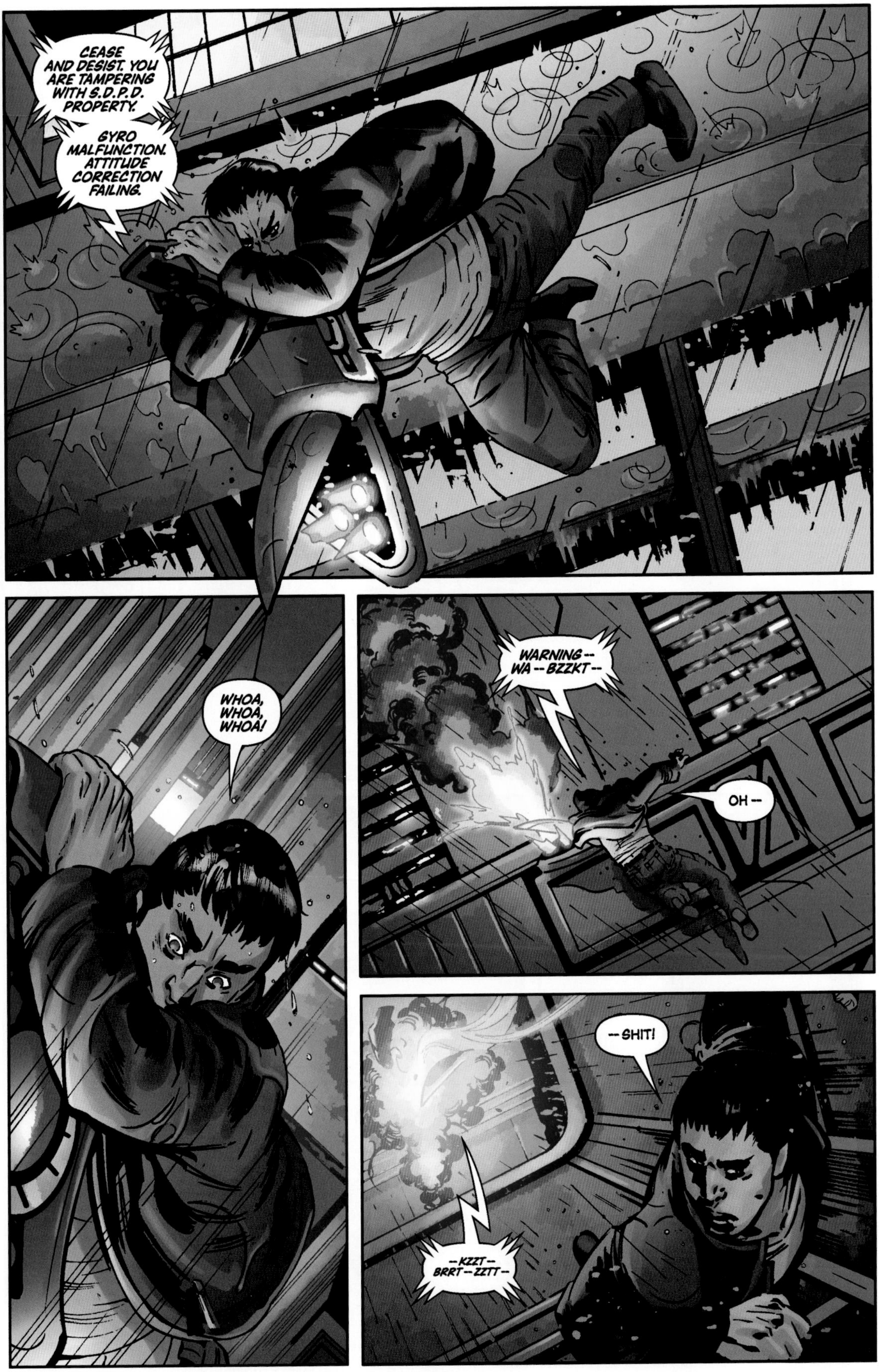
CEASE AND DESIST. YOU ARE TAMPERING WITH S.D.P.D. PROPERTY.
GYRO MALFUNCTION. ATTITUDE CORRECTION FAILING.
WHOA, WHOA, WHOA!
WARNING-- WA--BZZKT--
OH--
--SHIT!
--KZZT-- BRRT--ZZTT--

WEEOO WEEOO WEEOO

NUMBER TWO, NO MAYO, EXTRA ONIONS. BASKET OF FRIES.

ORDER UP.

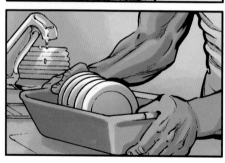

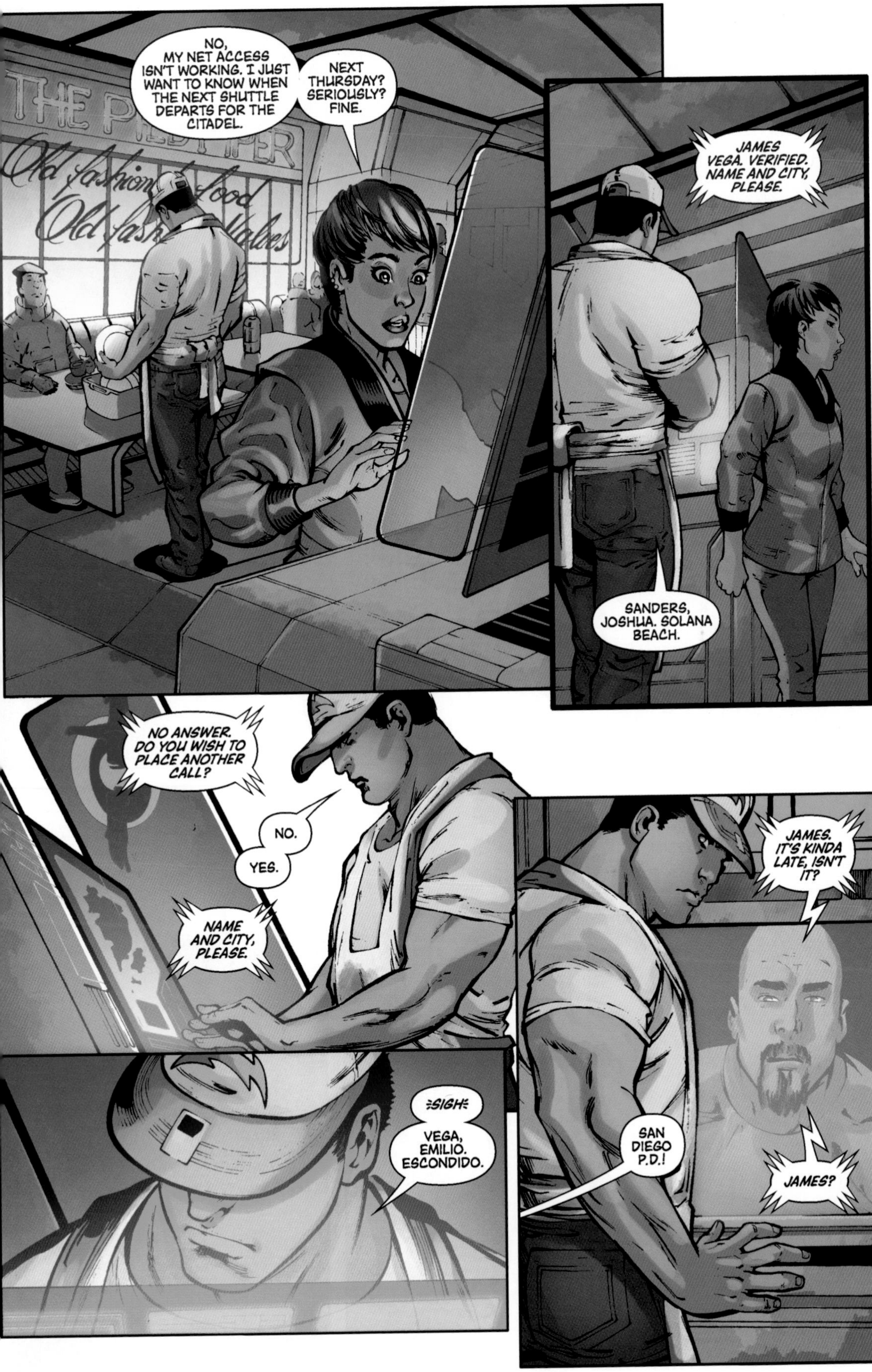
NO, MY NET ACCESS ISN'T WORKING. I JUST WANT TO KNOW WHEN THE NEXT SHUTTLE DEPARTS FOR THE CITADEL.
NEXT THURSDAY? SERIOUSLY? FINE.
JAMES VEGA. VERIFIED. NAME AND CITY, PLEASE.
SANDERS, JOSHUA. SOLANA BEACH.
NO ANSWER. DO YOU WISH TO PLACE ANOTHER CALL?
NO.
YES.
NAME AND CITY, PLEASE.
SIGH
VEGA, EMILIO. ESCONDIDO.
JAMES. IT'S KINDA LATE, ISN'T IT?
SAN DIEGO P.D.!
JAMES?

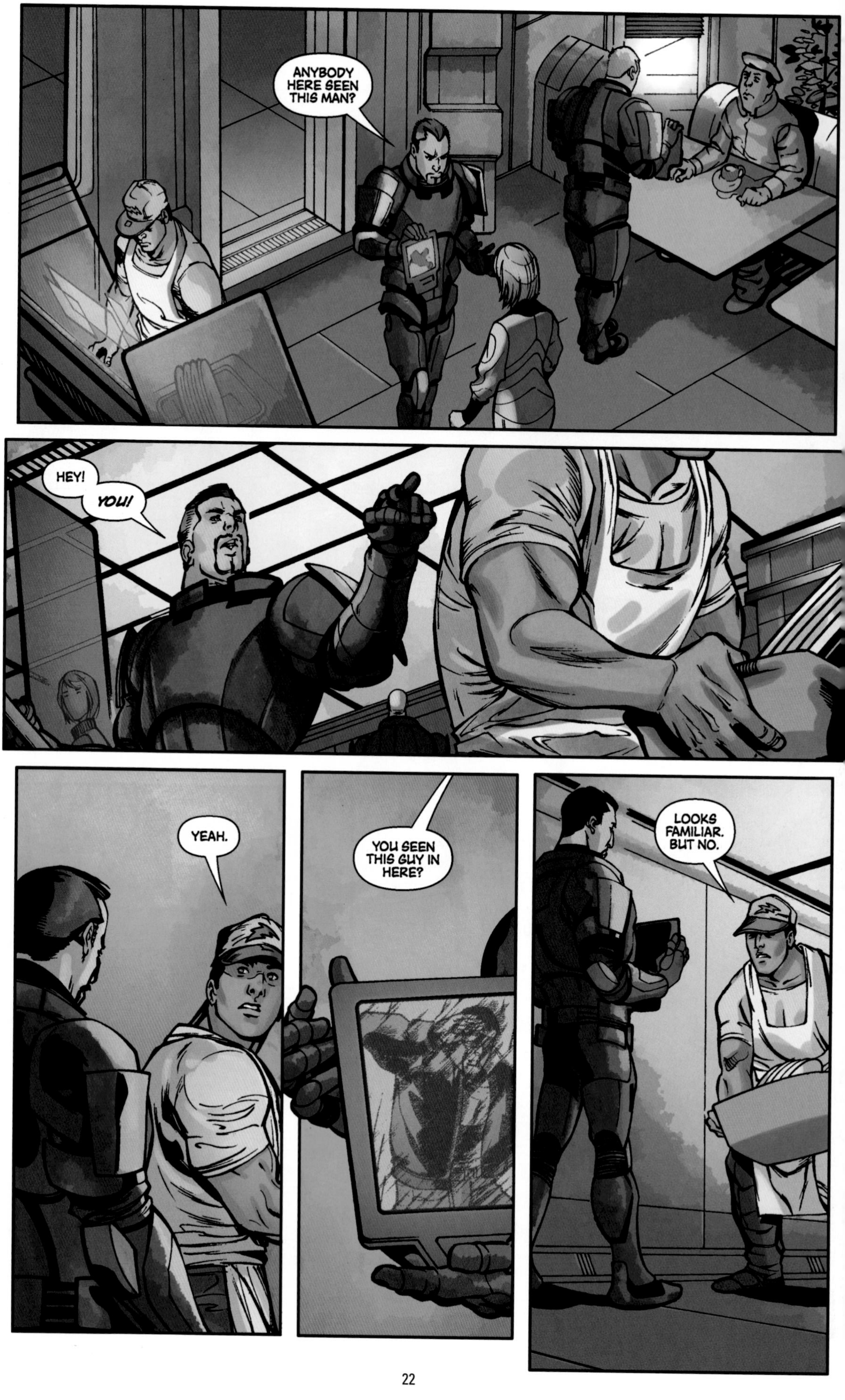
ANYBODY HERE SEEN THIS MAN?
HEY!
YOU!
YEAH.
YOU SEEN THIS GUY IN HERE?
LOOKS FAMILIAR. BUT NO.

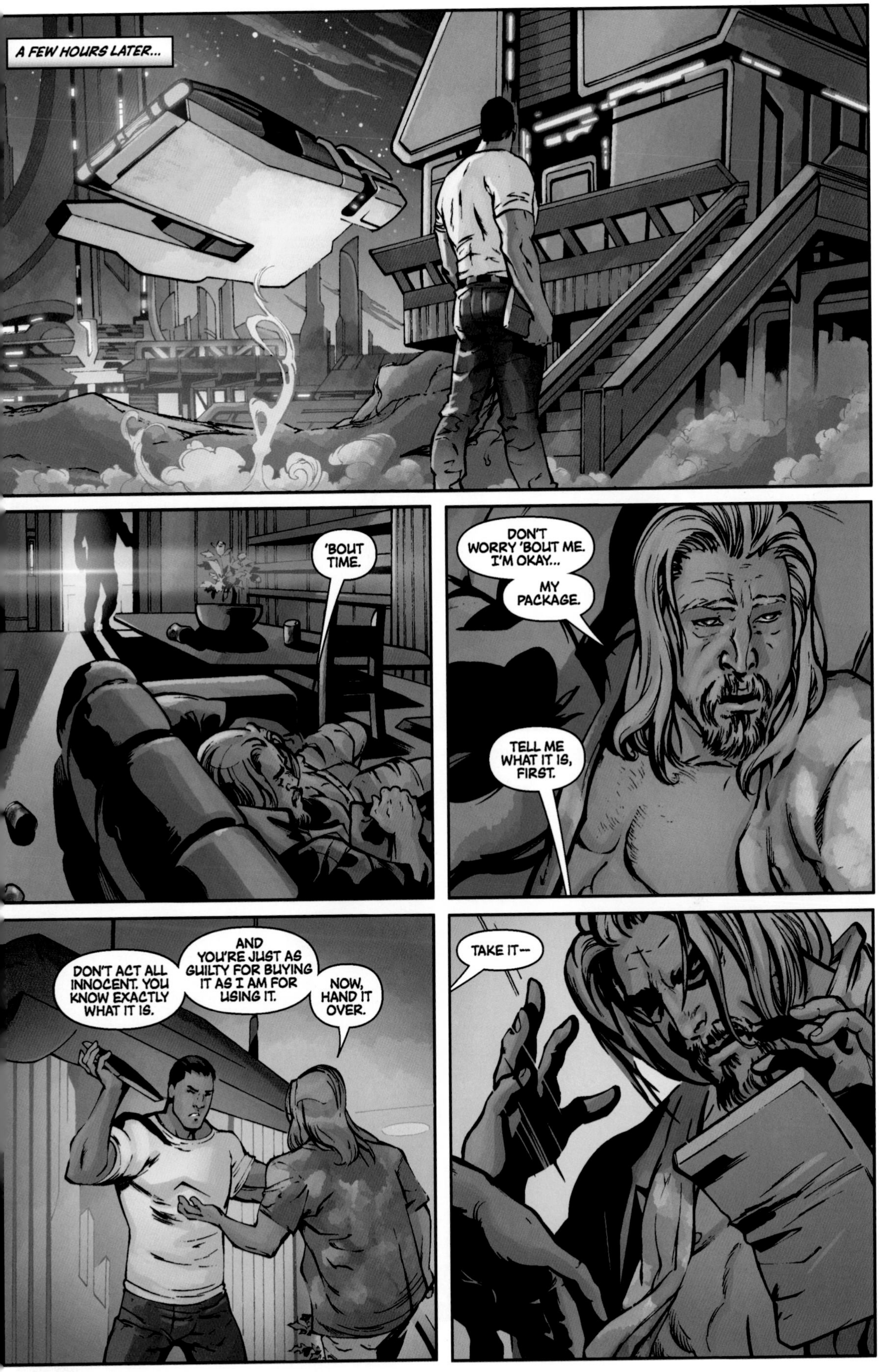
A FEW HOURS LATER...
'BOUT TIME.
DON'T WORRY 'BOUT ME. I'M OKAY...
MY PACKAGE.
TELL ME WHAT IT IS, FIRST.
DON'T ACT ALL INNOCENT. YOU KNOW EXACTLY WHAT IT IS.
AND YOU'RE JUST AS GUILTY FOR BUYING IT AS I AM FOR USING IT.
NOW, HAND IT OVER.
TAKE IT--

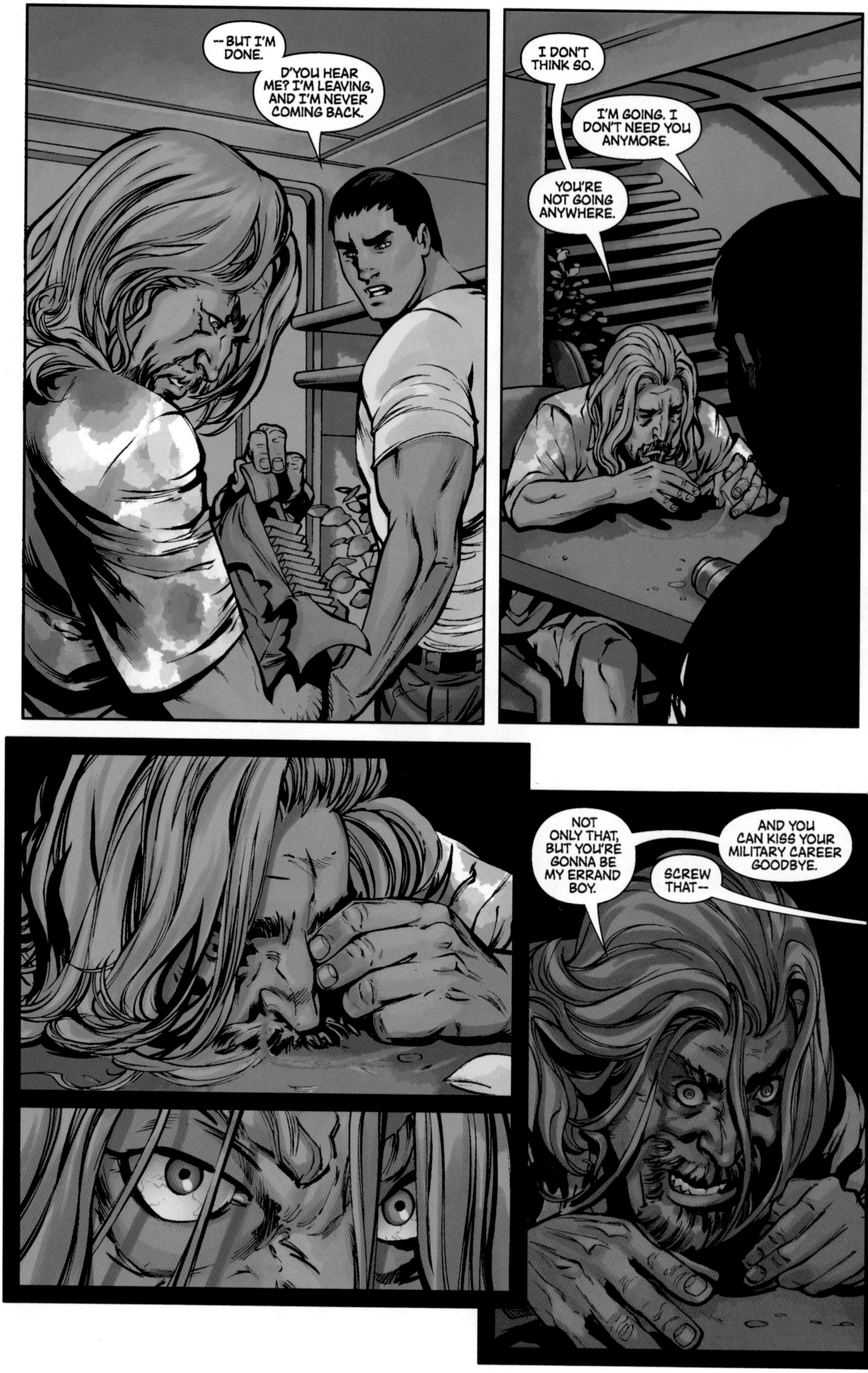
--BUT I'M DONE.
D'YOU HEAR ME? I'M LEAVING, AND I'M NEVER COMING BACK.
I DON'T THINK SO.
I'M GOING. I DON'T NEED YOU ANYMORE.
YOU'RE NOT GOING ANYWHERE.
NOT ONLY THAT, BUT YOU'RE GONNA BE MY ERRAND BOY.
SCREW THAT--
AND YOU CAN KISS YOUR MILITARY CAREER GOODBYE.

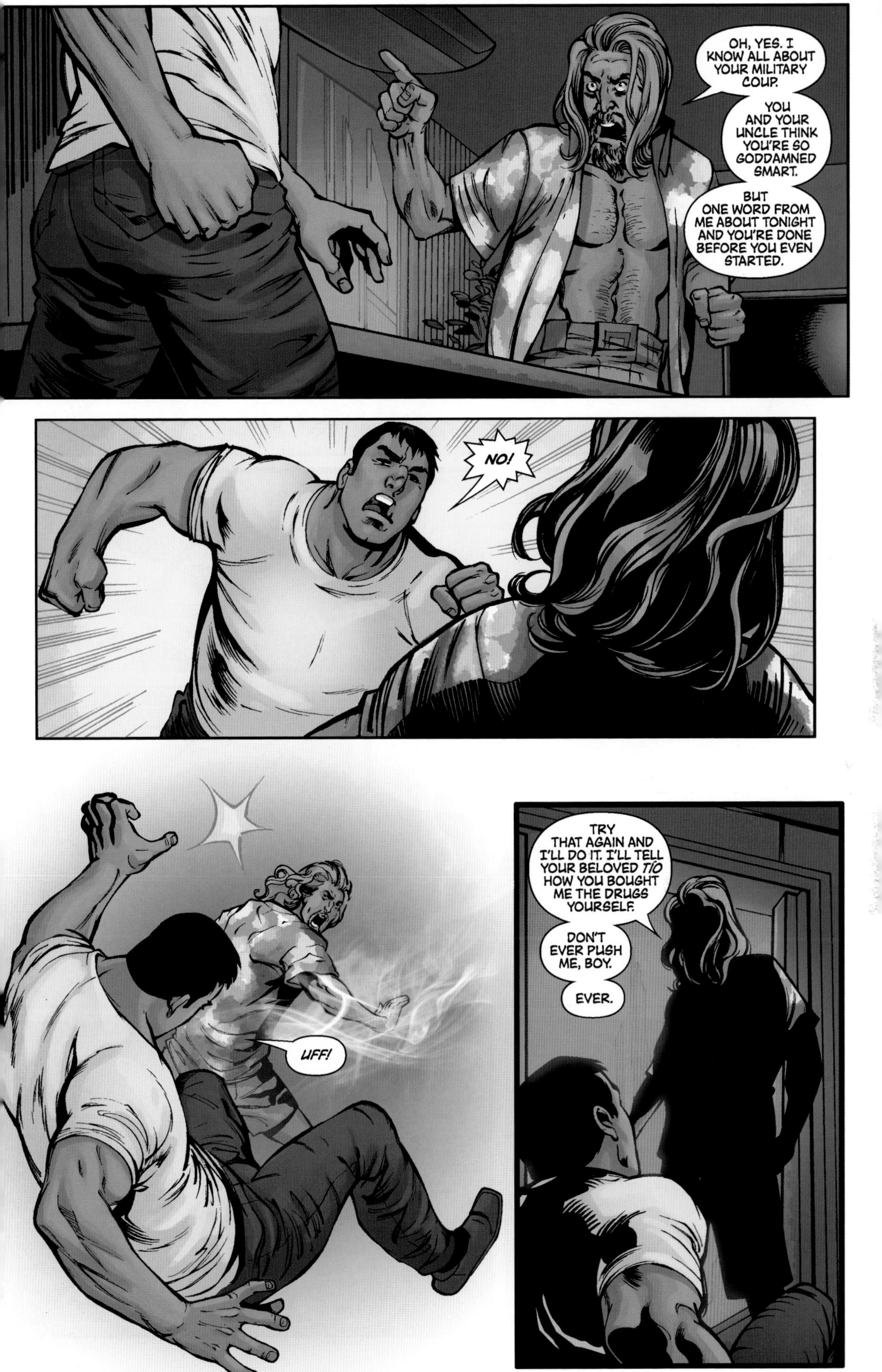
OH, YES. I KNOW ALL ABOUT YOUR MILITARY COUP.
YOU AND YOUR UNCLE THINK YOU'RE SO GODDAMNED SMART.
BUT ONE WORD FROM ME ABOUT TONIGHT AND YOU'RE DONE BEFORE YOU EVEN STARTED.
NO!
UFF!
TRY THAT AGAIN AND I'LL DO IT. I'LL TELL YOUR BELOVED *TÍO* HOW YOU BOUGHT ME THE DRUGS YOURSELF.
DON'T EVER PUSH ME, BOY.
EVER.

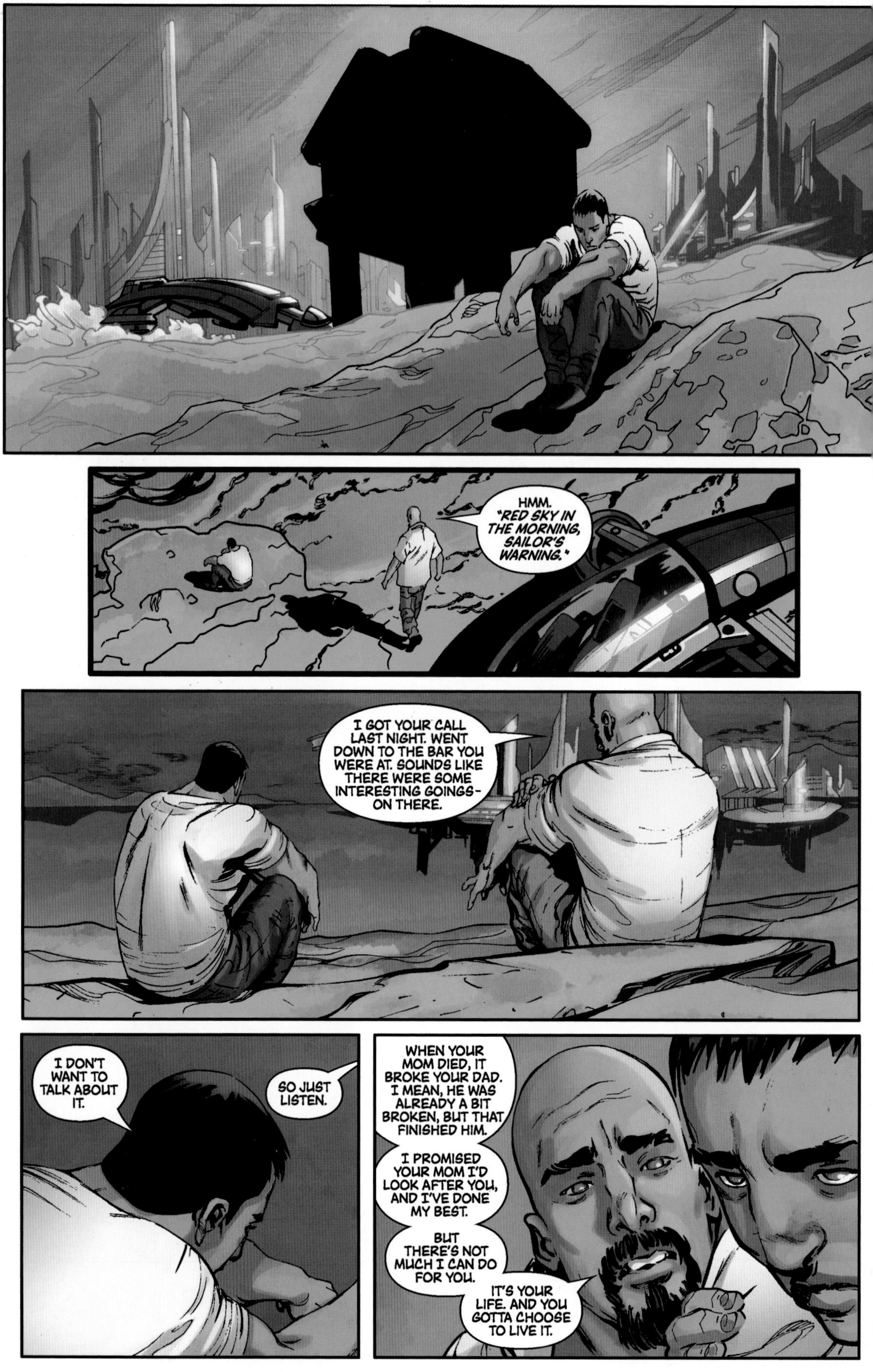
HMM. "RED SKY IN THE MORNING, SAILOR'S WARNING."
I GOT YOUR CALL LAST NIGHT. WENT DOWN TO THE BAR YOU WERE AT. SOUNDS LIKE THERE WERE SOME INTERESTING GOINGS-ON THERE.
I DON'T WANT TO TALK ABOUT IT.
SO JUST LISTEN.
WHEN YOUR MOM DIED, IT BROKE YOUR DAD. I MEAN, HE WAS ALREADY A BIT BROKEN, BUT THAT FINISHED HIM.
I PROMISED YOUR MOM I'D LOOK AFTER YOU, AND I'VE DONE MY BEST.
BUT THERE'S NOT MUCH I CAN DO FOR YOU.
IT'S YOUR LIFE. AND YOU GOTTA CHOOSE TO LIVE IT.

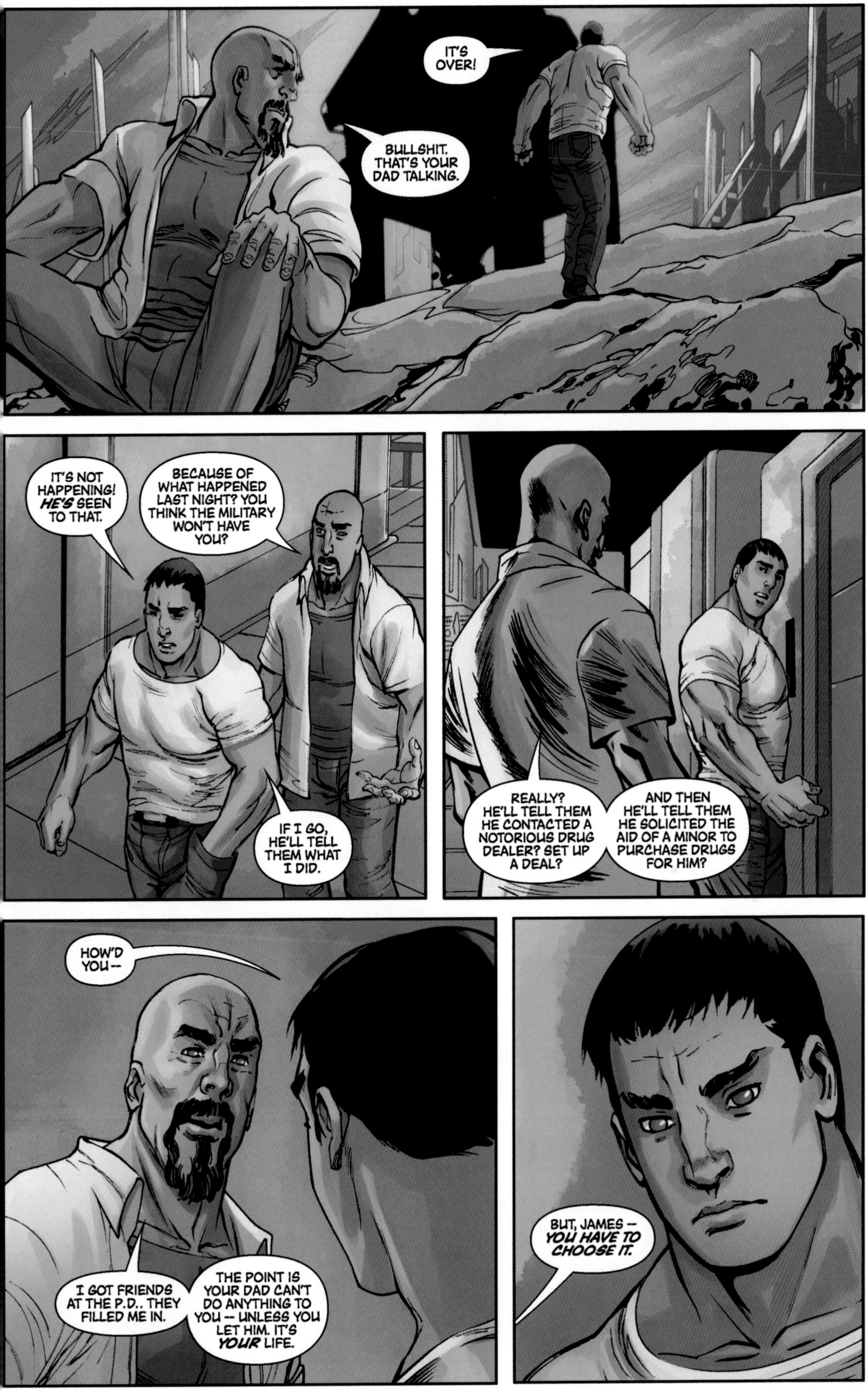
IT'S OVER!
BULLSHIT. THAT'S YOUR DAD TALKING.
IT'S NOT HAPPENING! *HE'S* SEEN TO THAT.
BECAUSE OF WHAT HAPPENED LAST NIGHT? YOU THINK THE MILITARY WON'T HAVE YOU?
IF I GO, HE'LL TELL THEM WHAT I DID.
REALLY? HE'LL TELL THEM HE CONTACTED A NOTORIOUS DRUG DEALER? SET UP A DEAL?
AND THEN HE'LL TELL THEM HE SOLICITED THE AID OF A MINOR TO PURCHASE DRUGS FOR HIM?
HOW'D YOU--
I GOT FRIENDS AT THE P.D.. THEY FILLED ME IN.
THE POINT IS YOUR DAD CAN'T DO ANYTHING TO YOU -- UNLESS YOU LET HIM. IT'S *YOUR* LIFE.
BUT, JAMES -- *YOU HAVE TO CHOOSE IT.*

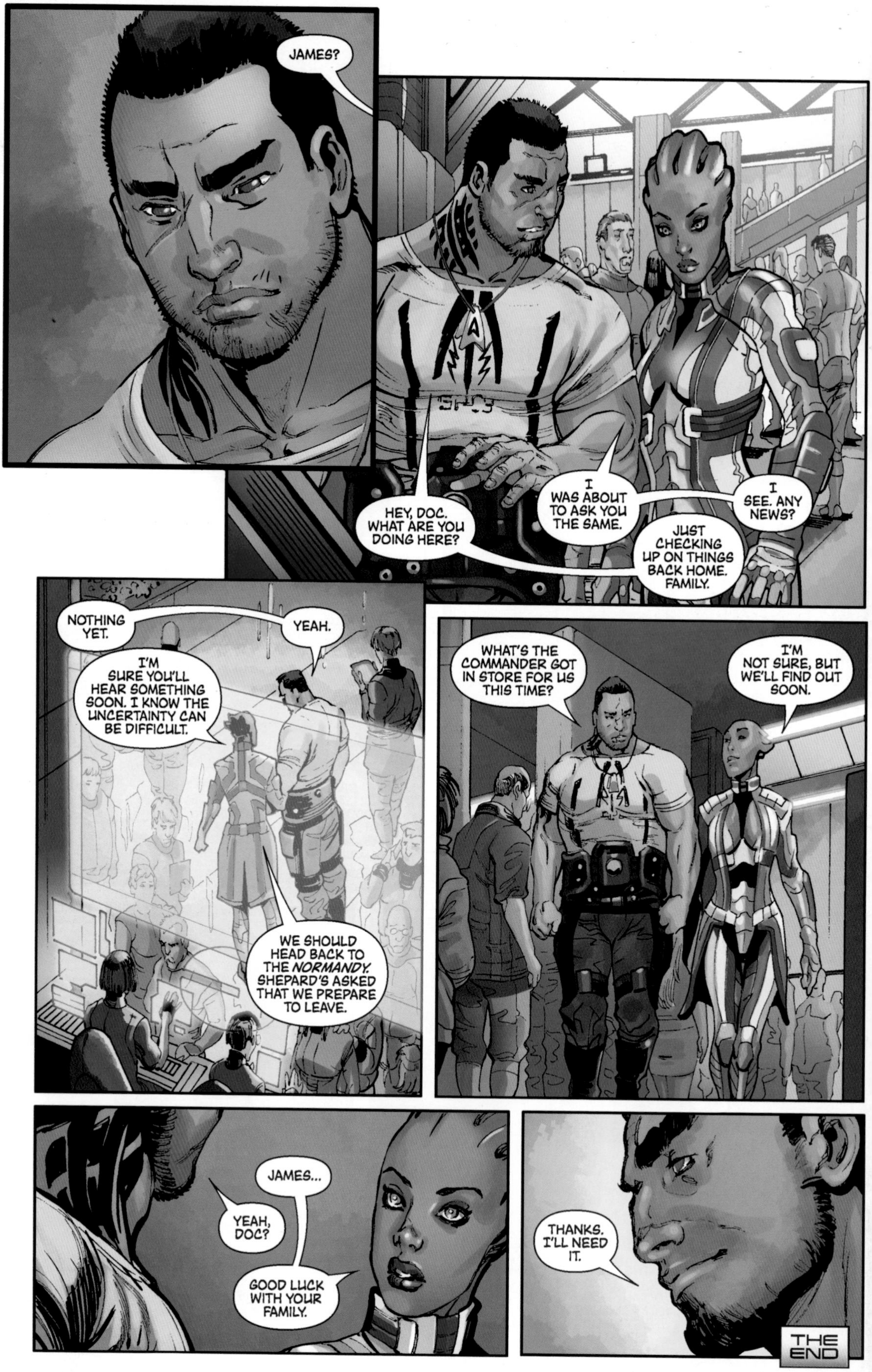
JAMES?
HEY, DOC. WHAT ARE YOU DOING HERE?
I WAS ABOUT TO ASK YOU THE SAME.
JUST CHECKING UP ON THINGS BACK HOME. FAMILY.
I SEE. ANY NEWS?
NOTHING YET.
YEAH.
I'M SURE YOU'LL HEAR SOMETHING SOON. I KNOW THE UNCERTAINTY CAN BE DIFFICULT.
WE SHOULD HEAD BACK TO THE *NORMANDY*. SHEPARD'S ASKED THAT WE PREPARE TO LEAVE.
WHAT'S THE COMMANDER GOT IN STORE FOR US THIS TIME?
I'M NOT SURE, BUT WE'LL FIND OUT SOON.
JAMES...
YEAH, DOC?
GOOD LUCK WITH YOUR FAMILY.
THANKS. I'LL NEED IT.
THE END

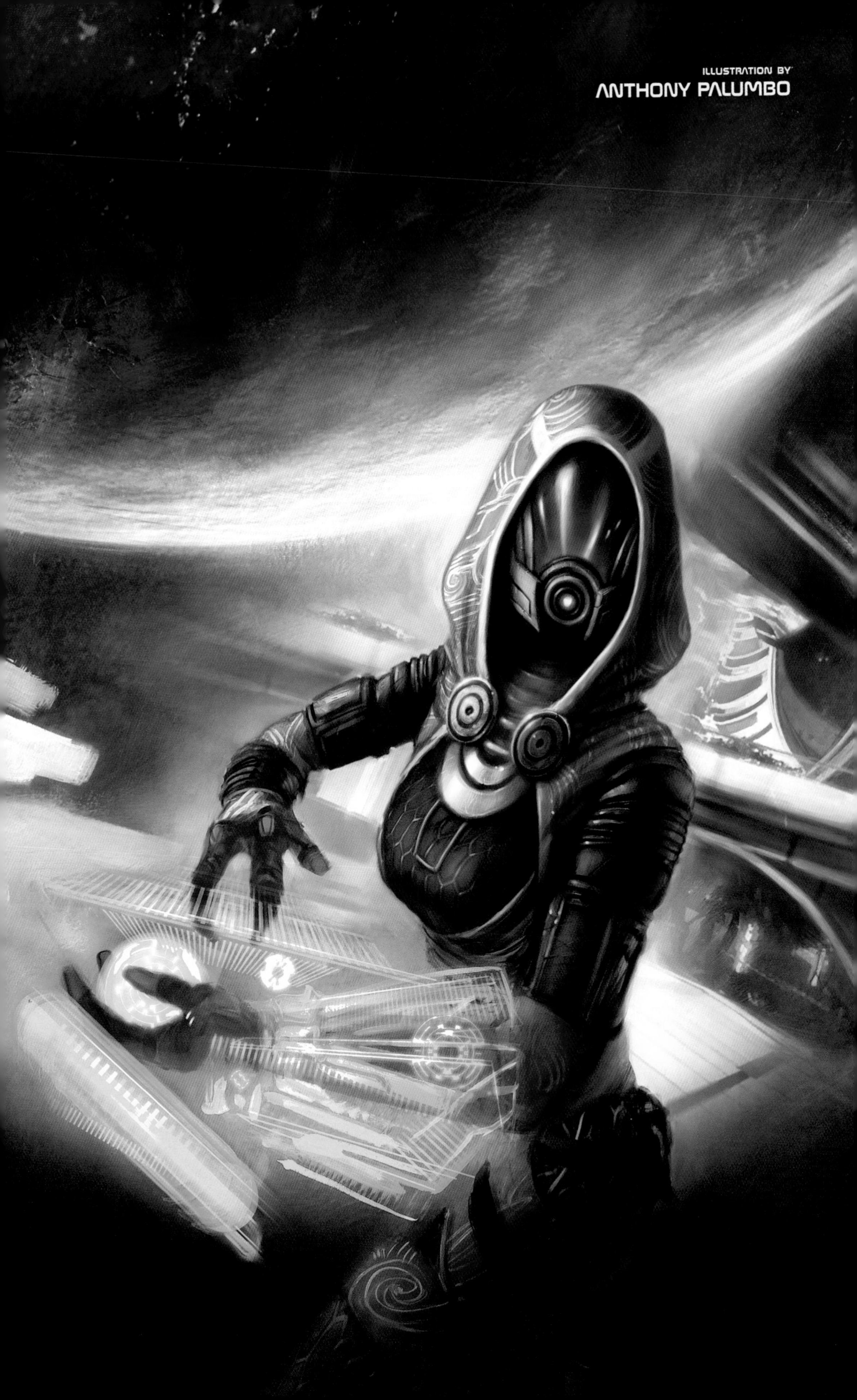
ILLUSTRATION BY
ANTHONY PALUMBO

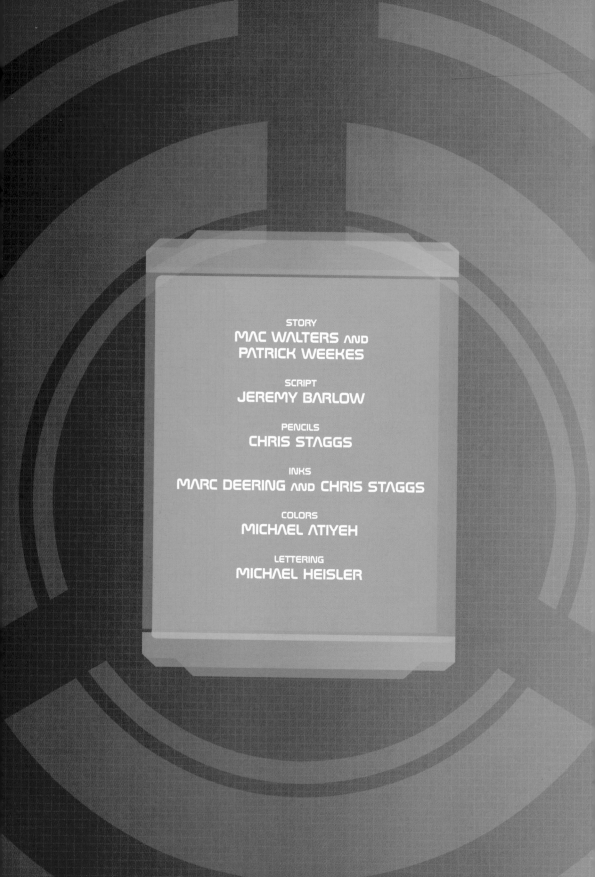

STORY
MAC WALTERS AND
PATRICK WEEKES

SCRIPT
JEREMY BARLOW

PENCILS
CHRIS STAGGS

INKS
MARC DEERING AND CHRIS STAGGS

COLORS
MICHAEL ATIYEH

LETTERING
MICHAEL HEISLER

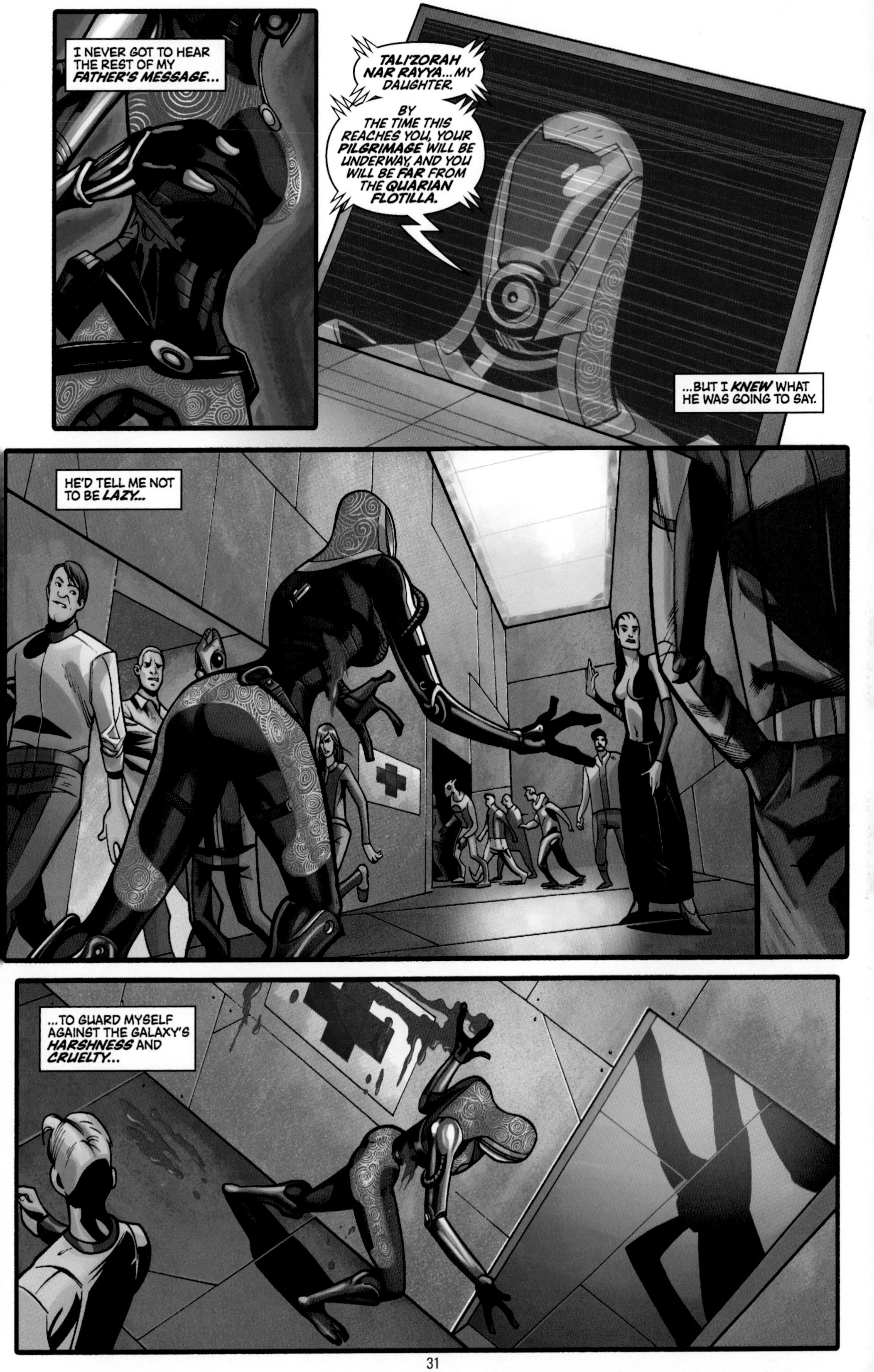
I NEVER GOT TO HEAR THE REST OF MY FATHER'S MESSAGE...
TALI'ZORAH NAR RAYYA...MY DAUGHTER.
BY THE TIME THIS REACHES YOU, YOUR PILGRIMAGE WILL BE UNDERWAY, AND YOU WILL BE FAR FROM THE QUARIAN FLOTILLA.
...BUT I KNEW WHAT HE WAS GOING TO SAY.
HE'D TELL ME NOT TO BE LAZY...
...TO GUARD MYSELF AGAINST THE GALAXY'S HARSHNESS AND CRUELTY...

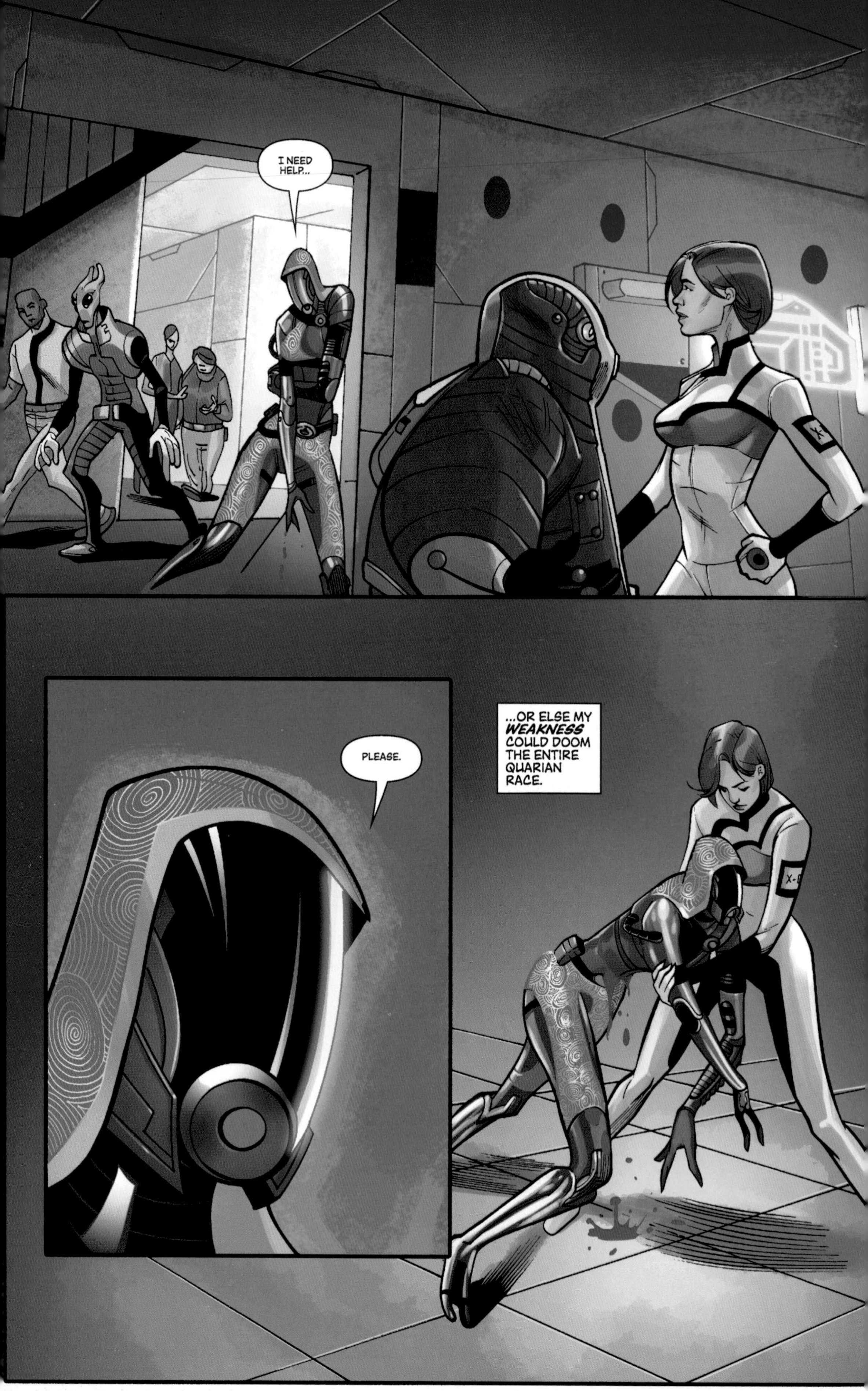
I NEED HELP...
PLEASE.
...OR ELSE MY WEAKNESS COULD DOOM THE ENTIRE QUARIAN RACE.

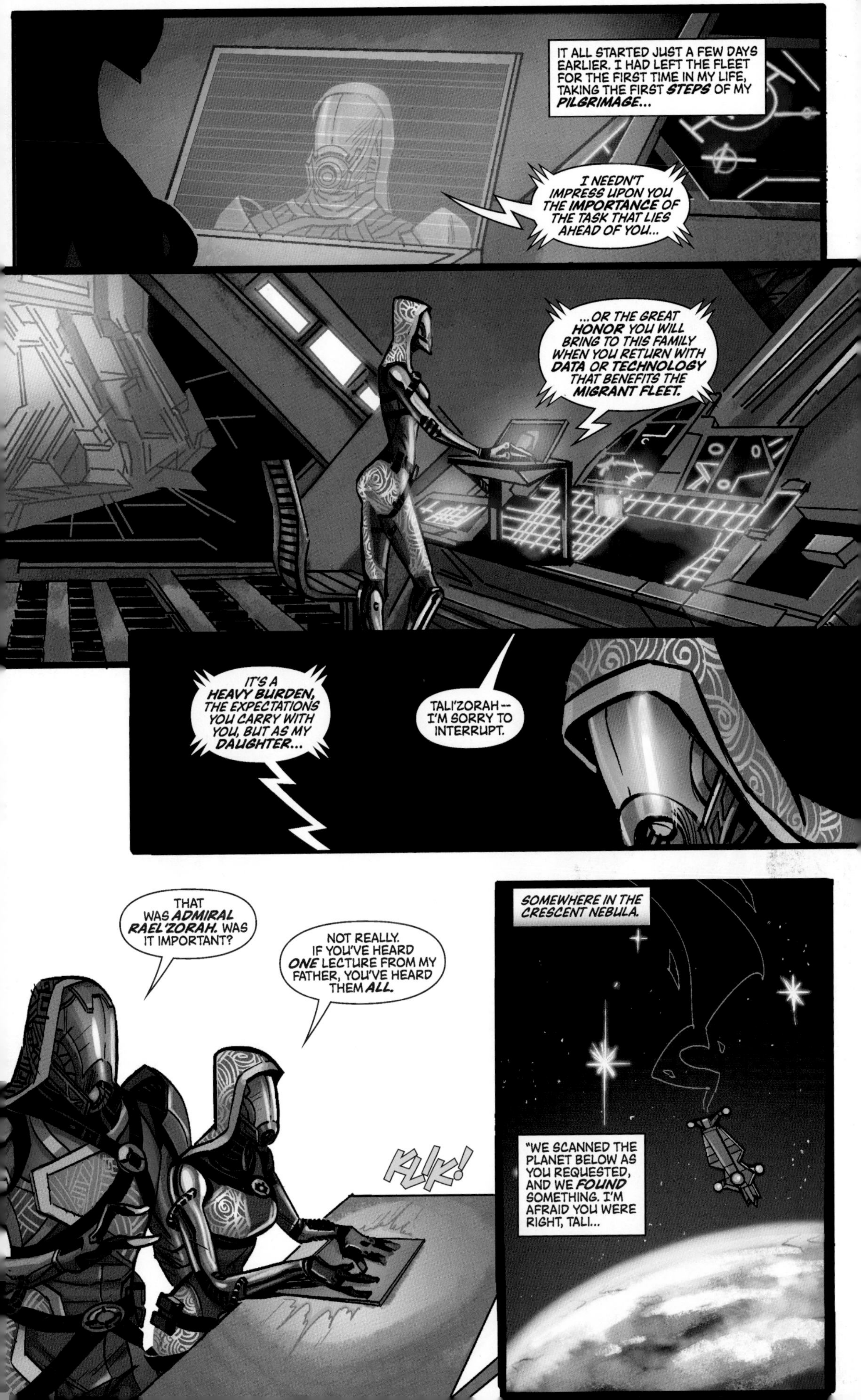

IT ALL STARTED JUST A FEW DAYS EARLIER. I HAD LEFT THE FLEET FOR THE FIRST TIME IN MY LIFE, TAKING THE FIRST STEPS OF MY PILGRIMAGE...
I NEEDN'T IMPRESS UPON YOU THE IMPORTANCE OF THE TASK THAT LIES AHEAD OF YOU...
...OR THE GREAT HONOR YOU WILL BRING TO THIS FAMILY WHEN YOU RETURN WITH DATA OR TECHNOLOGY THAT BENEFITS THE MIGRANT FLEET.
IT'S A HEAVY BURDEN, THE EXPECTATIONS YOU CARRY WITH YOU, BUT AS MY DAUGHTER...
TALI'ZORAH-- I'M SORRY TO INTERRUPT.
THAT WAS ADMIRAL RAEL'ZORAH. WAS IT IMPORTANT?
NOT REALLY. IF YOU'VE HEARD ONE LECTURE FROM MY FATHER, YOU'VE HEARD THEM ALL.
KLIK!
SOMEWHERE IN THE CRESCENT NEBULA.
"WE SCANNED THE PLANET BELOW AS YOU REQUESTED, AND WE FOUND SOMETHING. I'M AFRAID YOU WERE RIGHT, TALI...

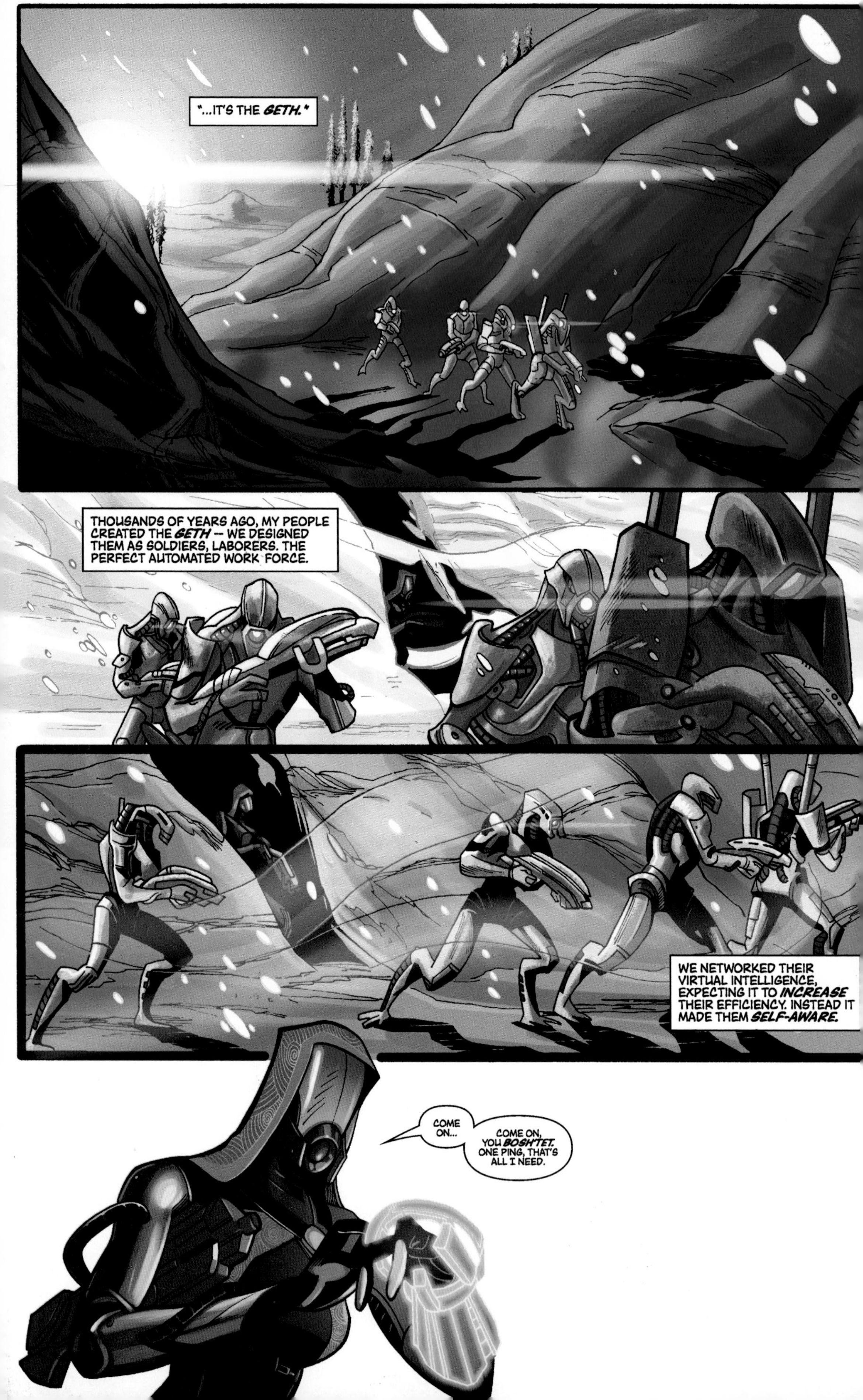
"...IT'S THE GETH."
THOUSANDS OF YEARS AGO, MY PEOPLE CREATED THE GETH -- WE DESIGNED THEM AS SOLDIERS, LABORERS. THE PERFECT AUTOMATED WORK FORCE.
WE NETWORKED THEIR VIRTUAL INTELLIGENCE, EXPECTING IT TO INCREASE THEIR EFFICIENCY. INSTEAD IT MADE THEM SELF-AWARE.
COME ON...
COME ON, YOU BOSH'TET. ONE PING, THAT'S ALL I NEED.

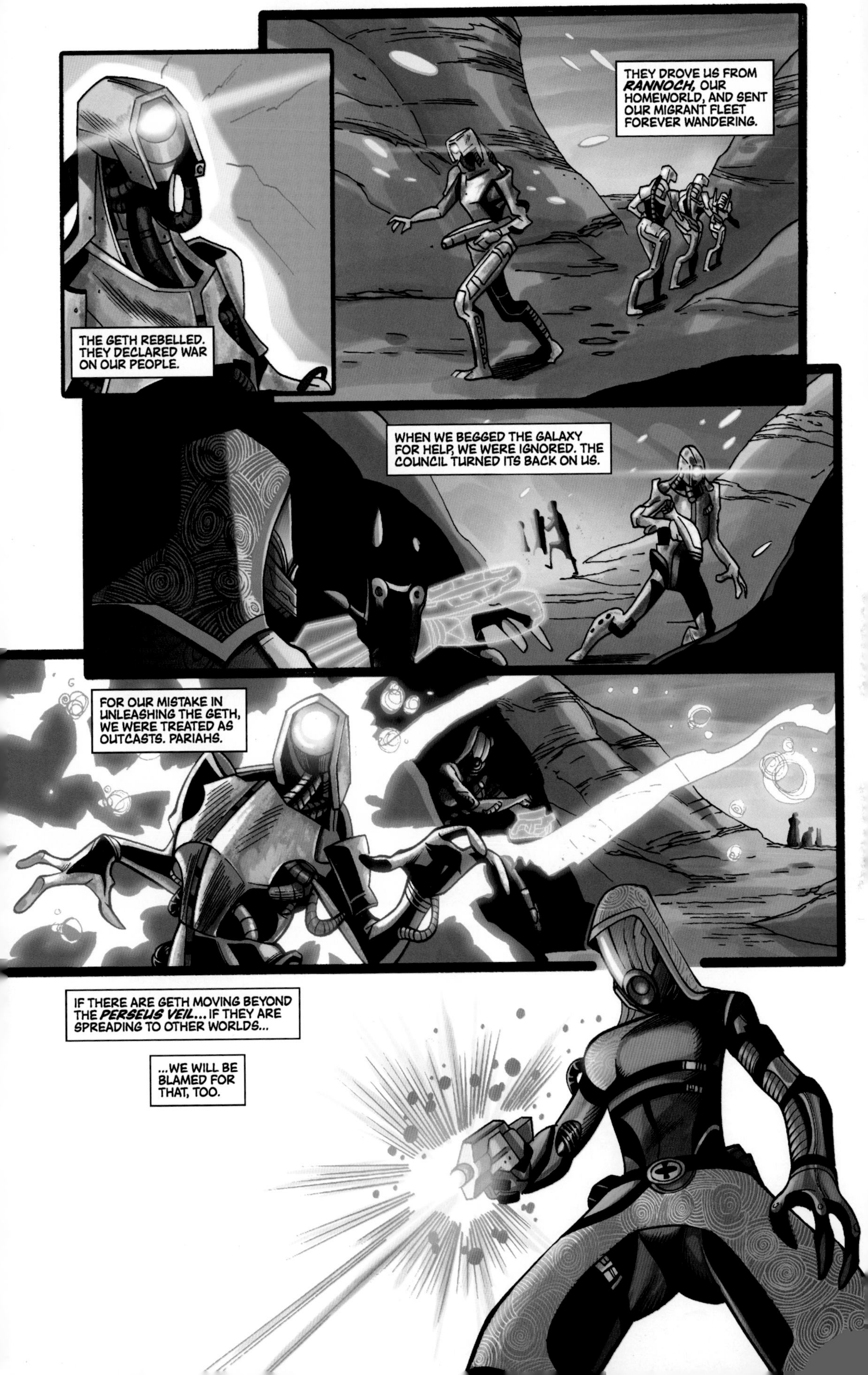
THE GETH REBELLED. THEY DECLARED WAR ON OUR PEOPLE.
THEY DROVE US FROM RANNOCH, OUR HOMEWORLD, AND SENT OUR MIGRANT FLEET FOREVER WANDERING.
WHEN WE BEGGED THE GALAXY FOR HELP, WE WERE IGNORED. THE COUNCIL TURNED ITS BACK ON US.
FOR OUR MISTAKE IN UNLEASHING THE GETH, WE WERE TREATED AS OUTCASTS. PARIAHS.
IF THERE ARE GETH MOVING BEYOND THE PERSEUS VEIL... IF THEY ARE SPREADING TO OTHER WORLDS...
...WE WILL BE BLAMED FOR THAT, TOO.

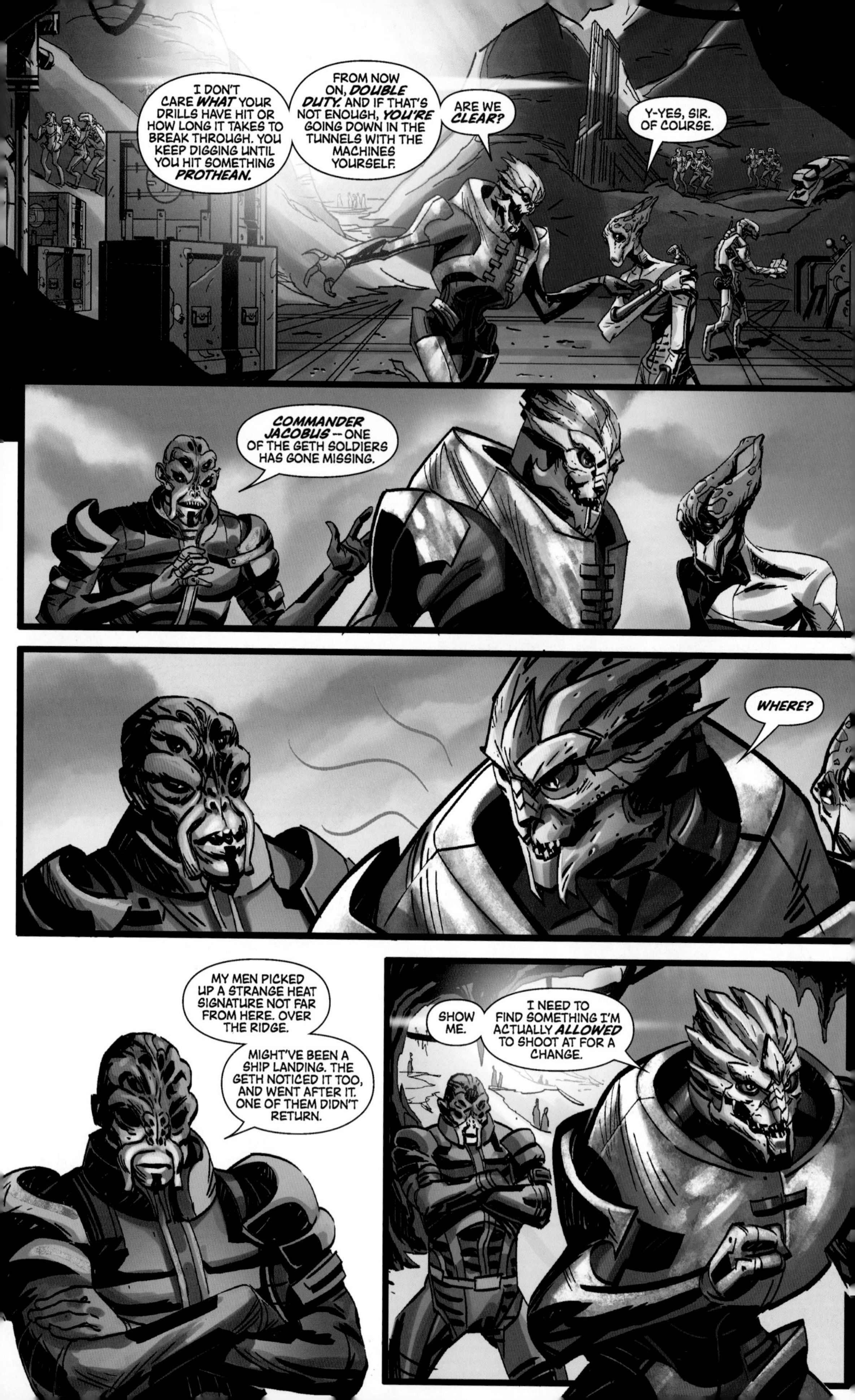
I DON'T CARE WHAT YOUR DRILLS HAVE HIT OR HOW LONG IT TAKES TO BREAK THROUGH. YOU KEEP DIGGING UNTIL YOU HIT SOMETHING PROTHEAN.
FROM NOW ON, DOUBLE DUTY. AND IF THAT'S NOT ENOUGH, YOU'RE GOING DOWN IN THE TUNNELS WITH THE MACHINES YOURSELF.
ARE WE CLEAR?
Y-YES, SIR. OF COURSE.
COMMANDER JACOBUS -- ONE OF THE GETH SOLDIERS HAS GONE MISSING.
WHERE?
MY MEN PICKED UP A STRANGE HEAT SIGNATURE NOT FAR FROM HERE. OVER THE RIDGE.
MIGHT'VE BEEN A SHIP LANDING. THE GETH NOTICED IT TOO, AND WENT AFTER IT. ONE OF THEM DIDN'T RETURN.
SHOW ME.
I NEED TO FIND SOMETHING I'M ACTUALLY ALLOWED TO SHOOT AT FOR A CHANGE.

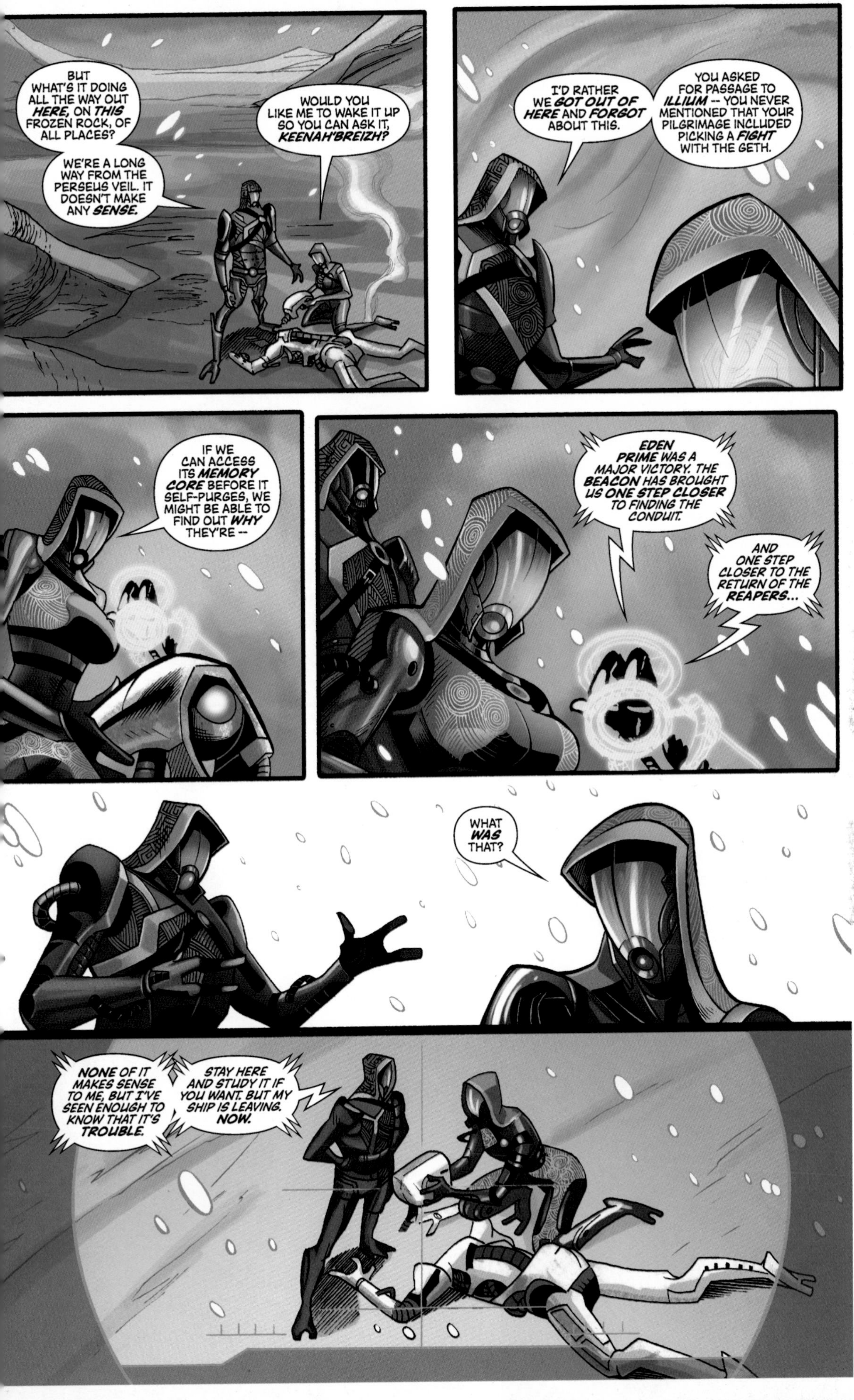

BUT WHAT'S IT DOING ALL THE WAY OUT HERE, ON THIS FROZEN ROCK, OF ALL PLACES?
WE'RE A LONG WAY FROM THE PERSEUS VEIL. IT DOESN'T MAKE ANY SENSE.
WOULD YOU LIKE ME TO WAKE IT UP SO YOU CAN ASK IT, KEENAH'BREIZH?
I'D RATHER WE GOT OUT OF HERE AND FORGOT ABOUT THIS.
YOU ASKED FOR PASSAGE TO ILLIUM -- YOU NEVER MENTIONED THAT YOUR PILGRIMAGE INCLUDED PICKING A FIGHT WITH THE GETH.
IF WE CAN ACCESS ITS MEMORY CORE BEFORE IT SELF-PURGES, WE MIGHT BE ABLE TO FIND OUT WHY THEY'RE --
EDEN PRIME WAS A MAJOR VICTORY. THE BEACON HAS BROUGHT US ONE STEP CLOSER TO FINDING THE CONDUIT.
AND ONE STEP CLOSER TO THE RETURN OF THE REAPERS...
WHAT WAS THAT?
NONE OF IT MAKES SENSE TO ME, BUT I'VE SEEN ENOUGH TO KNOW THAT IT'S TROUBLE.
STAY HERE AND STUDY IT IF YOU WANT. BUT MY SHIP IS LEAVING. NOW.

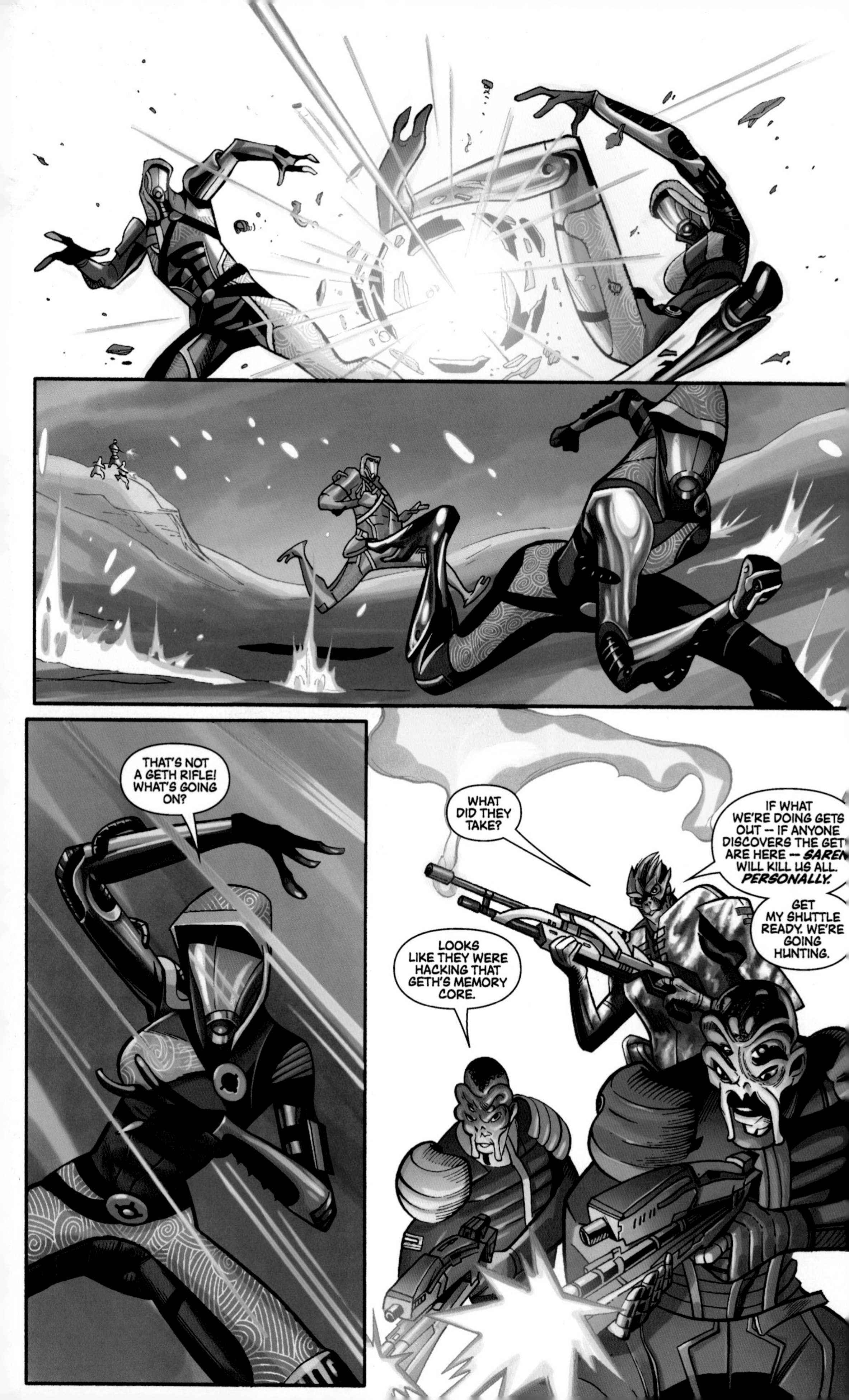
THAT'S NOT A GETH RIFLE! WHAT'S GOING ON?
WHAT DID THEY TAKE?
LOOKS LIKE THEY WERE HACKING THAT GETH'S MEMORY CORE.
IF WHAT WE'RE DOING GETS OUT -- IF ANYONE DISCOVERS THE GETH ARE HERE -- SAREN WILL KILL US ALL. PERSONALLY.
GET MY SHUTTLE READY. WE'RE GOING HUNTING.

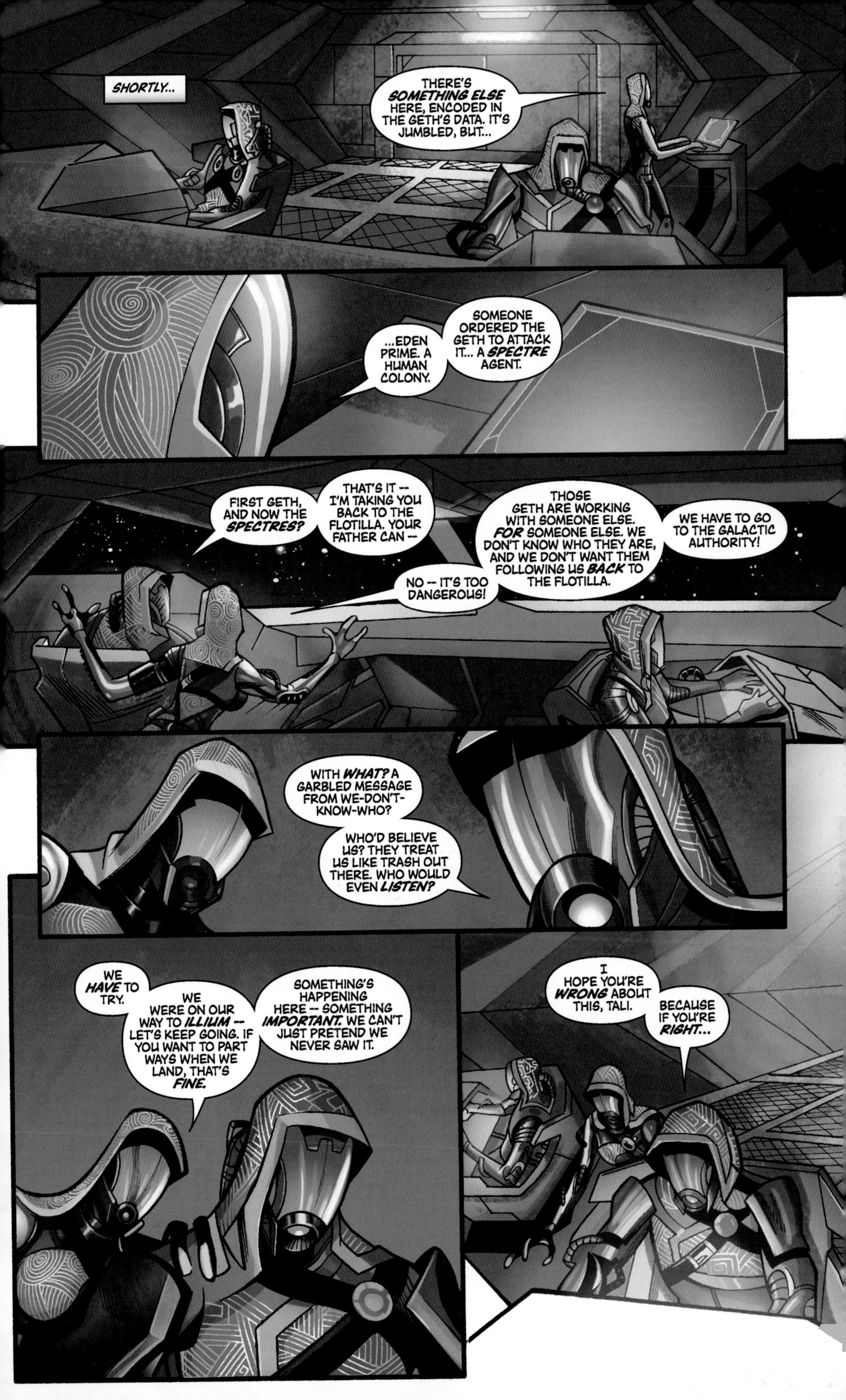
SHORTLY...
THERE'S SOMETHING ELSE HERE, ENCODED IN THE GETH'S DATA. IT'S JUMBLED, BUT...
SOMEONE ORDERED THE GETH TO ATTACK IT... A SPECTRE AGENT.
...EDEN PRIME. A HUMAN COLONY.
FIRST GETH, AND NOW THE SPECTRES?
THAT'S IT -- I'M TAKING YOU BACK TO THE FLOTILLA. YOUR FATHER CAN --
NO -- IT'S TOO DANGEROUS!
THOSE GETH ARE WORKING WITH SOMEONE ELSE. FOR SOMEONE ELSE. WE DON'T KNOW WHO THEY ARE, AND WE DON'T WANT THEM FOLLOWING US BACK TO THE FLOTILLA.
WE HAVE TO GO TO THE GALACTIC AUTHORITY!
WITH WHAT? A GARBLED MESSAGE FROM WE-DON'T-KNOW-WHO?
WHO'D BELIEVE US? THEY TREAT US LIKE TRASH OUT THERE. WHO WOULD EVEN LISTEN?
WE HAVE TO TRY.
SOMETHING'S HAPPENING HERE -- SOMETHING IMPORTANT. WE CAN'T JUST PRETEND WE NEVER SAW IT.
WE WERE ON OUR WAY TO ILLIUM -- LET'S KEEP GOING. IF YOU WANT TO PART WAYS WHEN WE LAND, THAT'S FINE.
I HOPE YOU'RE WRONG ABOUT THIS, TALI.
BECAUSE IF YOU'RE RIGHT...

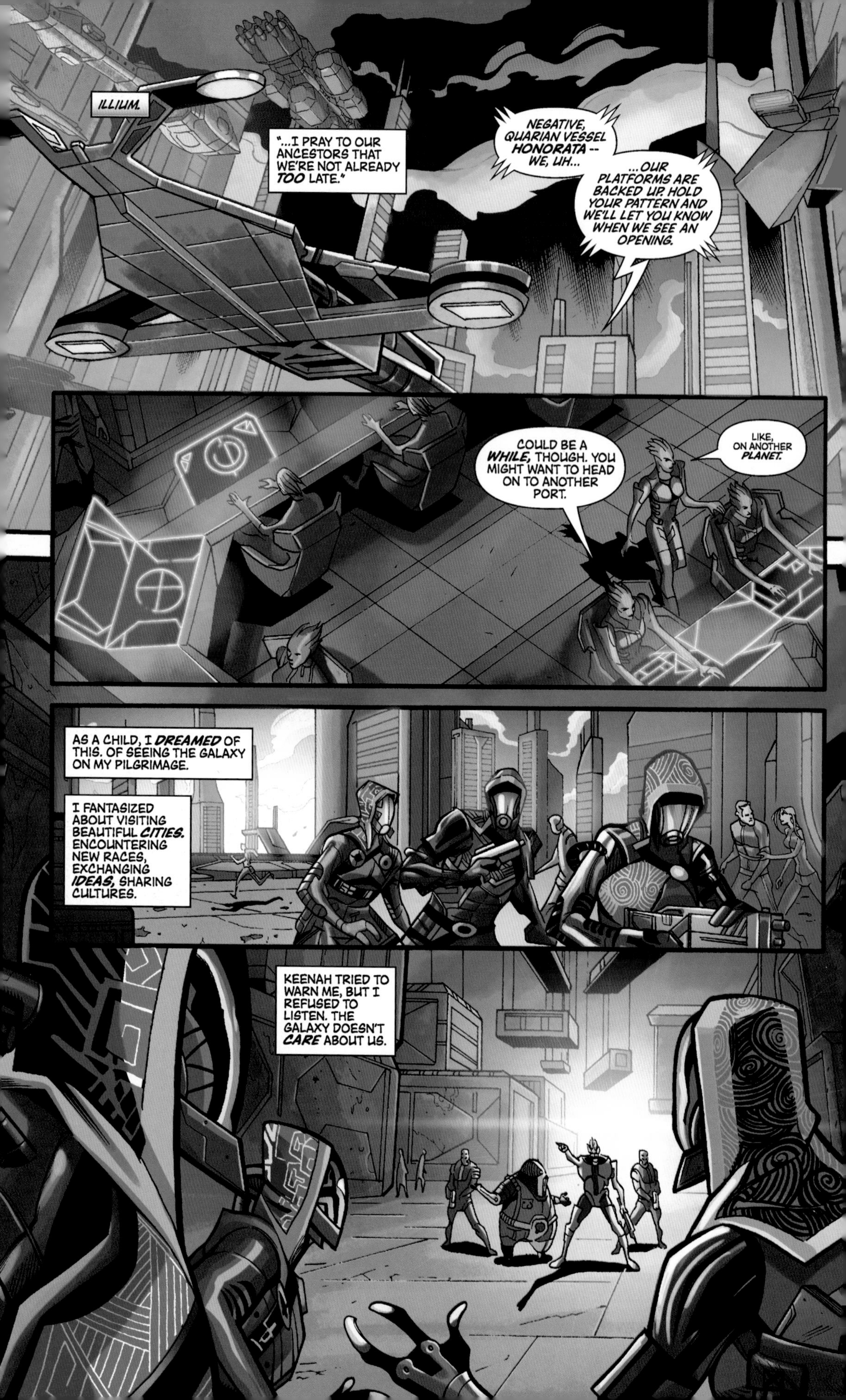

ILLIUM.
"...I PRAY TO OUR ANCESTORS THAT WE'RE NOT ALREADY TOO LATE."
NEGATIVE, QUARIAN VESSEL HONORATA -- WE, UH...
...OUR PLATFORMS ARE BACKED UP. HOLD YOUR PATTERN AND WE'LL LET YOU KNOW WHEN WE SEE AN OPENING.
COULD BE A WHILE, THOUGH. YOU MIGHT WANT TO HEAD ON TO ANOTHER PORT.
LIKE, ON ANOTHER PLANET.
AS A CHILD, I DREAMED OF THIS. OF SEEING THE GALAXY ON MY PILGRIMAGE.
I FANTASIZED ABOUT VISITING BEAUTIFUL CITIES. ENCOUNTERING NEW RACES, EXCHANGING IDEAS, SHARING CULTURES.
KEENAH TRIED TO WARN ME, BUT I REFUSED TO LISTEN. THE GALAXY DOESN'T CARE ABOUT US.

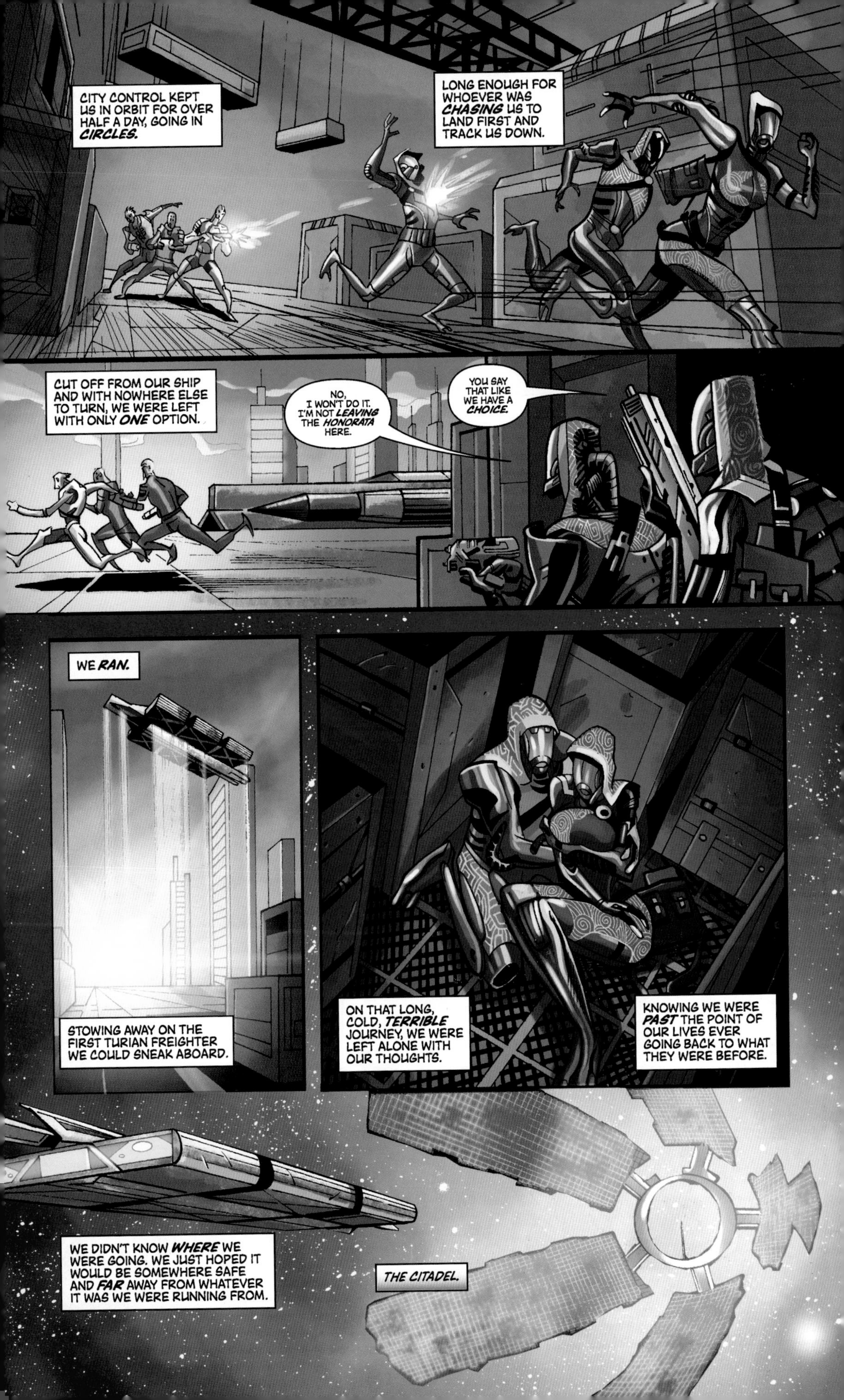

CITY CONTROL KEPT US IN ORBIT FOR OVER HALF A DAY, GOING IN CIRCLES.
LONG ENOUGH FOR WHOEVER WAS CHASING US TO LAND FIRST AND TRACK US DOWN.
CUT OFF FROM OUR SHIP AND WITH NOWHERE ELSE TO TURN, WE WERE LEFT WITH ONLY ONE OPTION.
NO, I WON'T DO IT. I'M NOT LEAVING THE HONORATA HERE.
YOU SAY THAT LIKE WE HAVE A CHOICE.
WE RAN.
STOWING AWAY ON THE FIRST TURIAN FREIGHTER WE COULD SNEAK ABOARD.
ON THAT LONG, COLD, TERRIBLE JOURNEY, WE WERE LEFT ALONE WITH OUR THOUGHTS.
KNOWING WE WERE PAST THE POINT OF OUR LIVES EVER GOING BACK TO WHAT THEY WERE BEFORE.
WE DIDN'T KNOW WHERE WE WERE GOING. WE JUST HOPED IT WOULD BE SOMEWHERE SAFE AND FAR AWAY FROM WHATEVER IT WAS WE WERE RUNNING FROM.
THE CITADEL.

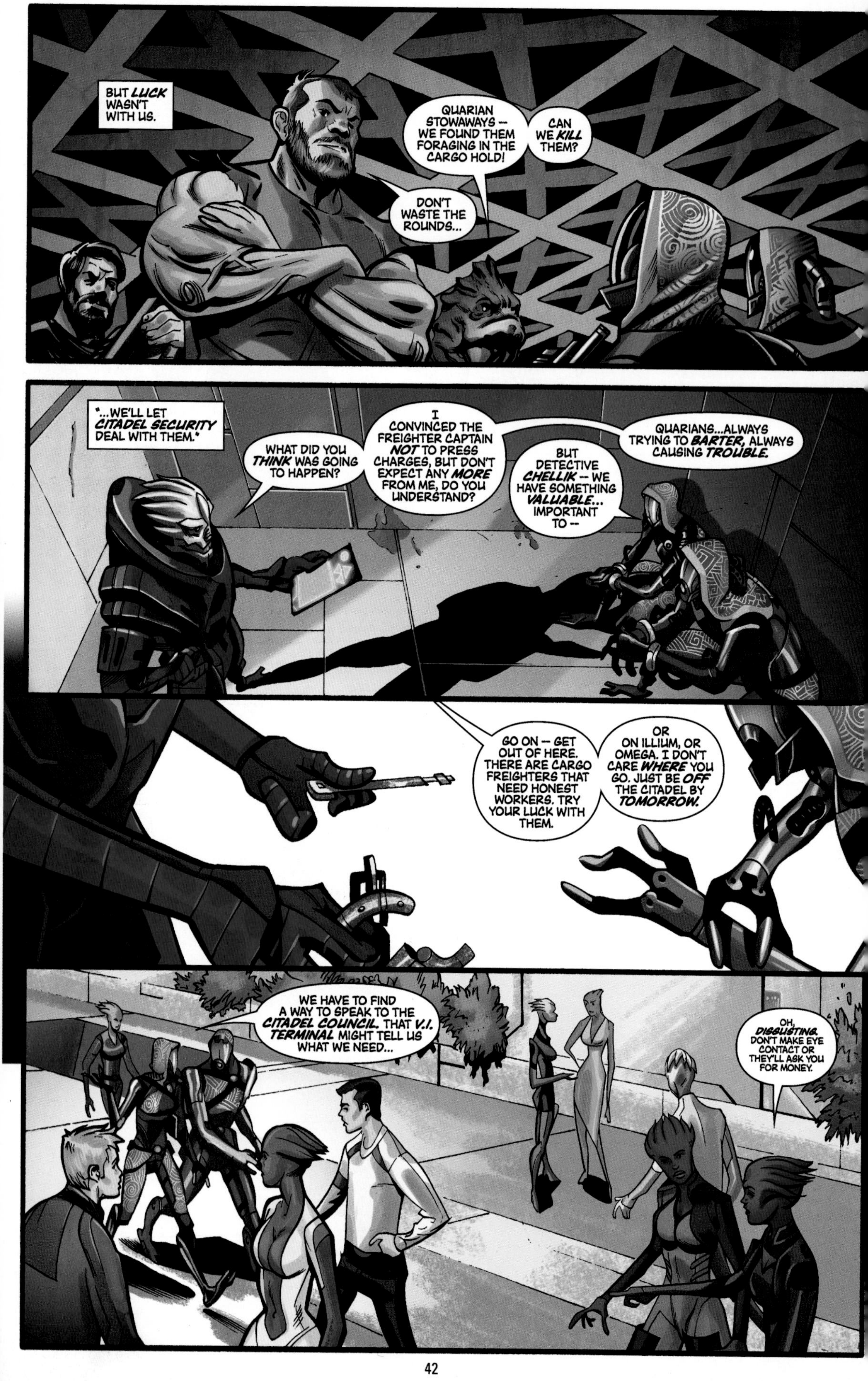
BUT LUCK WASN'T WITH US.
QUARIAN STOWAWAYS -- WE FOUND THEM FORAGING IN THE CARGO HOLD!
CAN WE KILL THEM?
DON'T WASTE THE ROUNDS...
"...WE'LL LET CITADEL SECURITY DEAL WITH THEM."
WHAT DID YOU THINK WAS GOING TO HAPPEN?
I CONVINCED THE FREIGHTER CAPTAIN NOT TO PRESS CHARGES, BUT DON'T EXPECT ANY MORE FROM ME, DO YOU UNDERSTAND?
QUARIANS...ALWAYS TRYING TO BARTER, ALWAYS CAUSING TROUBLE.
BUT DETECTIVE CHELLIK -- WE HAVE SOMETHING VALUABLE... IMPORTANT TO --
GO ON -- GET OUT OF HERE. THERE ARE CARGO FREIGHTERS THAT NEED HONEST WORKERS. TRY YOUR LUCK WITH THEM.
OR ON ILLIUM, OR OMEGA. I DON'T CARE WHERE YOU GO. JUST BE OFF THE CITADEL BY TOMORROW.
WE HAVE TO FIND A WAY TO SPEAK TO THE CITADEL COUNCIL. THAT V.I. TERMINAL MIGHT TELL US WHAT WE NEED...
OH, DISGUSTING. DON'T MAKE EYE CONTACT OR THEY'LL ASK YOU FOR MONEY.

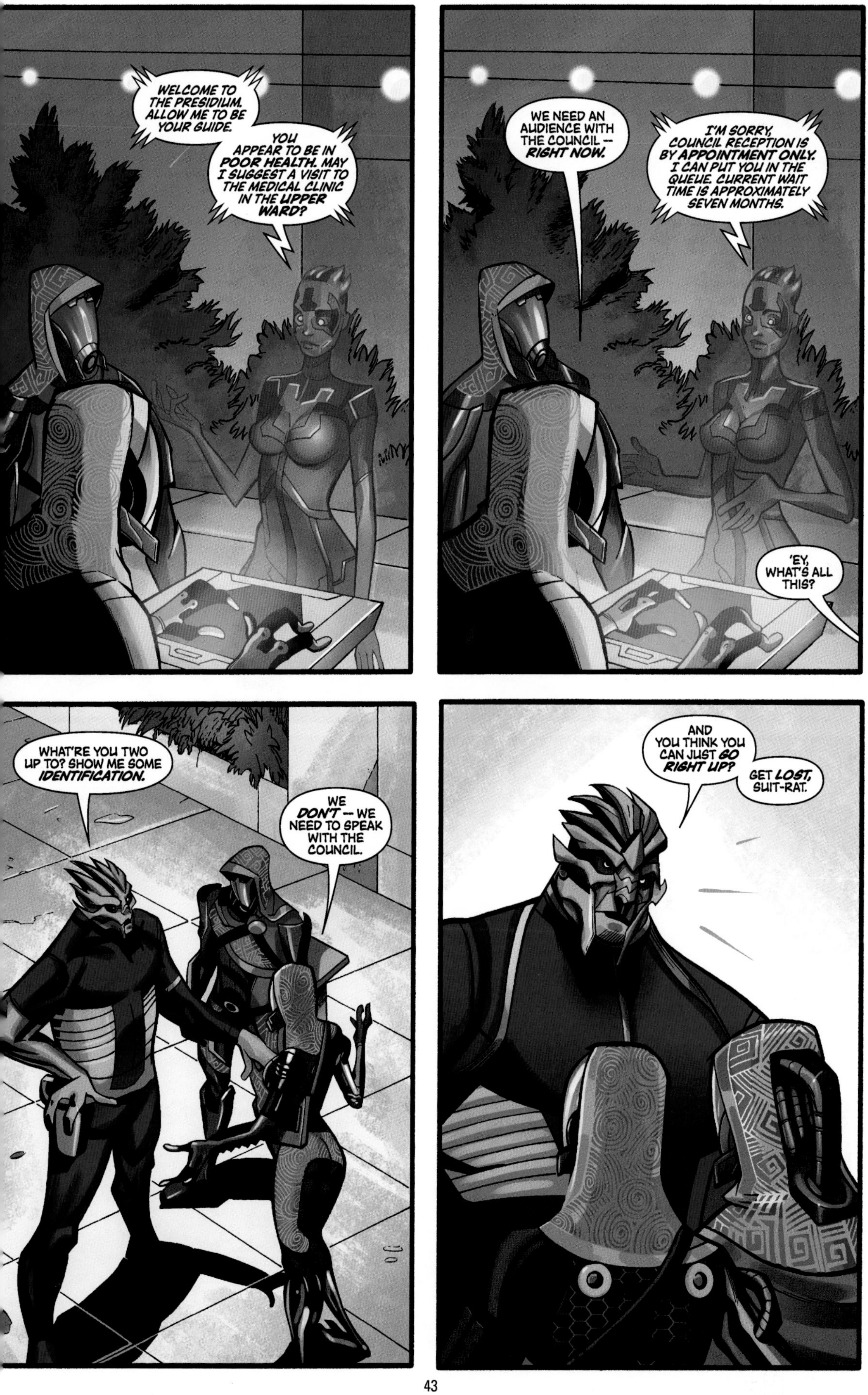
WELCOME TO THE PRESIDIUM. ALLOW ME TO BE YOUR GUIDE.
YOU APPEAR TO BE IN POOR HEALTH. MAY I SUGGEST A VISIT TO THE MEDICAL CLINIC IN THE UPPER WARD?
WE NEED AN AUDIENCE WITH THE COUNCIL -- RIGHT NOW.
I'M SORRY, COUNCIL RECEPTION IS BY APPOINTMENT ONLY. I CAN PUT YOU IN THE QUEUE. CURRENT WAIT TIME IS APPROXIMATELY SEVEN MONTHS.
'EY, WHAT'S ALL THIS?
WHAT'RE YOU TWO UP TO? SHOW ME SOME IDENTIFICATION.
WE DON'T -- WE NEED TO SPEAK WITH THE COUNCIL.
AND YOU THINK YOU CAN JUST GO RIGHT UP?
GET LOST, SUIT-RAT.

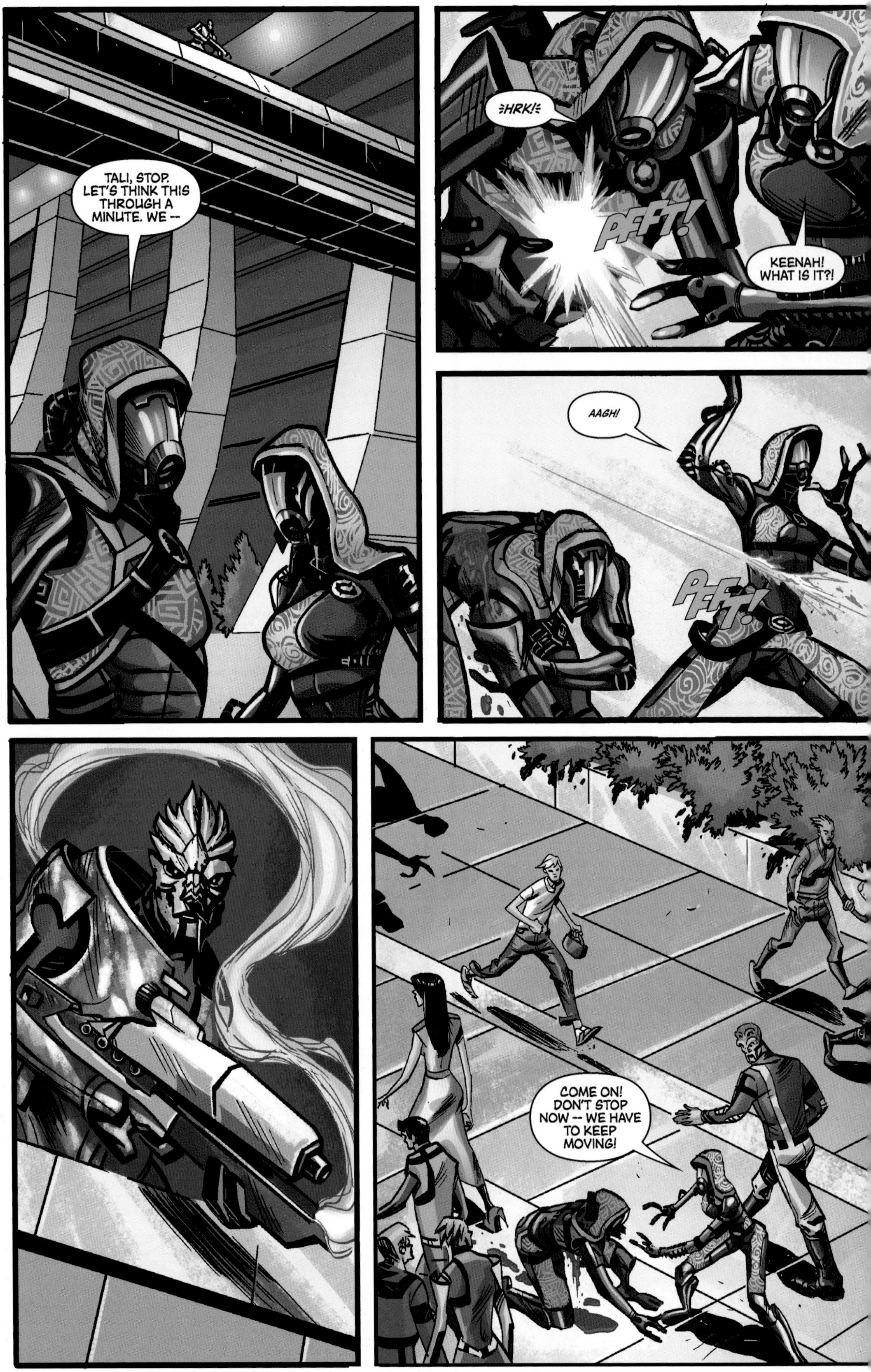

TALI, STOP. LET'S THINK THIS THROUGH A MINUTE. WE --
HRK!
PFFT!
KEENAH! WHAT IS IT?!
AAGH!
PFFT!
COME ON! DON'T STOP NOW -- WE HAVE TO KEEP MOVING!

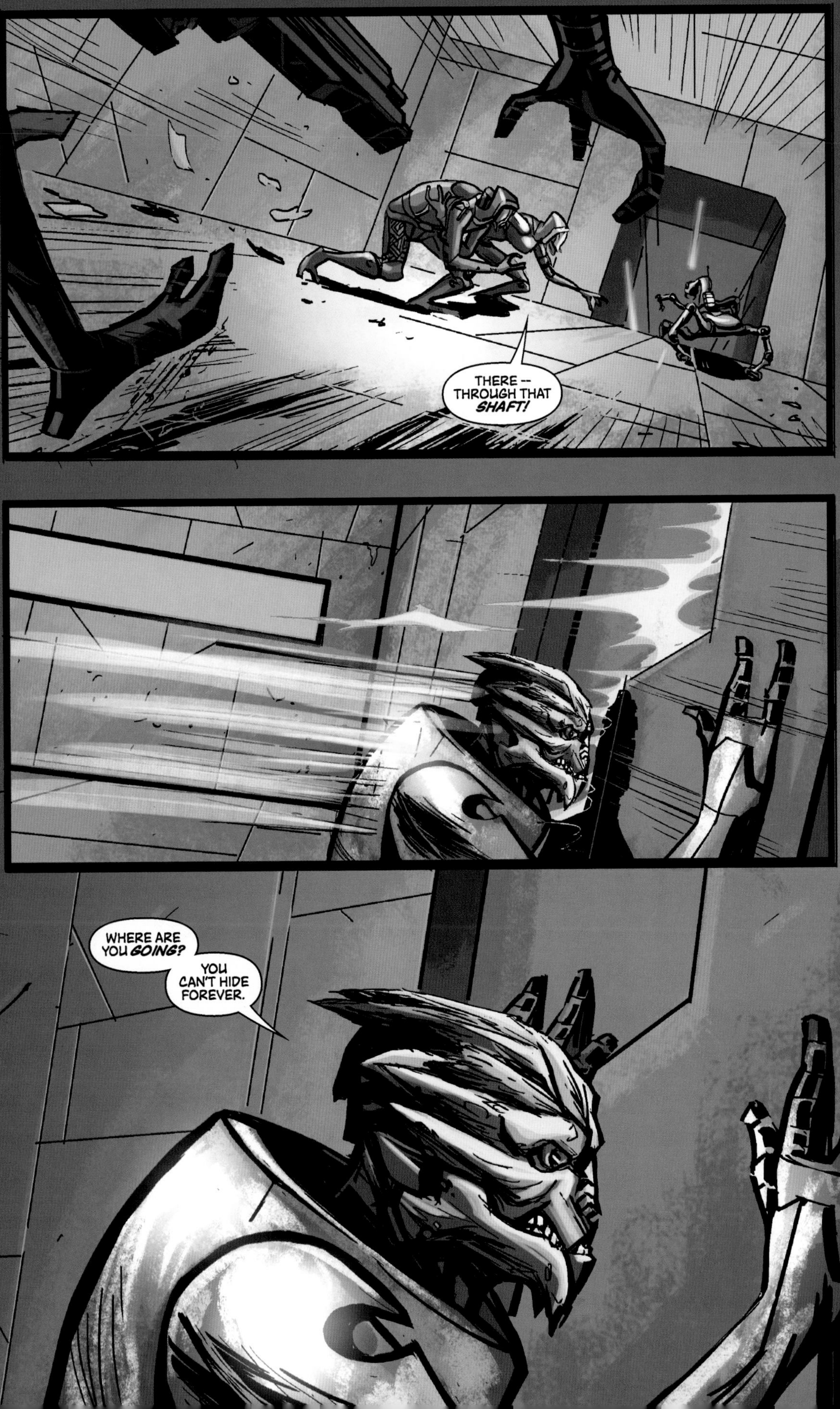
THERE -- THROUGH THAT *SHAFT!*
WHERE ARE YOU *GOING?*
YOU CAN'T HIDE FOREVER.

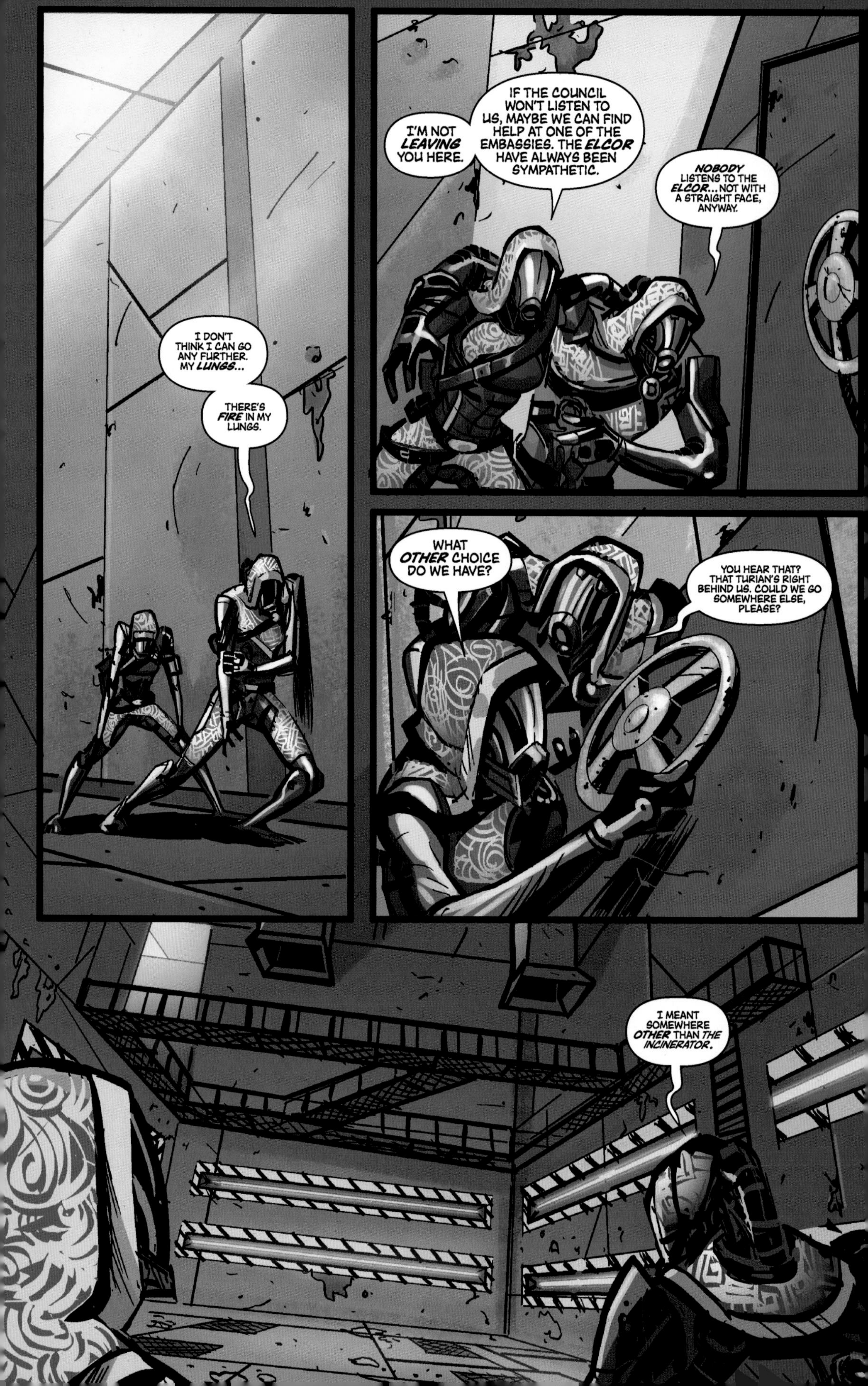
I DON'T THINK I CAN GO ANY FURTHER. MY *LUNGS...*
THERE'S *FIRE* IN MY LUNGS.
I'M NOT *LEAVING* YOU HERE.
IF THE COUNCIL WON'T LISTEN TO US, MAYBE WE CAN FIND HELP AT ONE OF THE EMBASSIES. THE *ELCOR* HAVE ALWAYS BEEN SYMPATHETIC.
NOBODY LISTENS TO THE *ELCOR...* NOT WITH A STRAIGHT FACE, ANYWAY.
WHAT *OTHER* CHOICE DO WE HAVE?
YOU HEAR THAT? THAT TURIAN'S RIGHT BEHIND US. COULD WE GO SOMEWHERE ELSE, PLEASE?
I MEANT SOMEWHERE *OTHER* THAN *THE INCINERATOR.*

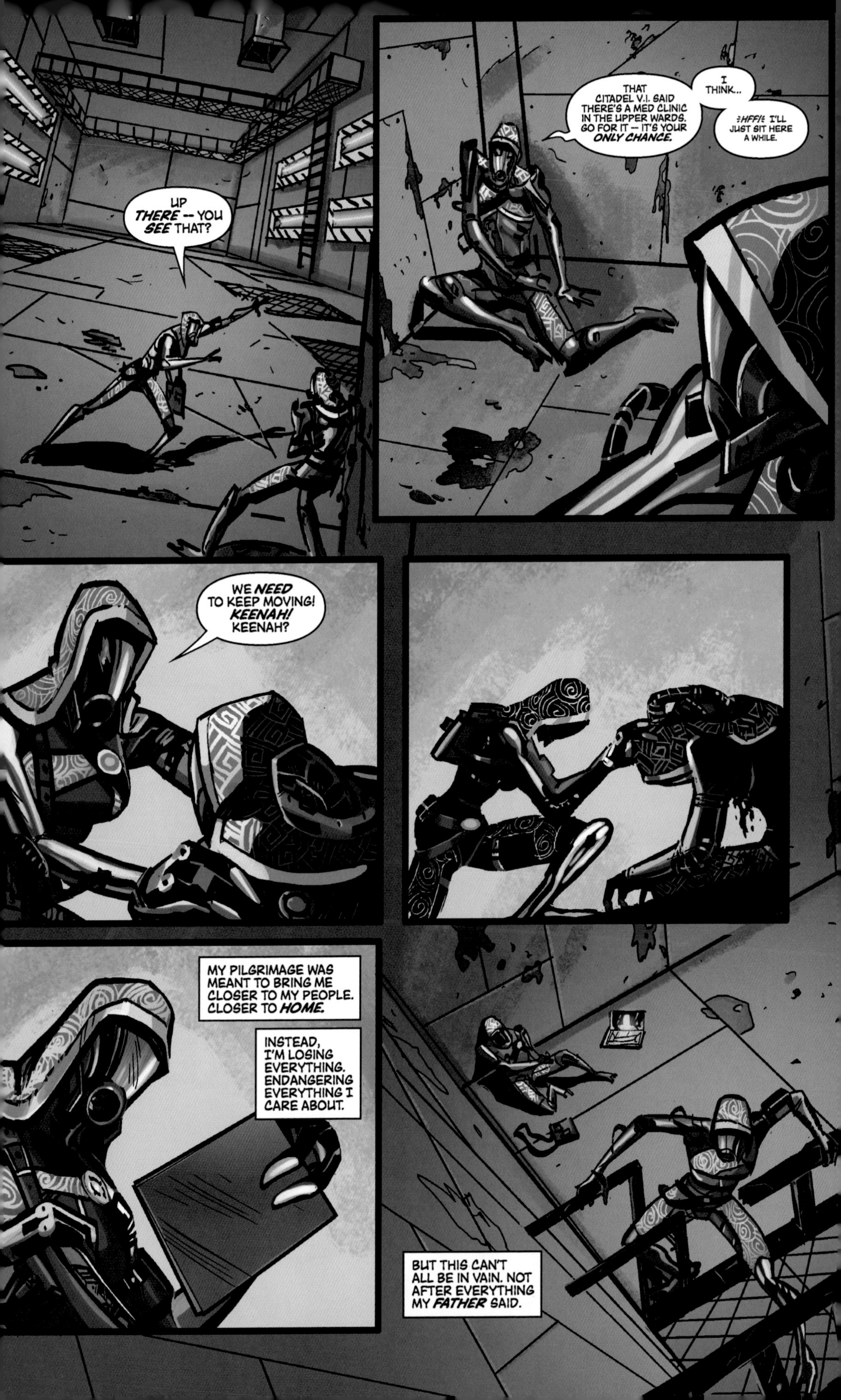
UP THERE -- YOU SEE THAT?
THAT CITADEL V.I. SAID THERE'S A MED CLINIC IN THE UPPER WARDS. GO FOR IT -- IT'S YOUR ONLY CHANCE.
I THINK...
HFF! I'LL JUST SIT HERE A WHILE.
WE NEED TO KEEP MOVING! KEENAH! KEENAH?
MY PILGRIMAGE WAS MEANT TO BRING ME CLOSER TO MY PEOPLE. CLOSER TO HOME.
INSTEAD, I'M LOSING EVERYTHING. ENDANGERING EVERYTHING I CARE ABOUT.
BUT THIS CAN'T ALL BE IN VAIN. NOT AFTER EVERYTHING MY FATHER SAID.

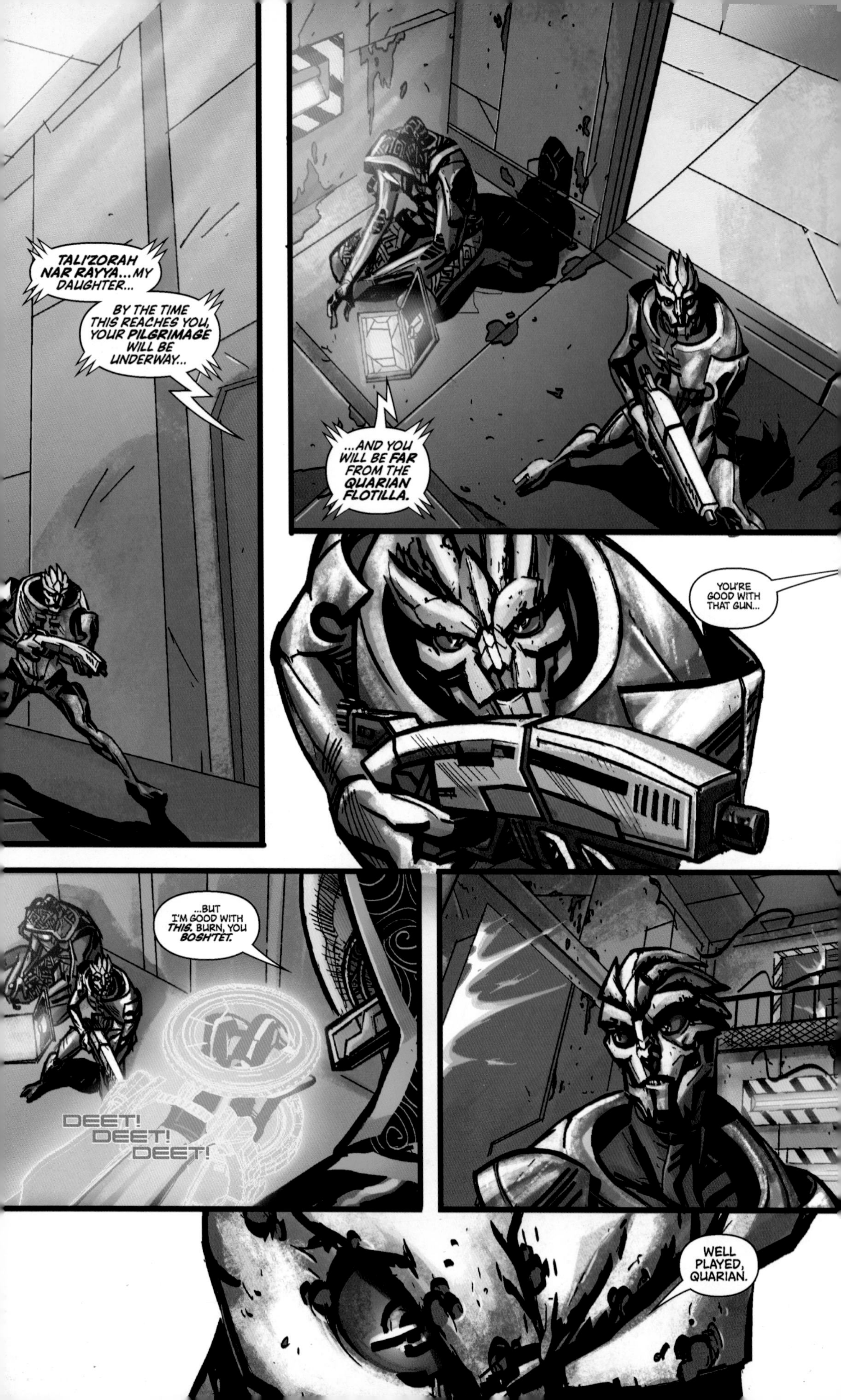
TALI'ZORAH NAR RAYYA... MY DAUGHTER...
BY THE TIME THIS REACHES YOU, YOUR PILGRIMAGE WILL BE UNDERWAY...
...AND YOU WILL BE FAR FROM THE QUARIAN FLOTILLA.
YOU'RE GOOD WITH THAT GUN...
...BUT I'M GOOD WITH THIS. BURN, YOU BOSH'TET.
DEET! DEET! DEET!
WELL PLAYED, QUARIAN.

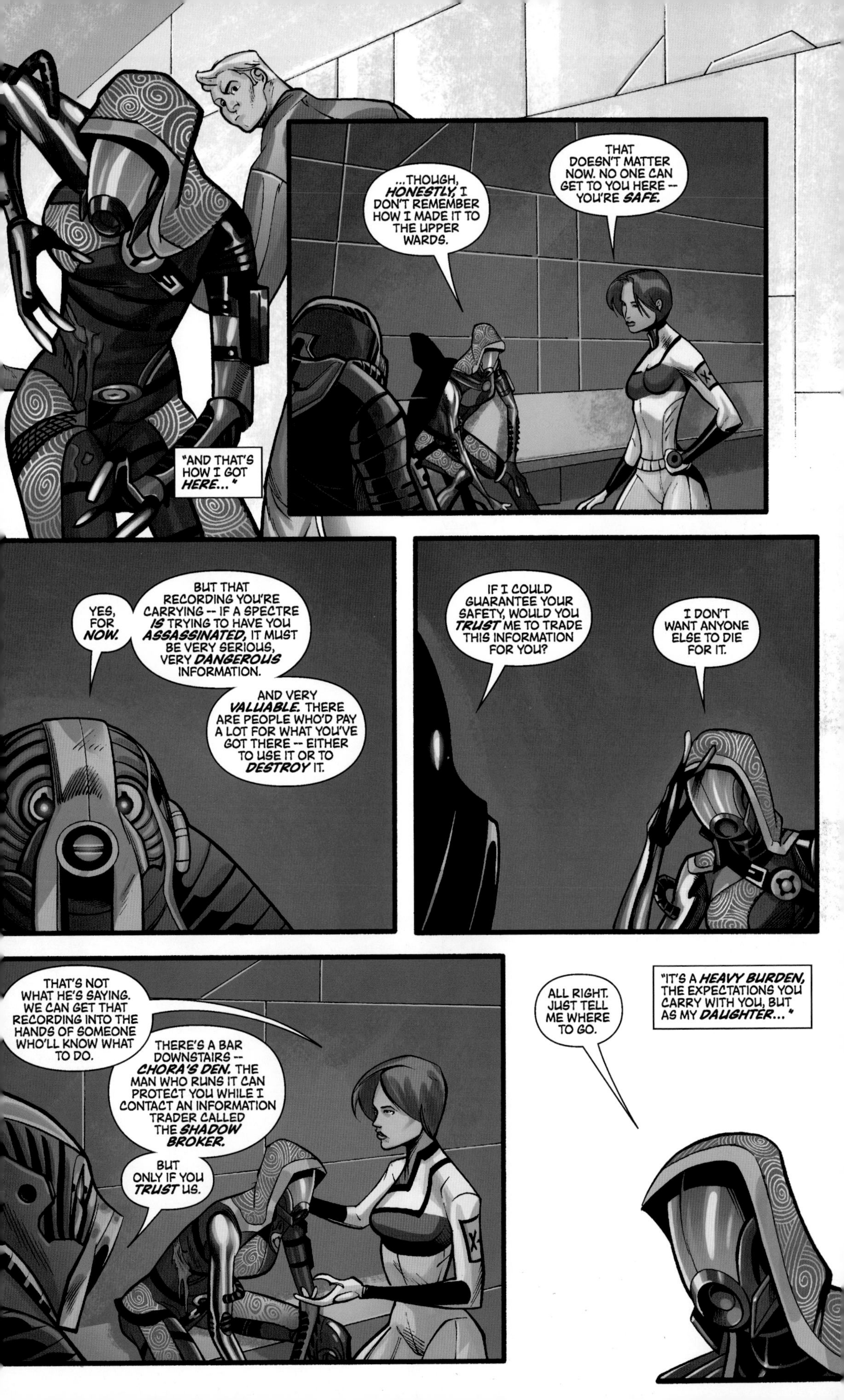
"AND THAT'S HOW I GOT *HERE...*"
...THOUGH, *HONESTLY,* I DON'T REMEMBER HOW I MADE IT TO THE UPPER WARDS.
THAT DOESN'T MATTER NOW. NO ONE CAN GET TO YOU HERE -- YOU'RE *SAFE.*
YES, FOR *NOW.*
BUT THAT RECORDING YOU'RE CARRYING -- IF A SPECTRE *IS* TRYING TO HAVE YOU *ASSASSINATED,* IT MUST BE VERY SERIOUS, VERY *DANGEROUS* INFORMATION.
AND VERY *VALUABLE.* THERE ARE PEOPLE WHO'D PAY A LOT FOR WHAT YOU'VE GOT THERE -- EITHER TO USE IT OR TO *DESTROY* IT.
IF I COULD GUARANTEE YOUR SAFETY, WOULD YOU *TRUST* ME TO TRADE THIS INFORMATION FOR YOU?
I DON'T WANT ANYONE ELSE TO DIE FOR IT.
THAT'S NOT WHAT HE'S SAYING. WE CAN GET THAT RECORDING INTO THE HANDS OF SOMEONE WHO'LL KNOW WHAT TO DO.
THERE'S A BAR DOWNSTAIRS -- *CHORA'S DEN.* THE MAN WHO RUNS IT CAN PROTECT YOU WHILE I CONTACT AN INFORMATION TRADER CALLED THE *SHADOW BROKER.*
BUT ONLY IF YOU *TRUST* US.
ALL RIGHT. JUST TELL ME WHERE TO GO.
"IT'S A *HEAVY BURDEN,* THE EXPECTATIONS YOU CARRY WITH YOU, BUT AS MY *DAUGHTER...*"

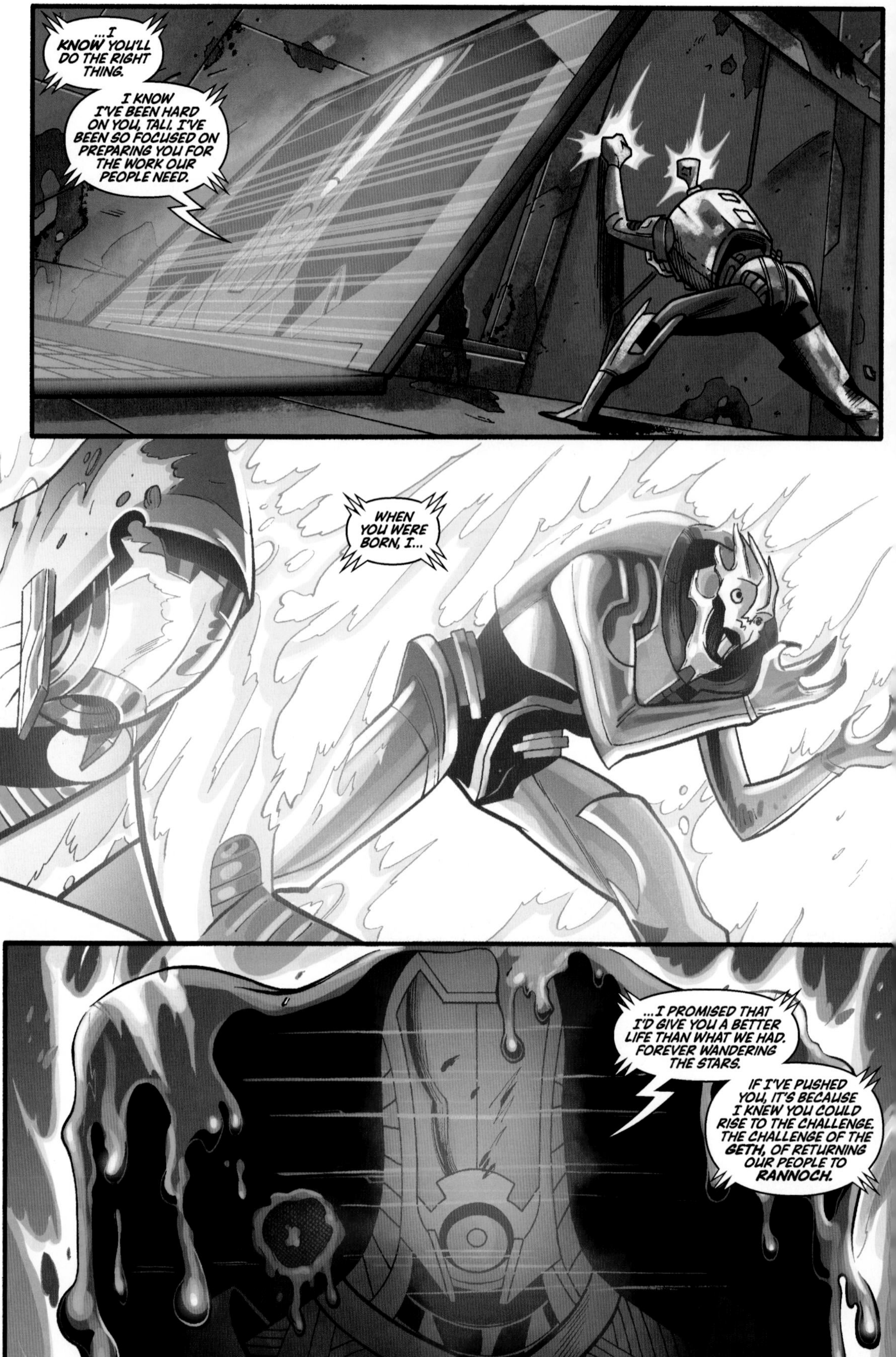
...I KNOW YOU'LL DO THE RIGHT THING.
I KNOW I'VE BEEN HARD ON YOU, TALI. I'VE BEEN SO FOCUSED ON PREPARING YOU FOR THE WORK OUR PEOPLE NEED.
WHEN YOU WERE BORN, I...
...I PROMISED THAT I'D GIVE YOU A BETTER LIFE THAN WHAT WE HAD. FOREVER WANDERING THE STARS.
IF I'VE PUSHED YOU, IT'S BECAUSE I KNEW YOU COULD RISE TO THE CHALLENGE. THE CHALLENGE OF THE GETH, OF RETURNING OUR PEOPLE TO RANNOCH.

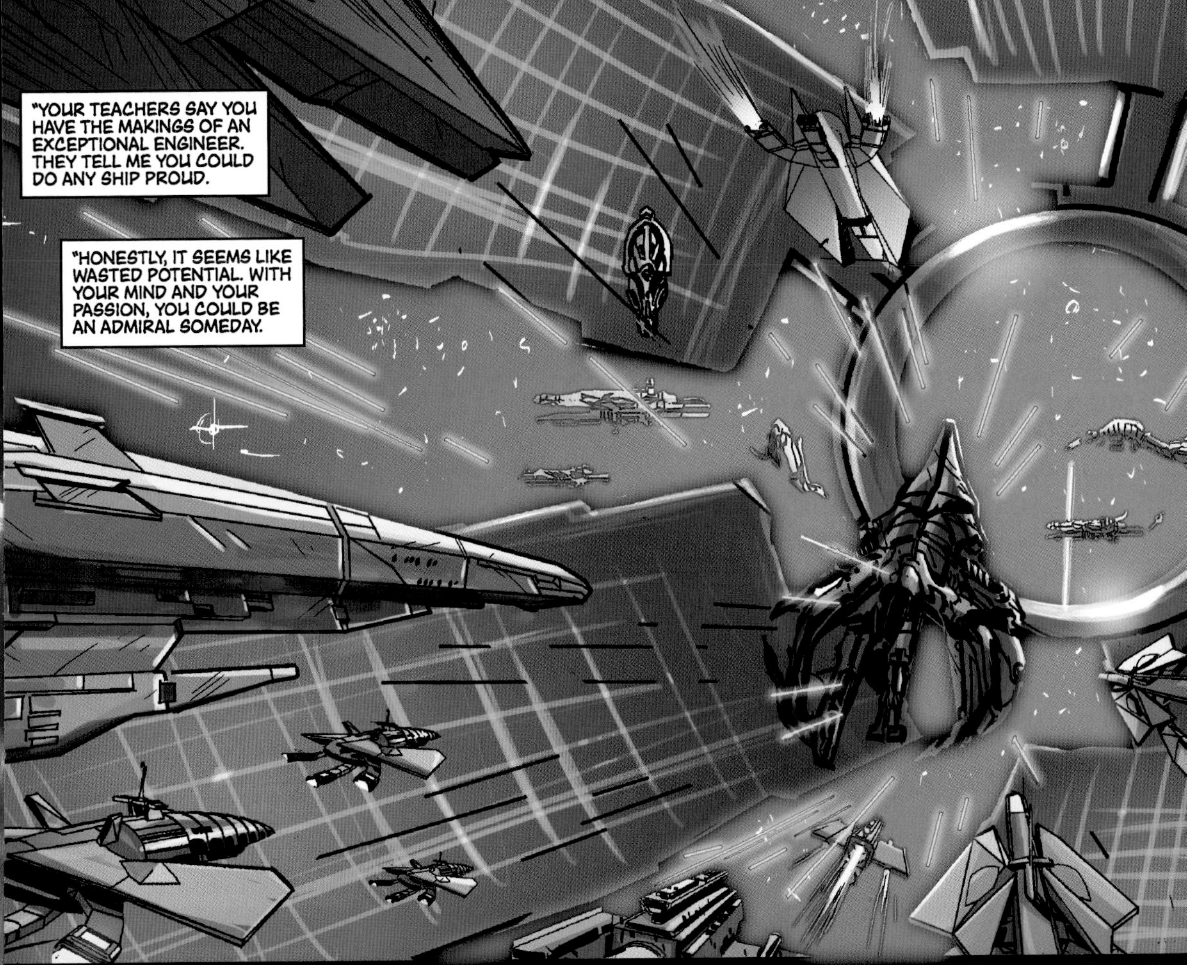
"YOUR TEACHERS SAY YOU HAVE THE MAKINGS OF AN EXCEPTIONAL ENGINEER. THEY TELL ME YOU COULD DO ANY SHIP PROUD.
"HONESTLY, IT SEEMS LIKE WASTED POTENTIAL. WITH YOUR MIND AND YOUR PASSION, YOU COULD BE AN ADMIRAL SOMEDAY.

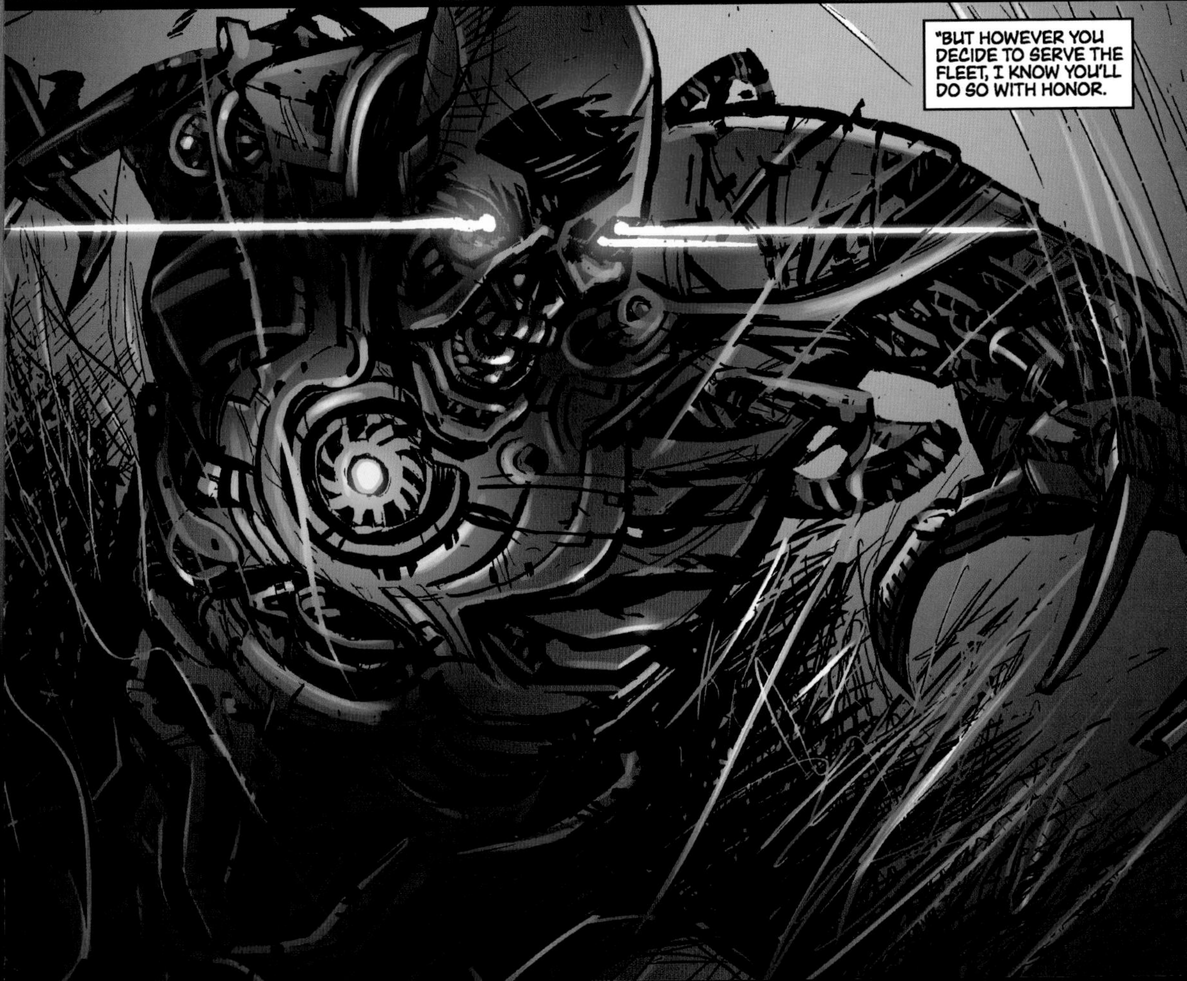
"BUT HOWEVER YOU DECIDE TO SERVE THE FLEET, I KNOW YOU'LL DO SO WITH HONOR.

STORY
MAC WALTERS AND
JOHN DOMBROW

SCRIPT
JEREMY BARLOW

ART
GARRY BROWN

COLORS
MICHAEL ATIYEH

LETTERING
MICHAEL HEISLER

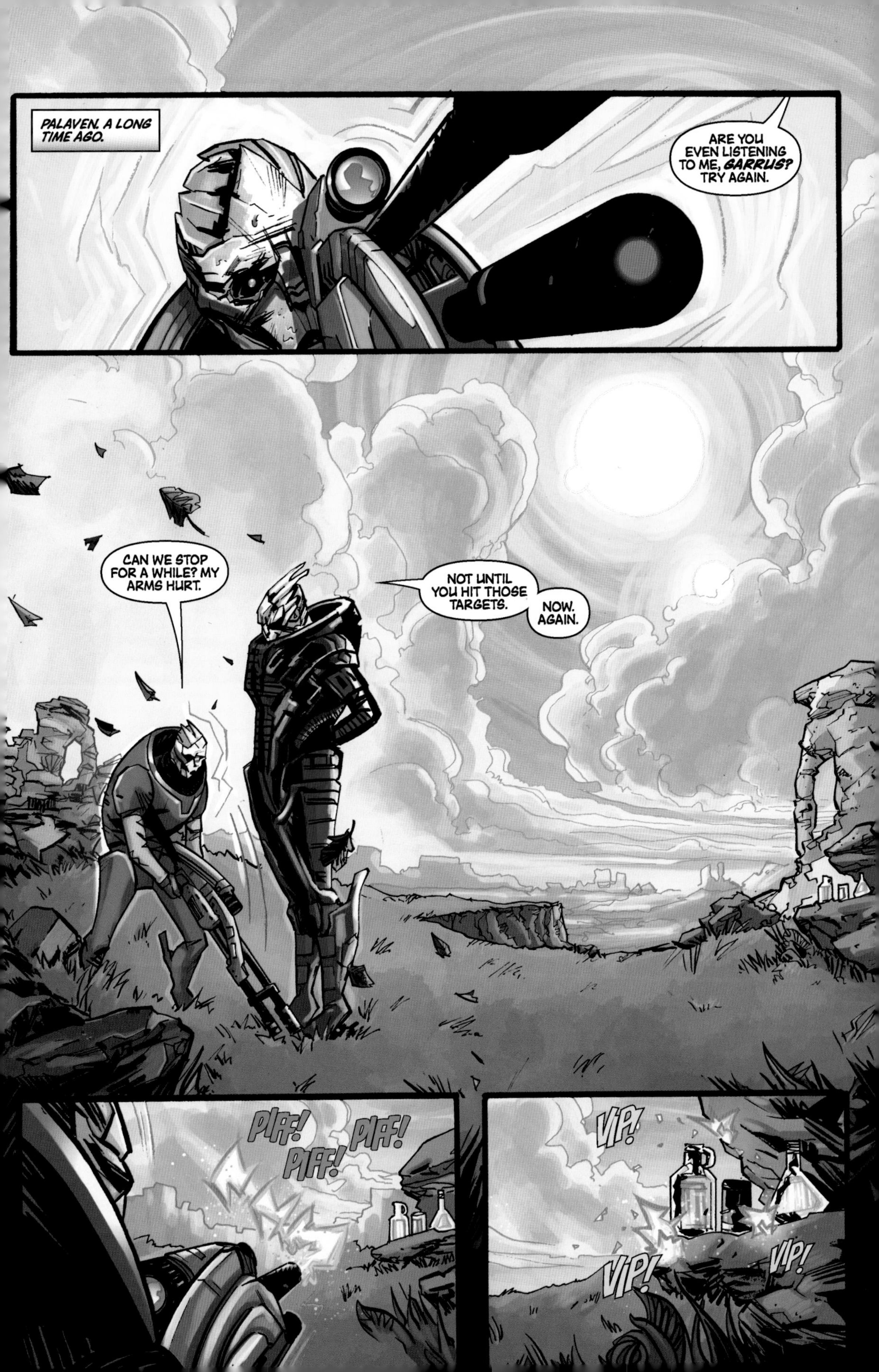
PALAVEN. A LONG TIME AGO.
ARE YOU EVEN LISTENING TO ME, GARRUS? TRY AGAIN.
CAN WE STOP FOR A WHILE? MY ARMS HURT.
NOT UNTIL YOU HIT THOSE TARGETS.
NOW. AGAIN.
PIFF! PIFF! PIFF!
VIP! VIP! VIP!

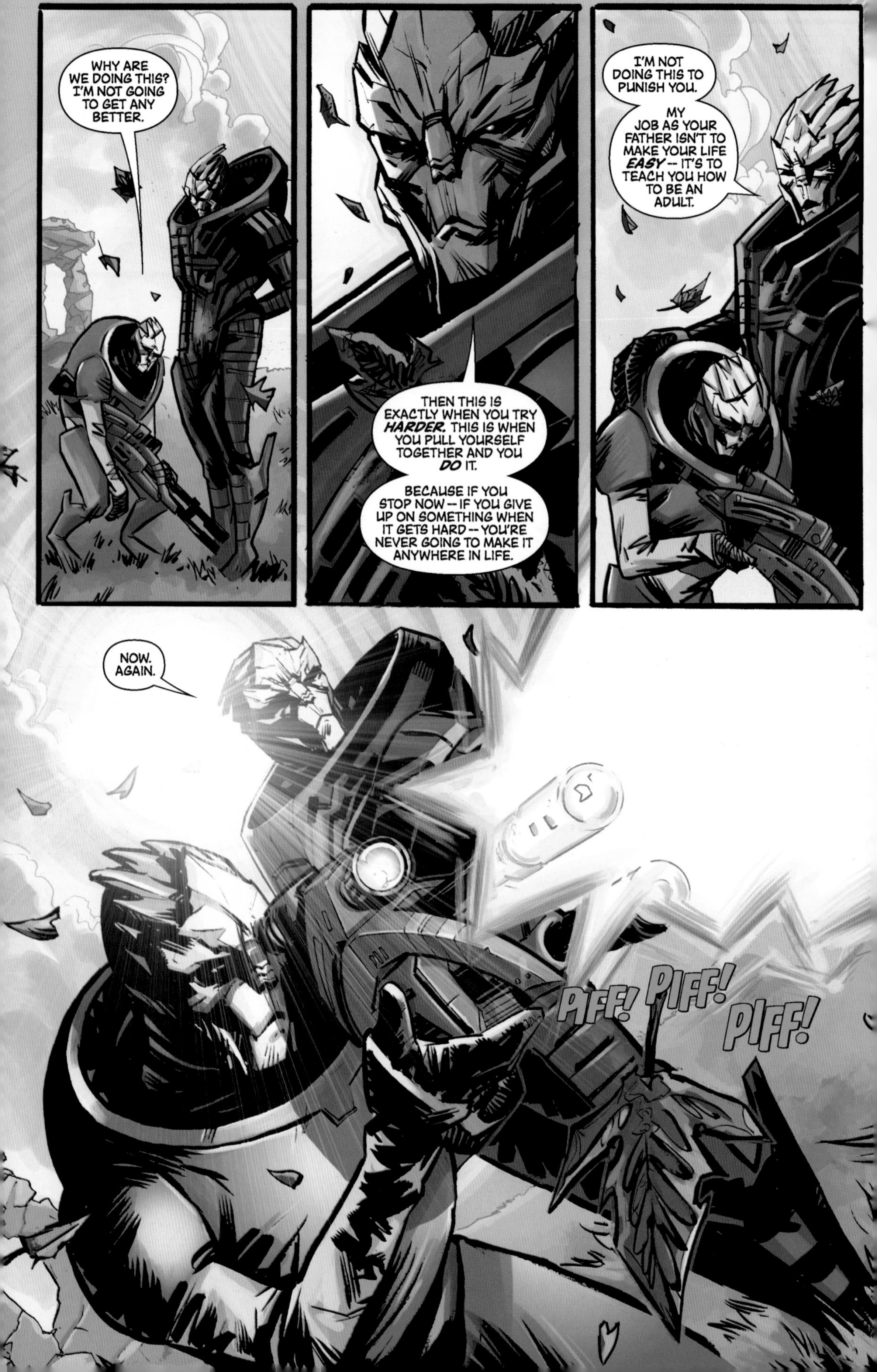
WHY ARE WE DOING THIS? I'M NOT GOING TO GET ANY BETTER.
THEN THIS IS EXACTLY WHEN YOU TRY HARDER. THIS IS WHEN YOU PULL YOURSELF TOGETHER AND YOU DO IT.
BECAUSE IF YOU STOP NOW -- IF YOU GIVE UP ON SOMETHING WHEN IT GETS HARD -- YOU'RE NEVER GOING TO MAKE IT ANYWHERE IN LIFE.
I'M NOT DOING THIS TO PUNISH YOU.
MY JOB AS YOUR FATHER ISN'T TO MAKE YOUR LIFE EASY -- IT'S TO TEACH YOU HOW TO BE AN ADULT.
NOW. AGAIN.
PIFF! PIFF! PIFF!

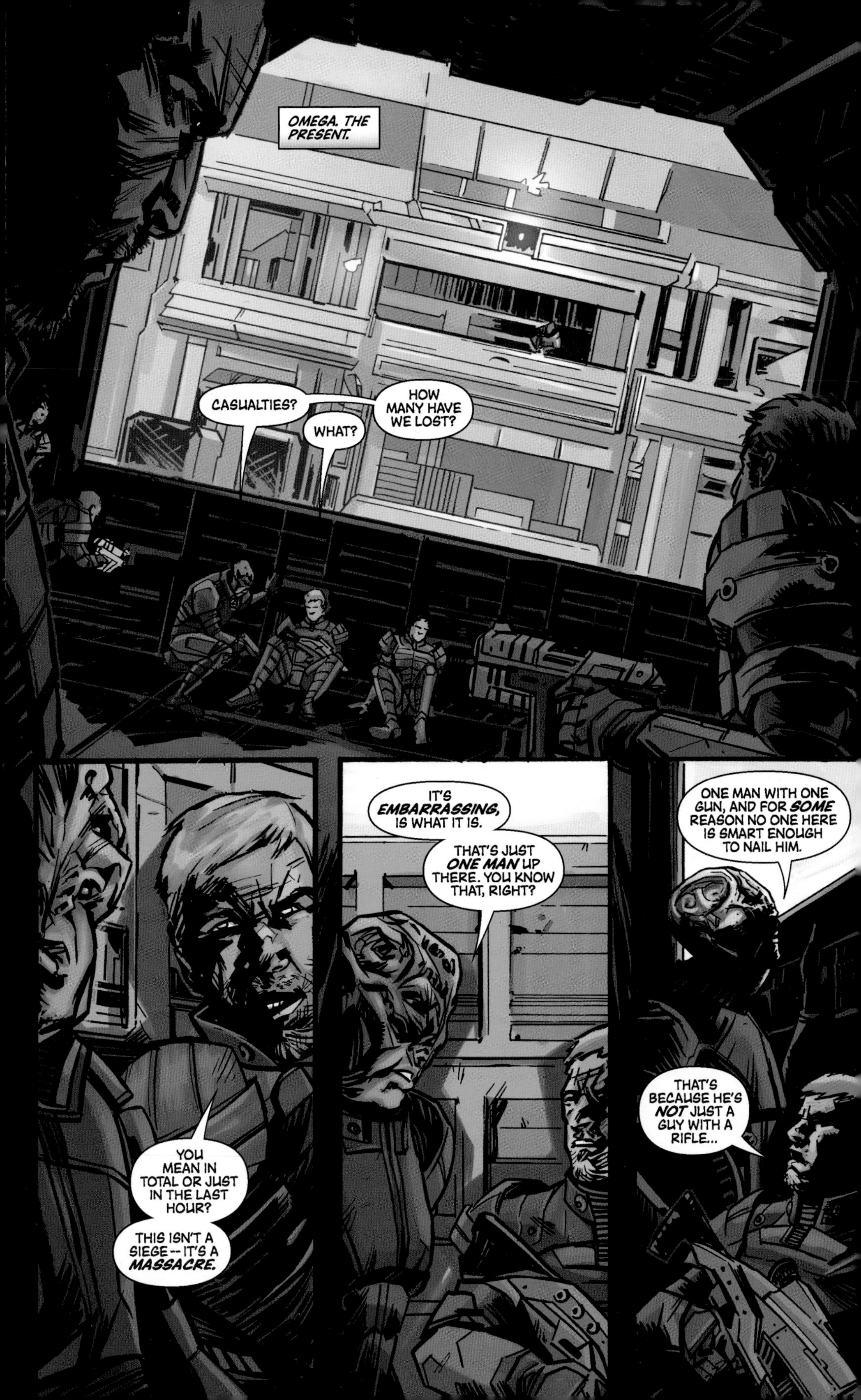
OMEGA. THE PRESENT.
CASUALTIES?
WHAT?
HOW MANY HAVE WE LOST?
YOU MEAN IN TOTAL OR JUST IN THE LAST HOUR?
THIS ISN'T A SIEGE -- IT'S A MASSACRE.
IT'S EMBARRASSING, IS WHAT IT IS.
THAT'S JUST ONE MAN UP THERE. YOU KNOW THAT, RIGHT?
ONE MAN WITH ONE GUN, AND FOR SOME REASON NO ONE HERE IS SMART ENOUGH TO NAIL HIM.
THAT'S BECAUSE HE'S NOT JUST A GUY WITH A RIFLE...

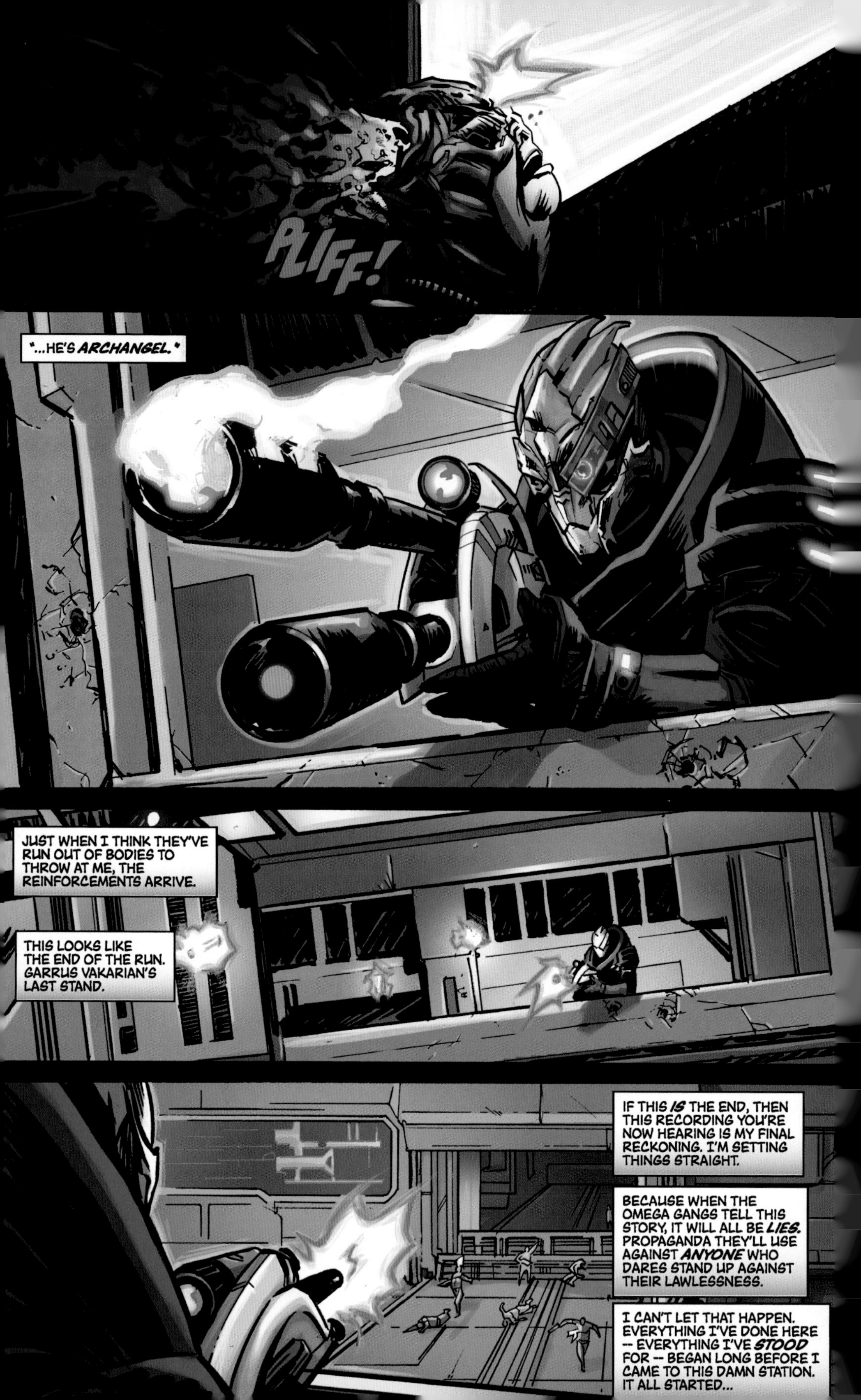
PLIFF!
"...HE'S ARCHANGEL."
JUST WHEN I THINK THEY'VE RUN OUT OF BODIES TO THROW AT ME, THE REINFORCEMENTS ARRIVE.
THIS LOOKS LIKE THE END OF THE RUN. GARRUS VAKARIAN'S LAST STAND.
IF THIS IS THE END, THEN THIS RECORDING YOU'RE NOW HEARING IS MY FINAL RECKONING. I'M SETTING THINGS STRAIGHT.
BECAUSE WHEN THE OMEGA GANGS TELL THIS STORY, IT WILL ALL BE LIES. PROPAGANDA THEY'LL USE AGAINST ANYONE WHO DARES STAND UP AGAINST THEIR LAWLESSNESS.
I CAN'T LET THAT HAPPEN. EVERYTHING I'VE DONE HERE -- EVERYTHING I'VE STOOD FOR -- BEGAN LONG BEFORE I CAME TO THIS DAMN STATION. IT ALL STARTED...

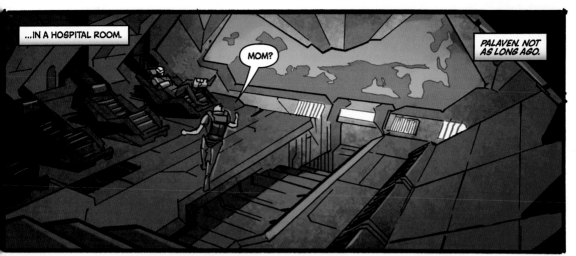

...IN A HOSPITAL ROOM.

MOM?

PALAVEN. NOT AS LONG AGO.

WHAT *HAPPENED?*

IT WAS A HIT AND RUN, THEY SAID. I DON'T REMEMBER.

DON'T WORRY ABOUT ME -- I'LL BE *FINE.*

WHAT ARE *YOU* DOING HERE? YOUR STUDY ABROAD SHUTTLE SHOULD'VE LEFT *HOURS* AGO.

I...I DIDN'T GO. I HEARD YOU WERE HERE AND I LEFT PORT.

IT DOESN'T MATTER. IT WAS JUST A *DUMB TRIP,* ANYWAY. I...

I CAN TAKE CARE OF YOU NOW. WE BOTH KNOW DAD WON'T LEAVE WORK TO BE HERE.

NOW, THAT'S NOT FAIR. HE CALLED HERE THE MOMENT HE HEARD, AND HE'S WORRIED SICK.

IN THE TIME IT WOULD TAKE FOR HIM TO TRAVEL ALL THE WAY BACK HERE FROM THE *CITADEL,* THESE OLD BONES WOULD BE *HEALED.* I TOLD HIM TO STAY PUT.

BUT, GARRUS...

...YOUR SCHOLARSHIP WAS FOR *THIS SUMMER* ONLY. IF YOU DON'T GO, YOU LOSE IT. YOU WON'T QUALIFY AGAIN.

THIS WAS YOUR *DREAM.* I WON'T LET YOU WASTE IT. YOU *GET BACK THERE* AND --

IT'S TOO LATE, THEY'RE GONE. AND IF I LEFT YOU HERE, LIKE THIS, I WOULDN'T DESERVE IT.

I WOULDN'T FORGIVE MYSELF.

DAD WAS *RIGHT.* HE ALWAYS SAID HE'D SUPPORT ME IN WHATEVER I WANTED TO DO...

...BUT HE *MEANT* AS LONG AS IT'S WHAT HE WANTED ME TO DO.

IT'S TIME I FACED FACTS. I'M AN OFFICER'S SON...

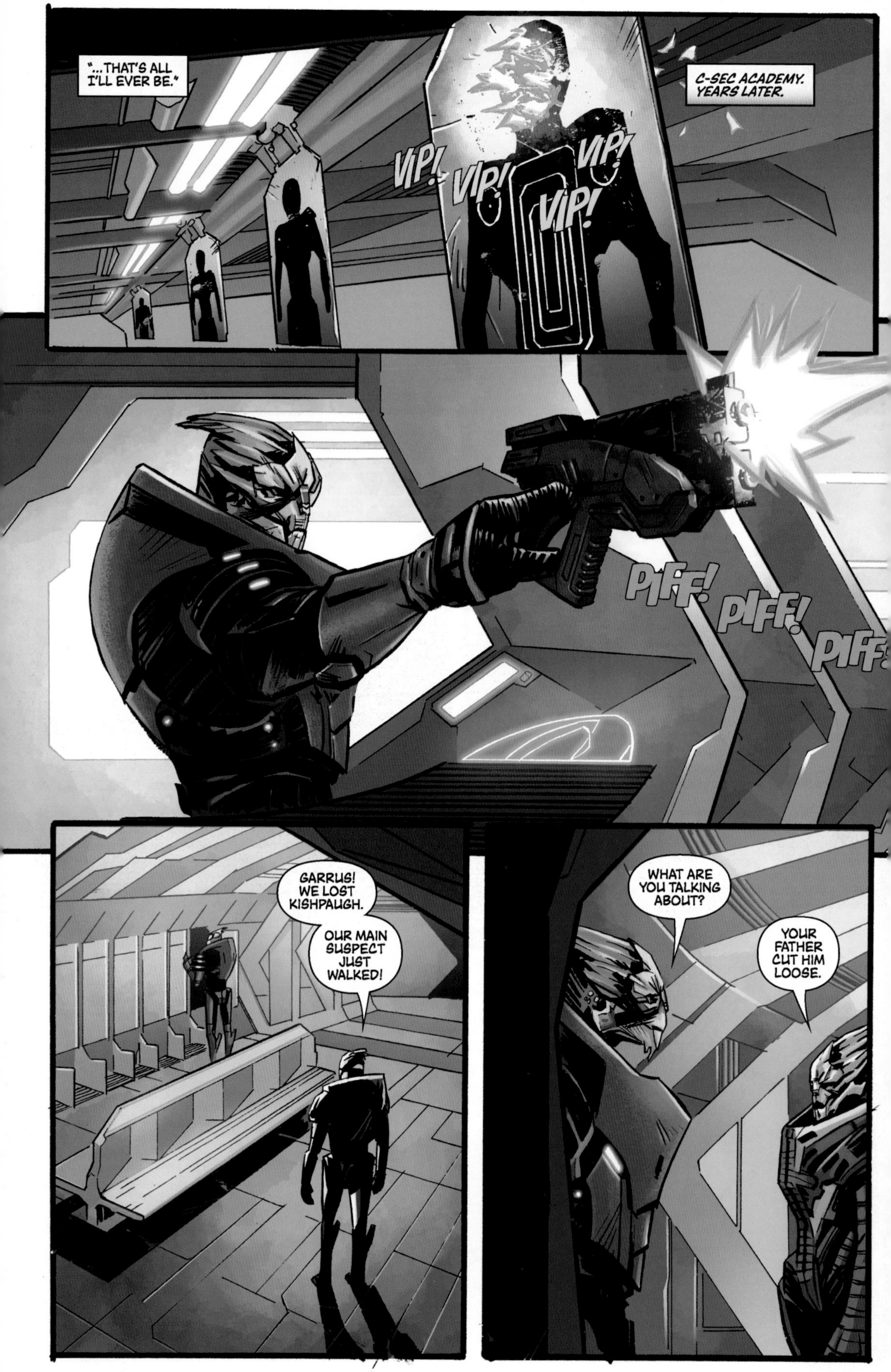
"...THAT'S ALL I'LL EVER BE."
C-SEC ACADEMY. YEARS LATER.
VIP!
VIP!
VIP!
VIP!
PIFF!
PIFF!
PIFF!
GARRUS! WE LOST KISHPAUGH.
OUR MAIN SUSPECT JUST WALKED!
WHAT ARE YOU TALKING ABOUT?
YOUR FATHER CUT HIM LOOSE.

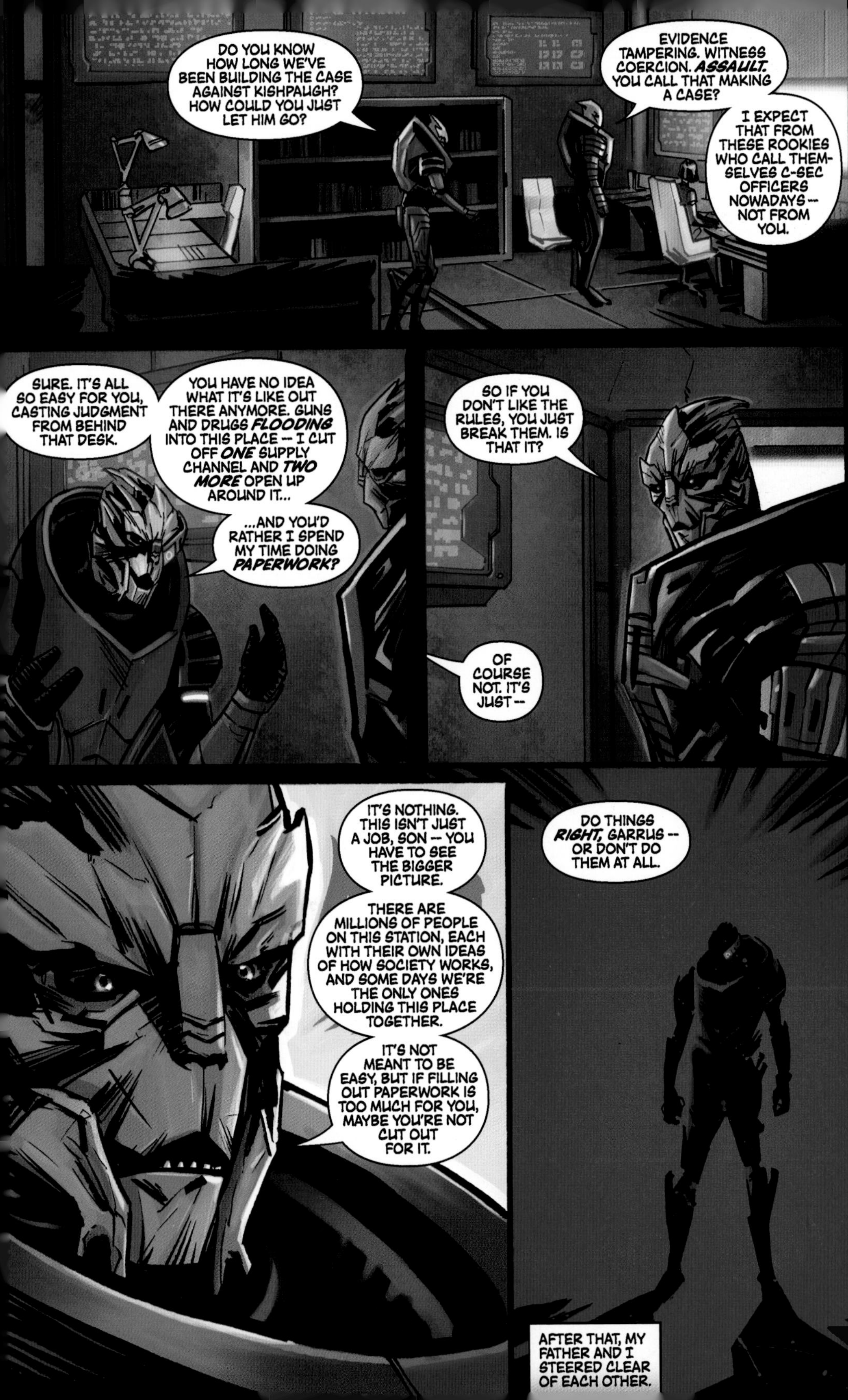

DO YOU KNOW HOW LONG WE'VE BEEN BUILDING THE CASE AGAINST KISHPAUGH? HOW COULD YOU JUST LET HIM GO?
EVIDENCE TAMPERING. WITNESS COERCION. ***ASSAULT.*** YOU CALL THAT MAKING A CASE?
I EXPECT THAT FROM THESE ROOKIES WHO CALL THEM-SELVES C-SEC OFFICERS NOWADAYS -- NOT FROM YOU.
SURE. IT'S ALL SO EASY FOR YOU, CASTING JUDGMENT FROM BEHIND THAT DESK.
YOU HAVE NO IDEA WHAT IT'S LIKE OUT THERE ANYMORE. GUNS AND DRUGS ***FLOODING*** INTO THIS PLACE -- I CUT OFF ***ONE*** SUPPLY CHANNEL AND ***TWO MORE*** OPEN UP AROUND IT...
...AND YOU'D RATHER I SPEND MY TIME DOING ***PAPERWORK?***
SO IF YOU DON'T LIKE THE RULES, YOU JUST BREAK THEM. IS THAT IT?
OF COURSE NOT. IT'S JUST --
IT'S NOTHING. THIS ISN'T JUST A JOB, SON -- YOU HAVE TO SEE THE BIGGER PICTURE.
THERE ARE MILLIONS OF PEOPLE ON THIS STATION, EACH WITH THEIR OWN IDEAS OF HOW SOCIETY WORKS, AND SOME DAYS WE'RE THE ONLY ONES HOLDING THIS PLACE TOGETHER.
IT'S NOT MEANT TO BE EASY, BUT IF FILLING OUT PAPERWORK IS TOO MUCH FOR YOU, MAYBE YOU'RE NOT CUT OUT FOR IT.
DO THINGS ***RIGHT,*** GARRUS -- OR DON'T DO THEM AT ALL.
AFTER THAT, MY FATHER AND I STEERED CLEAR OF EACH OTHER.

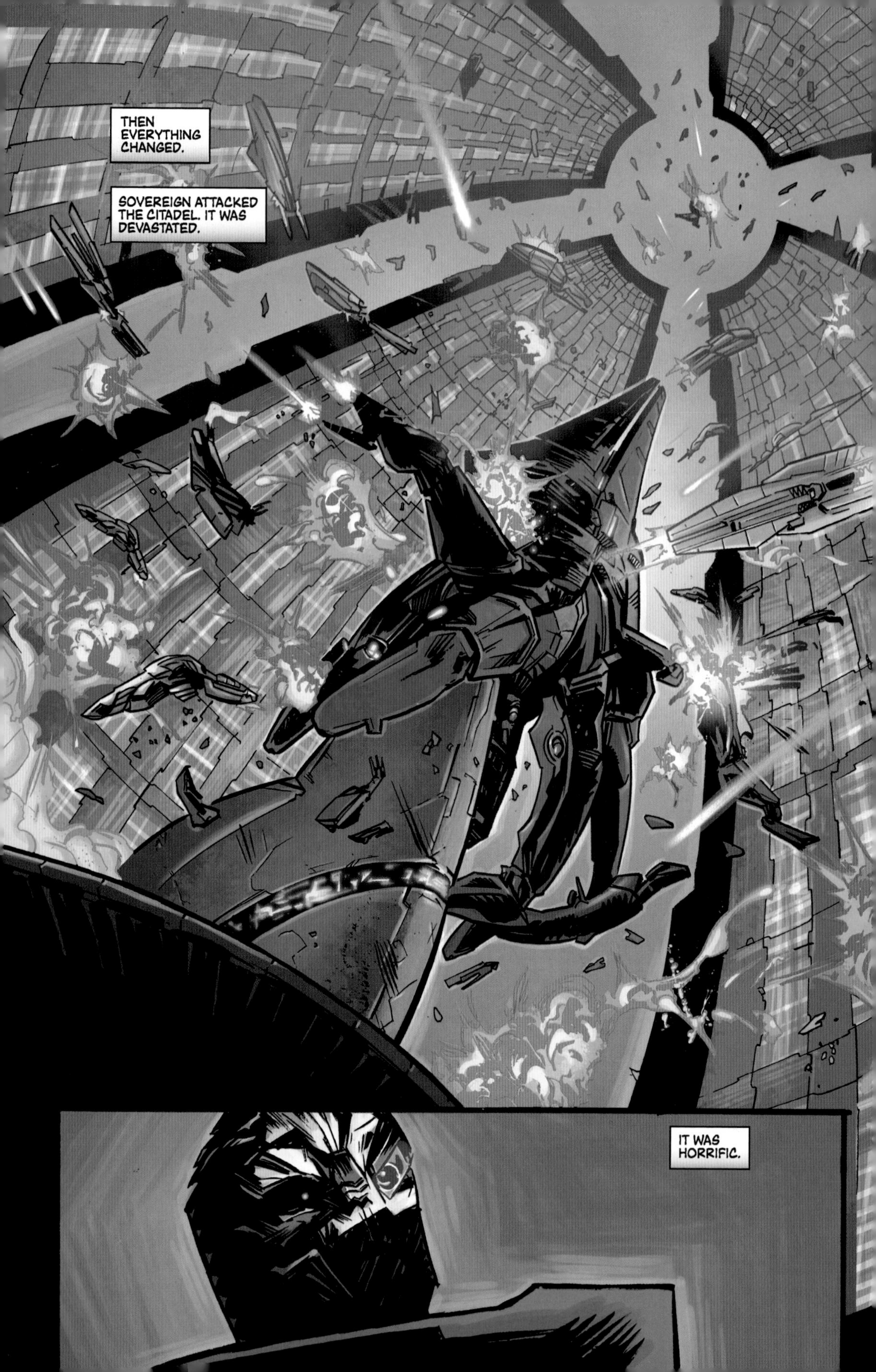
THEN EVERYTHING CHANGED.
SOVEREIGN ATTACKED THE CITADEL. IT WAS DEVASTATED.
IT WAS HORRIFIC.

AT THE TIME, IT WAS HARD TO SEE A WAY FORWARD.

THE CITADEL WOULD BE REPAIRED, BUT HOW COULD LIFE EVER GO BACK TO WHAT IT WAS BEFORE?

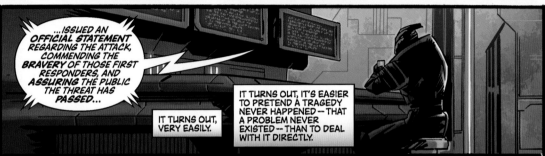

...ISSUED AN *OFFICIAL STATEMENT* REGARDING THE ATTACK, COMMENDING THE *BRAVERY* OF THOSE FIRST RESPONDERS, AND *ASSURING* THE PUBLIC THE THREAT HAS *PASSED*...

IT TURNS OUT, VERY EASILY.

IT TURNS OUT, IT'S EASIER TO PRETEND A TRAGEDY NEVER HAPPENED -- THAT A PROBLEM NEVER EXISTED -- THAN TO DEAL WITH IT DIRECTLY.

EASIER FOR *SOME.* FED UP WITH ALL THE CITADEL'S *RED TAPE,* I TOOK MATTERS INTO MY OWN HANDS.

YOU CAN'T DO THIS TO ME. YOU'RE C-SEC!

NOT ANYMORE, *KISHPAUGH.* I'M FREE TO BREAK THE LAW JUST LIKE *YOU,* AND I'M *LOOKING* FOR A REASON TO DO IT.

THAT POISON YOU PUSH -- WHERE DO YOU GET IT? WHO'S YOUR SUPPLIER?

OMEGA. IT ALL COMES FROM OMEGA.

YOU DON'T WANT TO WORK WITH US ANYMORE, THAT'S *FINE.*

BUT YOU KEEP PUSHING THE *LINE* LIKE THIS, VAKARIAN, AND I'LL LOCK YOU UP *MYSELF.* YOU HEAR ME?

LOUD AND CLEAR. DON'T WORRY -- I'M NOT YOUR PROBLEM ANYMORE...

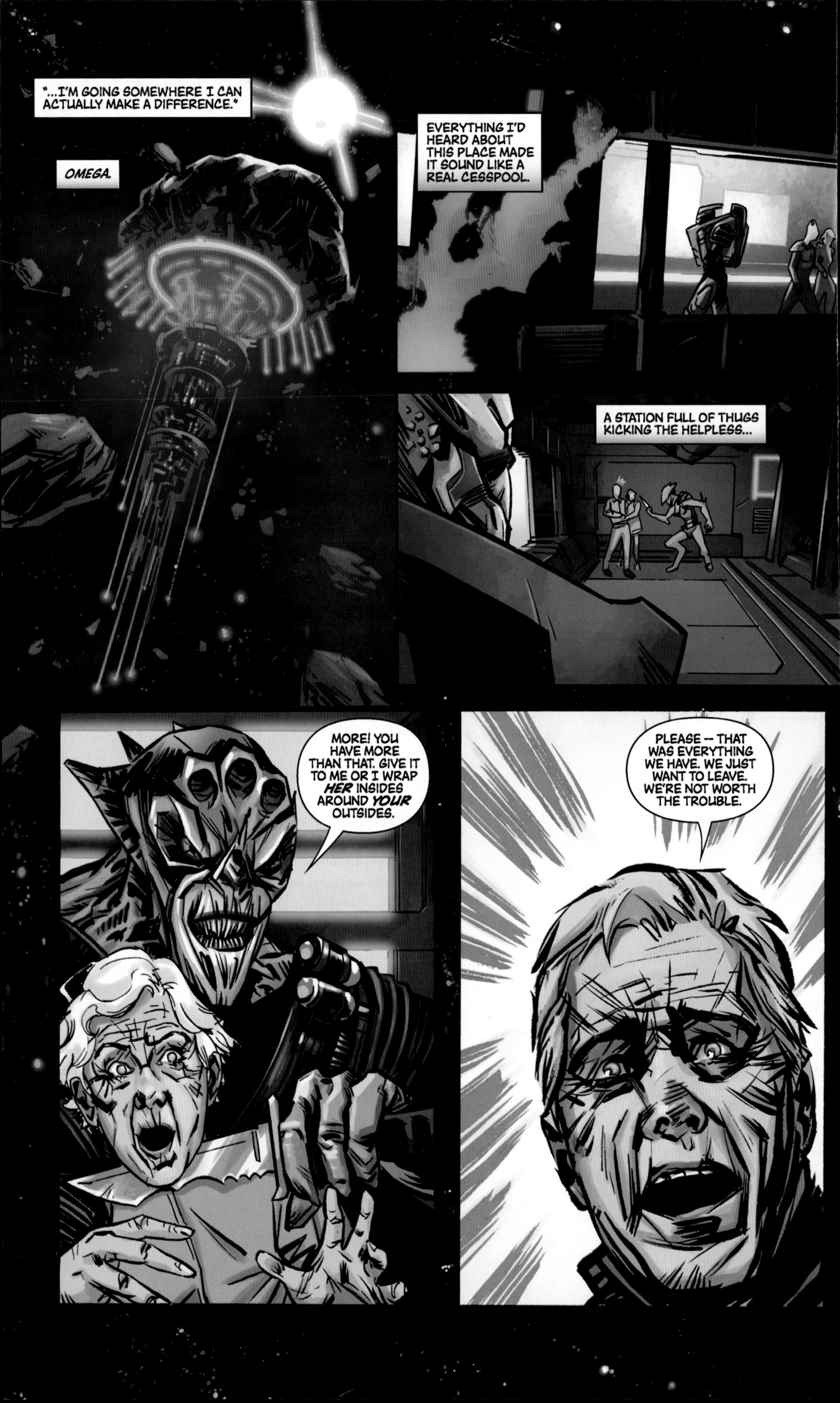

"...I'M GOING SOMEWHERE I CAN ACTUALLY MAKE A DIFFERENCE."
OMEGA.
EVERYTHING I'D HEARD ABOUT THIS PLACE MADE IT SOUND LIKE A REAL CESSPOOL.
A STATION FULL OF THUGS KICKING THE HELPLESS...
MORE! YOU HAVE MORE THAN THAT. GIVE IT TO ME OR I WRAP HER INSIDES AROUND YOUR OUTSIDES.
PLEASE -- THAT WAS EVERYTHING WE HAVE. WE JUST WANT TO LEAVE. WE'RE NOT WORTH THE TROUBLE.

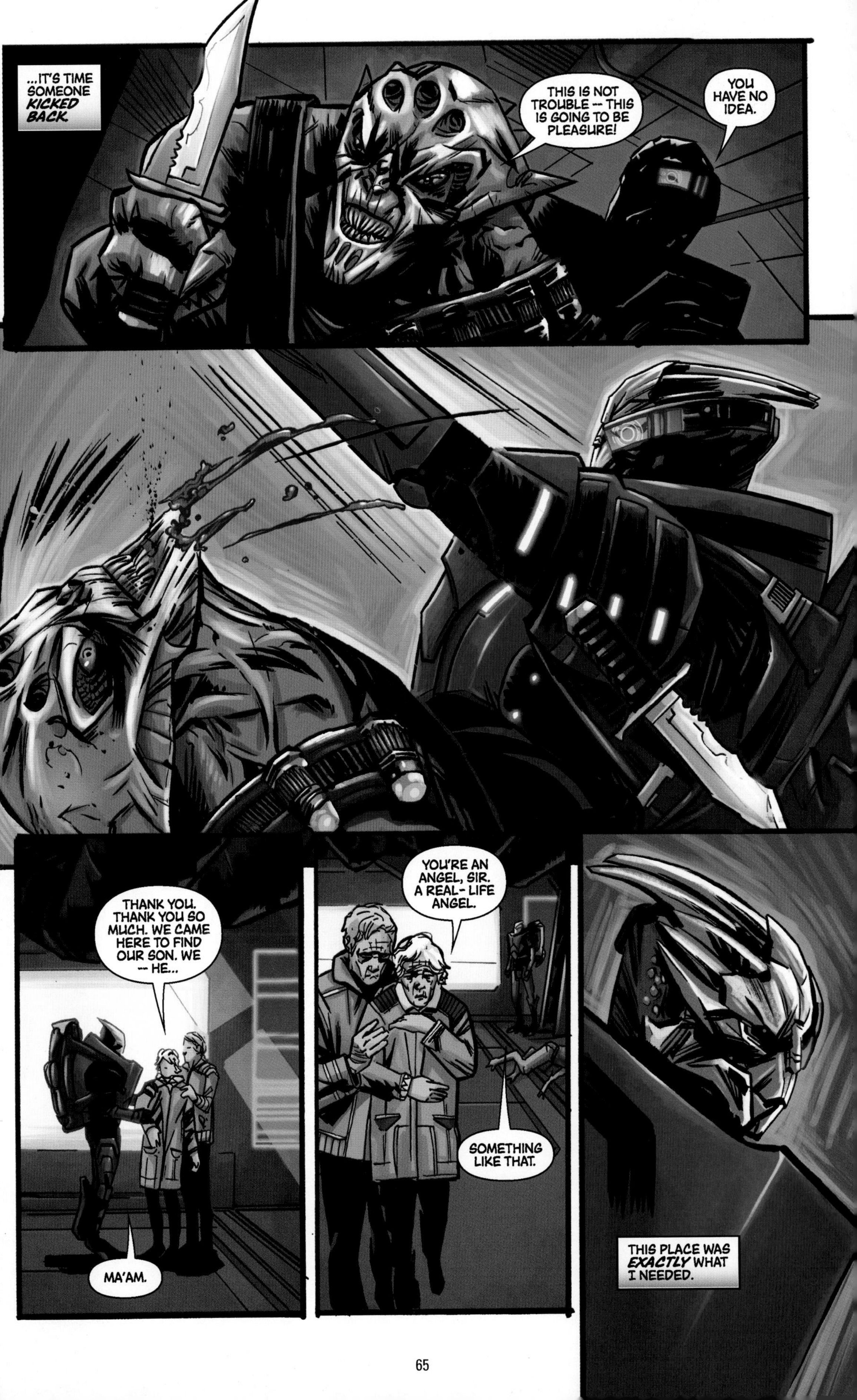
...IT'S TIME SOMEONE *KICKED BACK.*
THIS IS NOT TROUBLE -- THIS IS GOING TO BE PLEASURE!
YOU HAVE NO IDEA.
THANK YOU. THANK YOU SO MUCH. WE CAME HERE TO FIND OUR SON. WE -- HE...
MA'AM.
YOU'RE AN ANGEL, SIR. A REAL-LIFE ANGEL.
SOMETHING LIKE THAT.
THIS PLACE WAS *EXACTLY* WHAT I NEEDED.

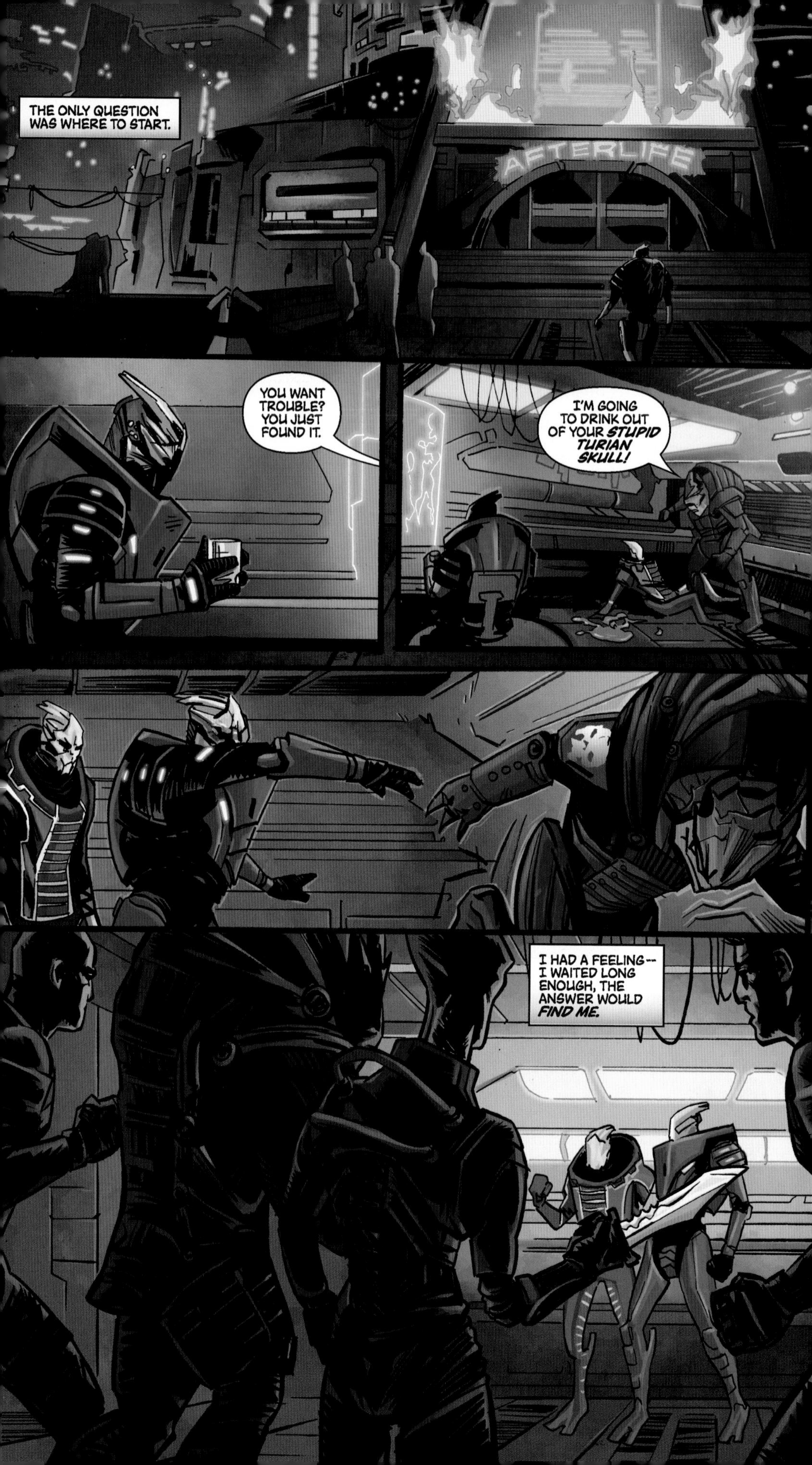
THE ONLY QUESTION WAS WHERE TO START.
AFTERLIFE
YOU WANT TROUBLE? YOU JUST FOUND IT.
I'M GOING TO DRINK OUT OF YOUR STUPID TURIAN SKULL!
I HAD A FEELING-- I WAITED LONG ENOUGH, THE ANSWER WOULD FIND ME.

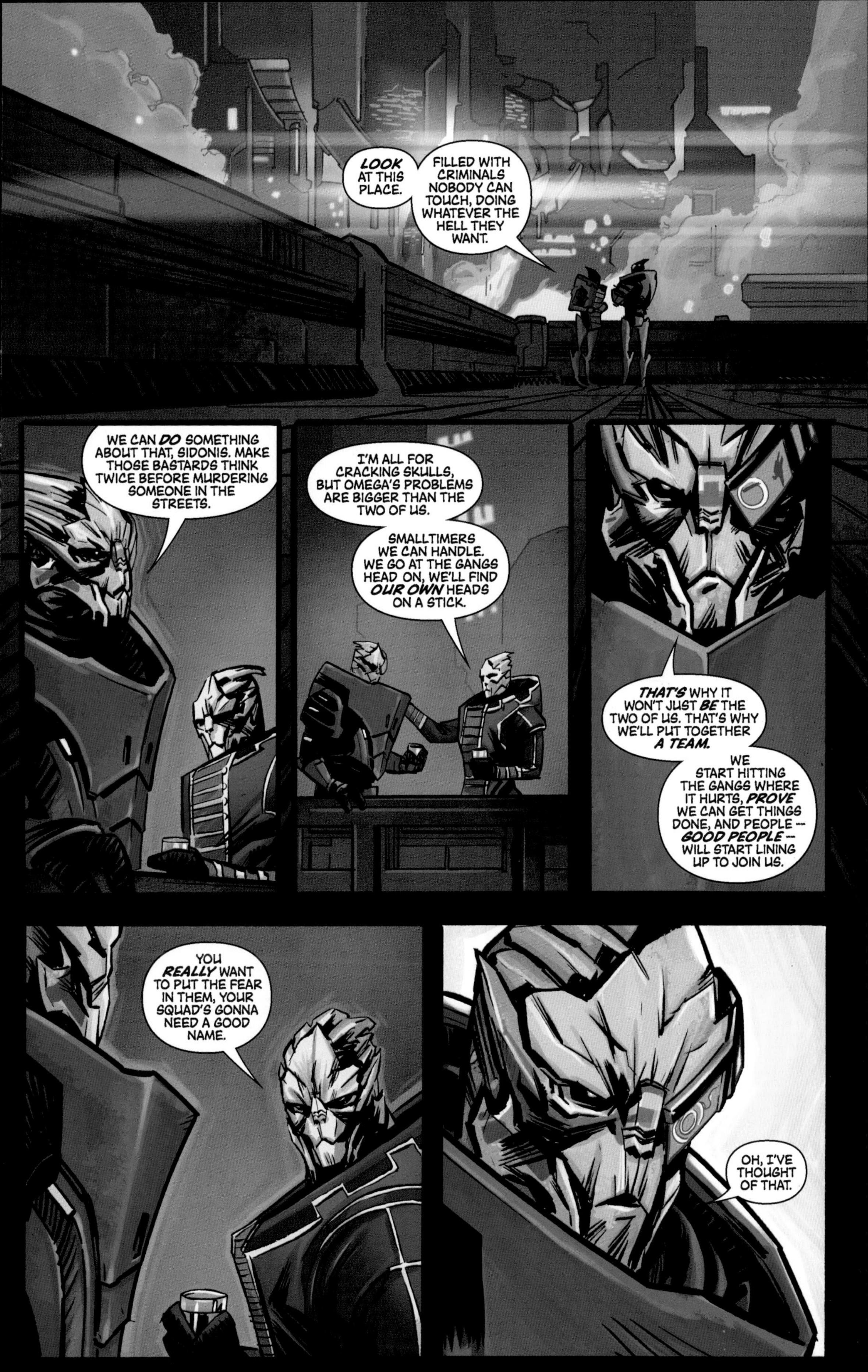
LOOK AT THIS PLACE.
FILLED WITH CRIMINALS NOBODY CAN TOUCH, DOING WHATEVER THE HELL THEY WANT.
WE CAN DO SOMETHING ABOUT THAT, SIDONIS. MAKE THOSE BASTARDS THINK TWICE BEFORE MURDERING SOMEONE IN THE STREETS.
I'M ALL FOR CRACKING SKULLS, BUT OMEGA'S PROBLEMS ARE BIGGER THAN THE TWO OF US.
SMALLTIMERS WE CAN HANDLE. WE GO AT THE GANGS HEAD ON, WE'LL FIND OUR OWN HEADS ON A STICK.
THAT'S WHY IT WON'T JUST BE THE TWO OF US. THAT'S WHY WE'LL PUT TOGETHER A TEAM.
WE START HITTING THE GANGS WHERE IT HURTS, PROVE WE CAN GET THINGS DONE, AND PEOPLE -- GOOD PEOPLE -- WILL START LINING UP TO JOIN US.
YOU REALLY WANT TO PUT THE FEAR IN THEM, YOUR SQUAD'S GONNA NEED A GOOD NAME.
OH, I'VE THOUGHT OF THAT.

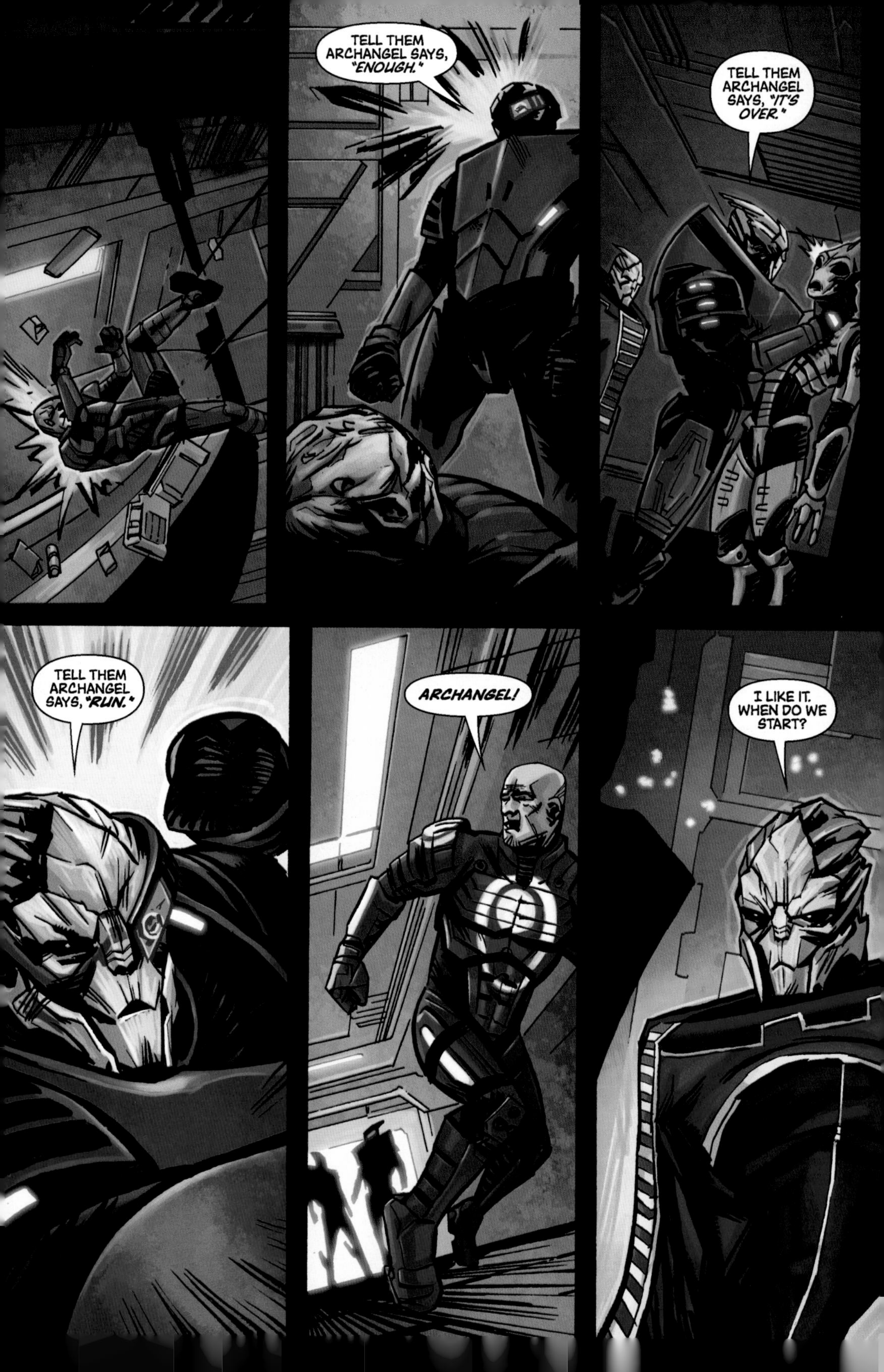
TELL THEM ARCHANGEL SAYS, "ENOUGH."
TELL THEM ARCHANGEL SAYS, "IT'S OVER."
TELL THEM ARCHANGEL SAYS, "RUN."
ARCHANGEL!
I LIKE IT. WHEN DO WE START?

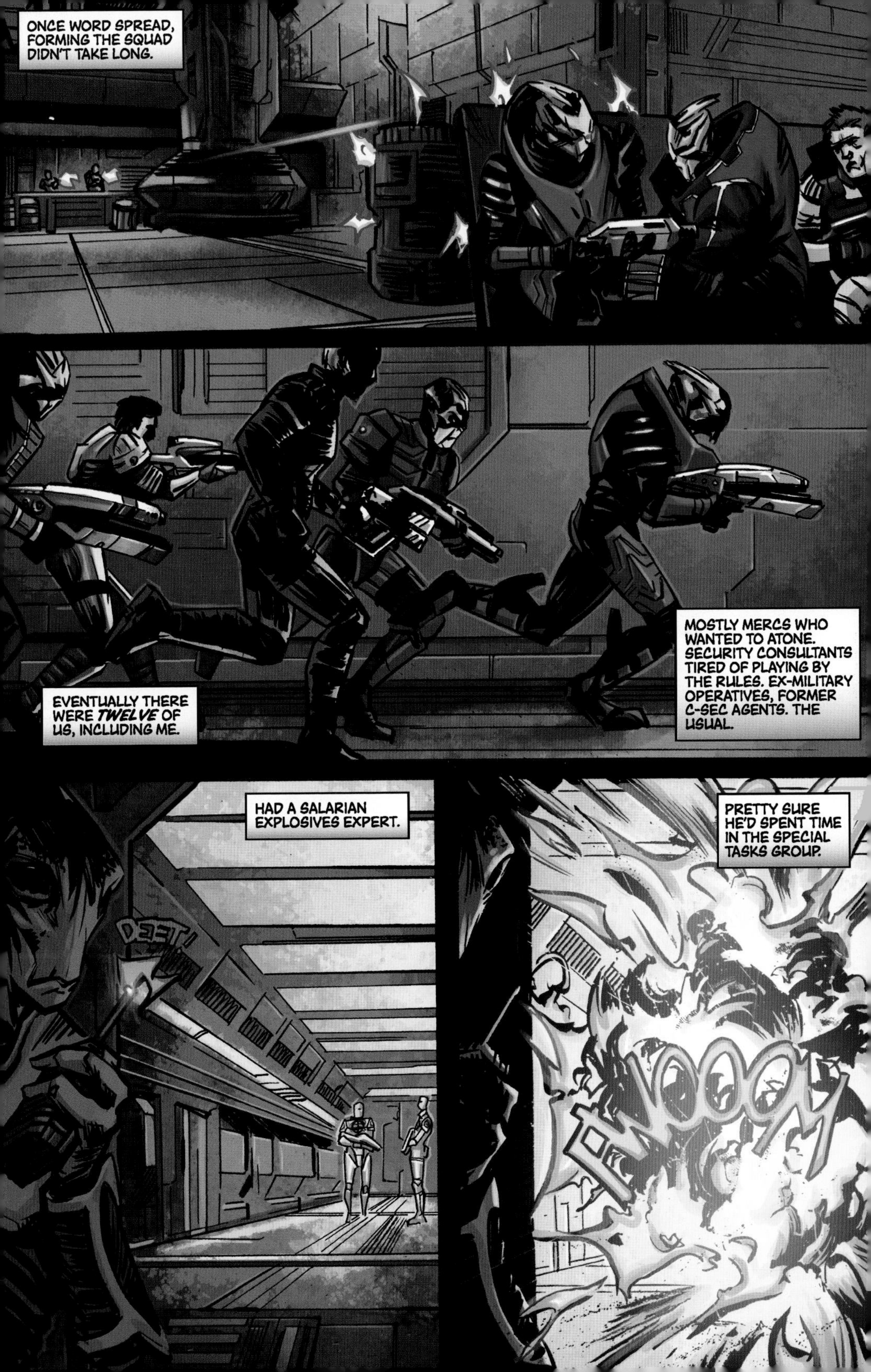
ONCE WORD SPREAD, FORMING THE SQUAD DIDN'T TAKE LONG.
EVENTUALLY THERE WERE *TWELVE* OF US, INCLUDING ME.
MOSTLY MERCS WHO WANTED TO ATONE. SECURITY CONSULTANTS TIRED OF PLAYING BY THE RULES. EX-MILITARY OPERATIVES, FORMER C-SEC AGENTS. THE USUAL.
HAD A SALARIAN EXPLOSIVES EXPERT.
PRETTY SURE HE'D SPENT TIME IN THE SPECIAL TASKS GROUP.

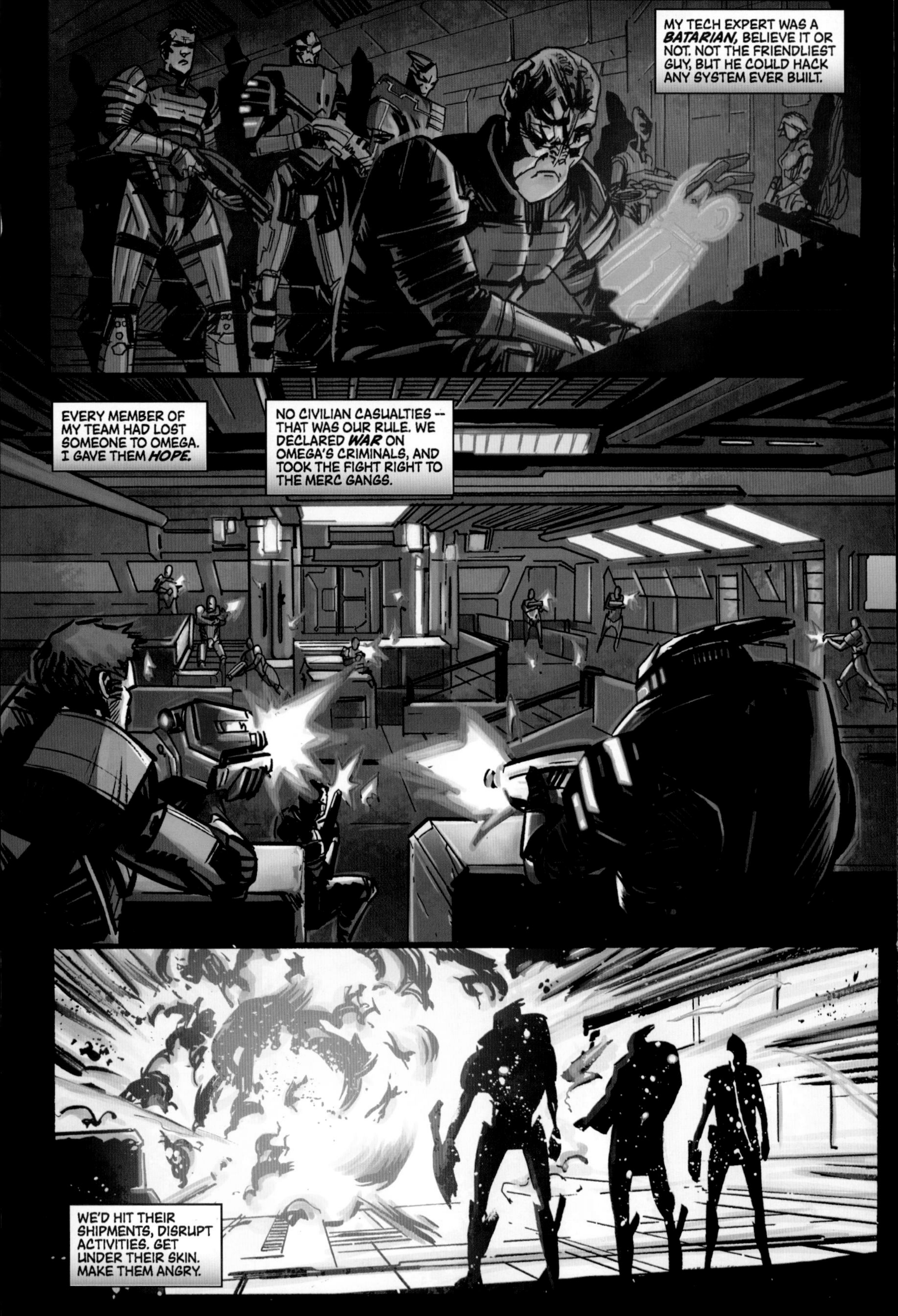
MY TECH EXPERT WAS A BATARIAN, BELIEVE IT OR NOT. NOT THE FRIENDLIEST GUY, BUT HE COULD HACK ANY SYSTEM EVER BUILT.
EVERY MEMBER OF MY TEAM HAD LOST SOMEONE TO OMEGA. I GAVE THEM HOPE.
NO CIVILIAN CASUALTIES -- THAT WAS OUR RULE. WE DECLARED WAR ON OMEGA'S CRIMINALS, AND TOOK THE FIGHT RIGHT TO THE MERC GANGS.
WE'D HIT THEIR SHIPMENTS, DISRUPT ACTIVITIES. GET UNDER THEIR SKIN. MAKE THEM ANGRY.

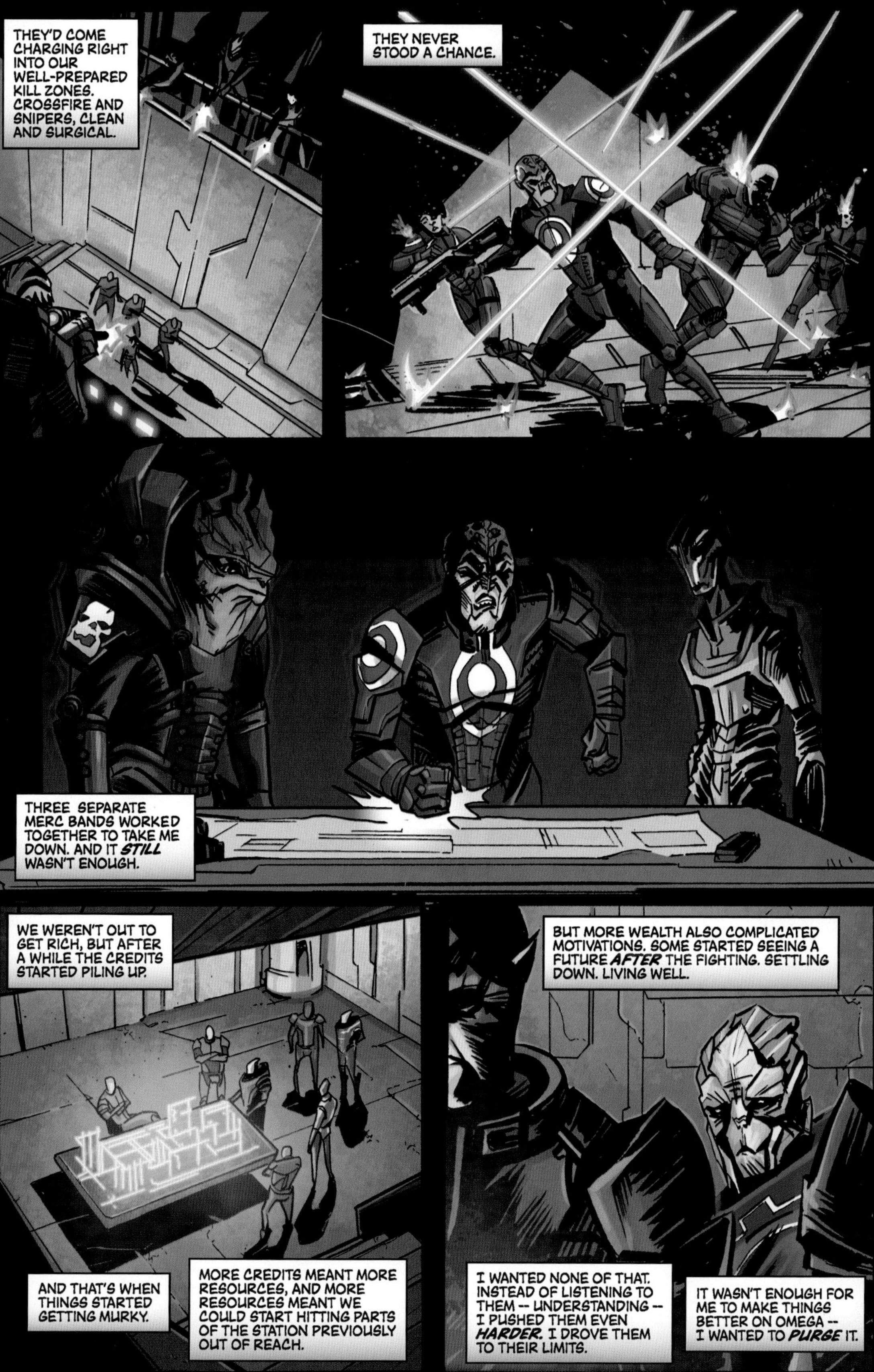
THEY'D COME CHARGING RIGHT INTO OUR WELL-PREPARED KILL ZONES. CROSSFIRE AND SNIPERS, CLEAN AND SURGICAL.
THEY NEVER STOOD A CHANCE.
THREE SEPARATE MERC BANDS WORKED TOGETHER TO TAKE ME DOWN. AND IT *STILL* WASN'T ENOUGH.
WE WEREN'T OUT TO GET RICH, BUT AFTER A WHILE THE CREDITS STARTED PILING UP.
AND THAT'S WHEN THINGS STARTED GETTING MURKY.
MORE CREDITS MEANT MORE RESOURCES, AND MORE RESOURCES MEANT WE COULD START HITTING PARTS OF THE STATION PREVIOUSLY OUT OF REACH.
BUT MORE WEALTH ALSO COMPLICATED MOTIVATIONS. SOME STARTED SEEING A FUTURE *AFTER* THE FIGHTING. SETTLING DOWN. LIVING WELL.
I WANTED NONE OF THAT. INSTEAD OF LISTENING TO THEM -- UNDERSTANDING -- I PUSHED THEM EVEN *HARDER*. I DROVE THEM TO THEIR LIMITS.
IT WASN'T ENOUGH FOR ME TO MAKE THINGS BETTER ON OMEGA -- I WANTED TO *PURGE* IT.

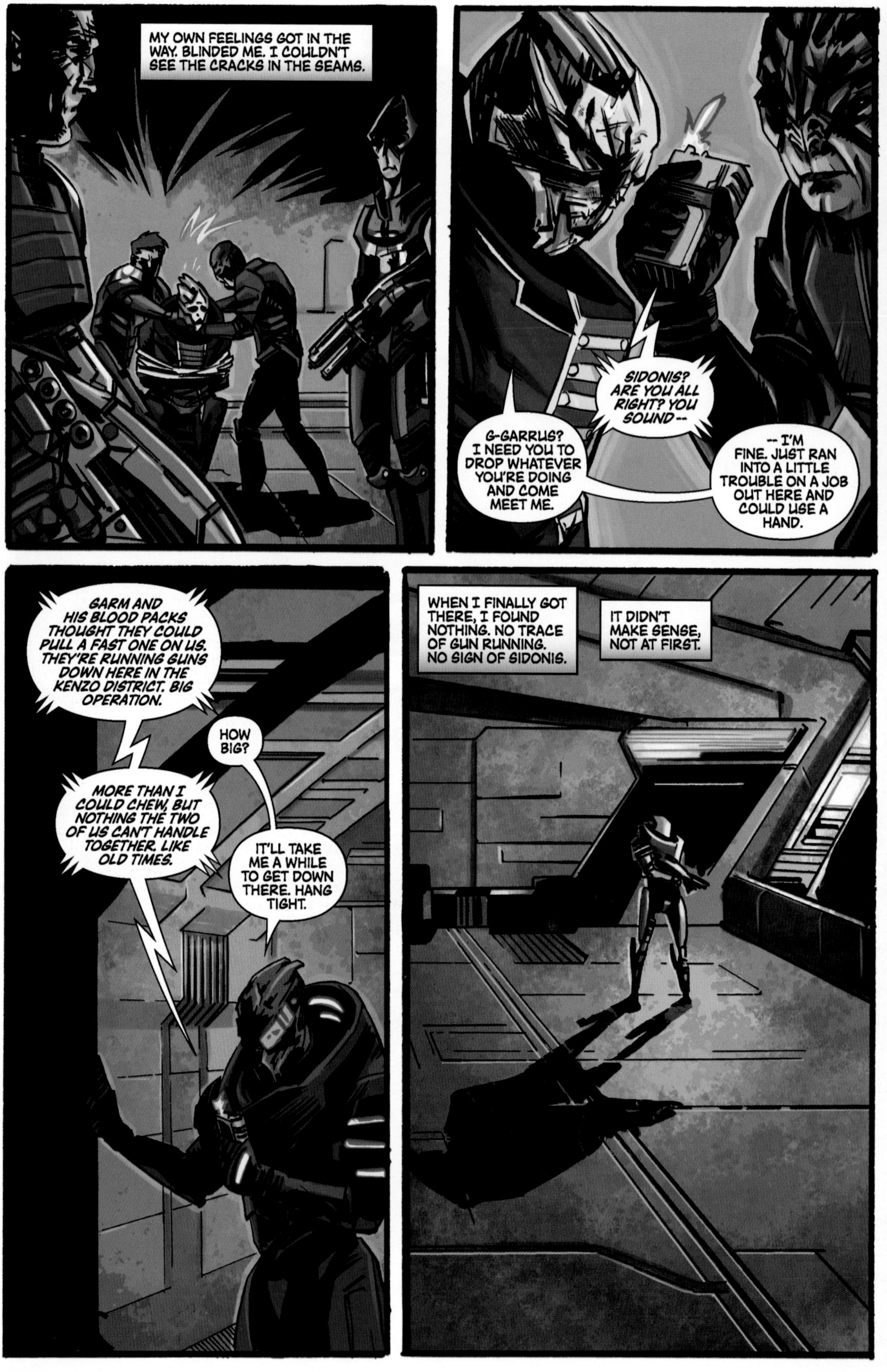
MY OWN FEELINGS GOT IN THE WAY. BLINDED ME. I COULDN'T SEE THE CRACKS IN THE SEAMS.
SIDONIS? ARE YOU ALL RIGHT? YOU SOUND --
G-GARRUS? I NEED YOU TO DROP WHATEVER YOU'RE DOING AND COME MEET ME.
-- I'M FINE. JUST RAN INTO A LITTLE TROUBLE ON A JOB OUT HERE AND COULD USE A HAND.
GARM AND HIS BLOOD PACKS THOUGHT THEY COULD PULL A FAST ONE ON US. THEY'RE RUNNING GUNS DOWN HERE IN THE KENZO DISTRICT. BIG OPERATION.
HOW BIG?
MORE THAN I COULD CHEW, BUT NOTHING THE TWO OF US CAN'T HANDLE TOGETHER. LIKE OLD TIMES.
IT'LL TAKE ME A WHILE TO GET DOWN THERE. HANG TIGHT.
WHEN I FINALLY GOT THERE, I FOUND NOTHING. NO TRACE OF GUN RUNNING. NO SIGN OF SIDONIS.
IT DIDN'T MAKE SENSE, NOT AT FIRST.

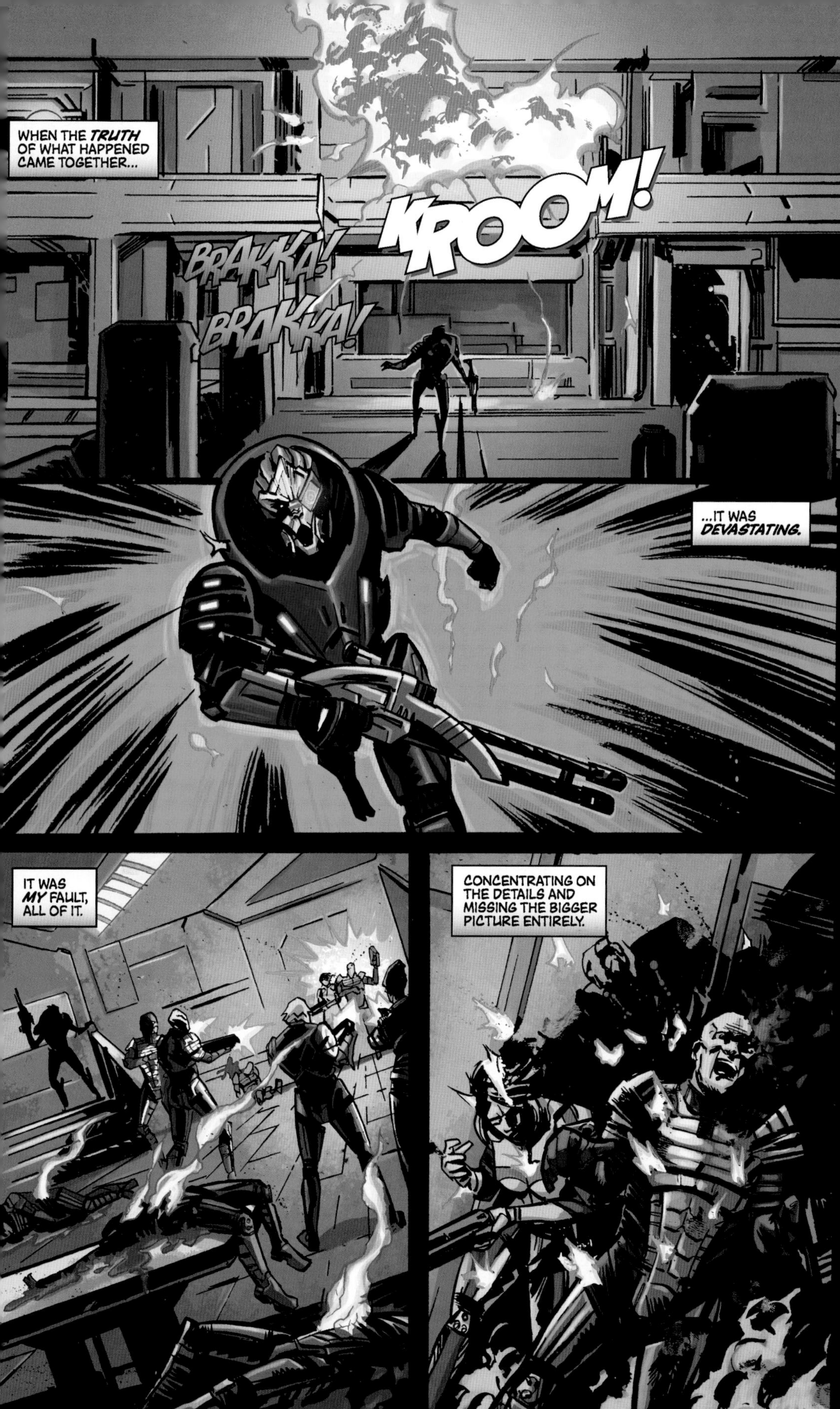
WHEN THE TRUTH OF WHAT HAPPENED CAME TOGETHER...
BRAKKA! BRAKKA!
KROOM!
...IT WAS DEVASTATING.
IT WAS MY FAULT, ALL OF IT.
CONCENTRATING ON THE DETAILS AND MISSING THE BIGGER PICTURE ENTIRELY.

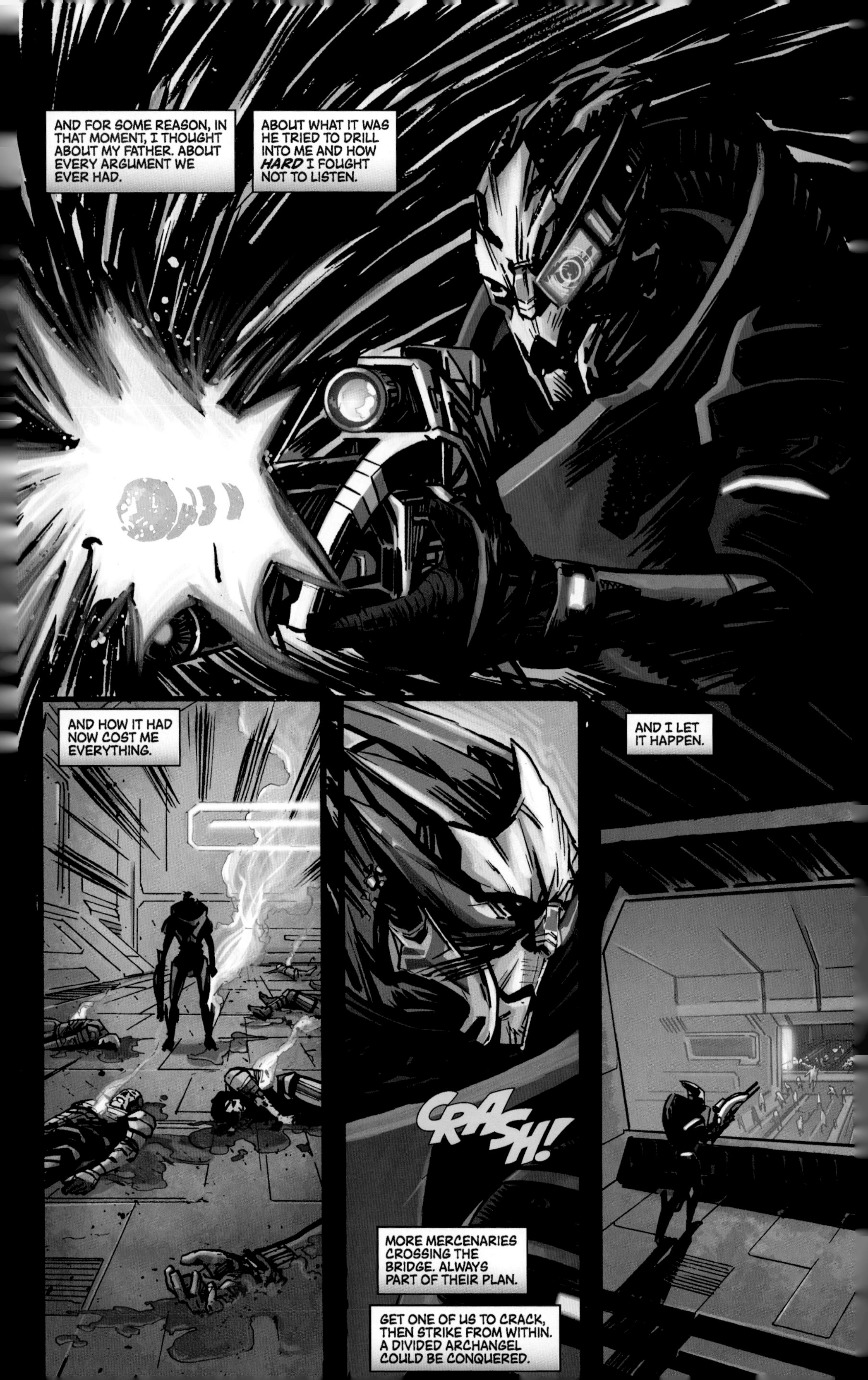
AND FOR SOME REASON, IN THAT MOMENT, I THOUGHT ABOUT MY FATHER. ABOUT EVERY ARGUMENT WE EVER HAD.
ABOUT WHAT IT WAS HE TRIED TO DRILL INTO ME AND HOW HARD I FOUGHT NOT TO LISTEN.
AND HOW IT HAD NOW COST ME EVERYTHING.
AND I LET IT HAPPEN.
CRASH!
MORE MERCENARIES CROSSING THE BRIDGE. ALWAYS PART OF THEIR PLAN.
GET ONE OF US TO CRACK, THEN STRIKE FROM WITHIN. A DIVIDED ARCHANGEL COULD BE CONQUERED.

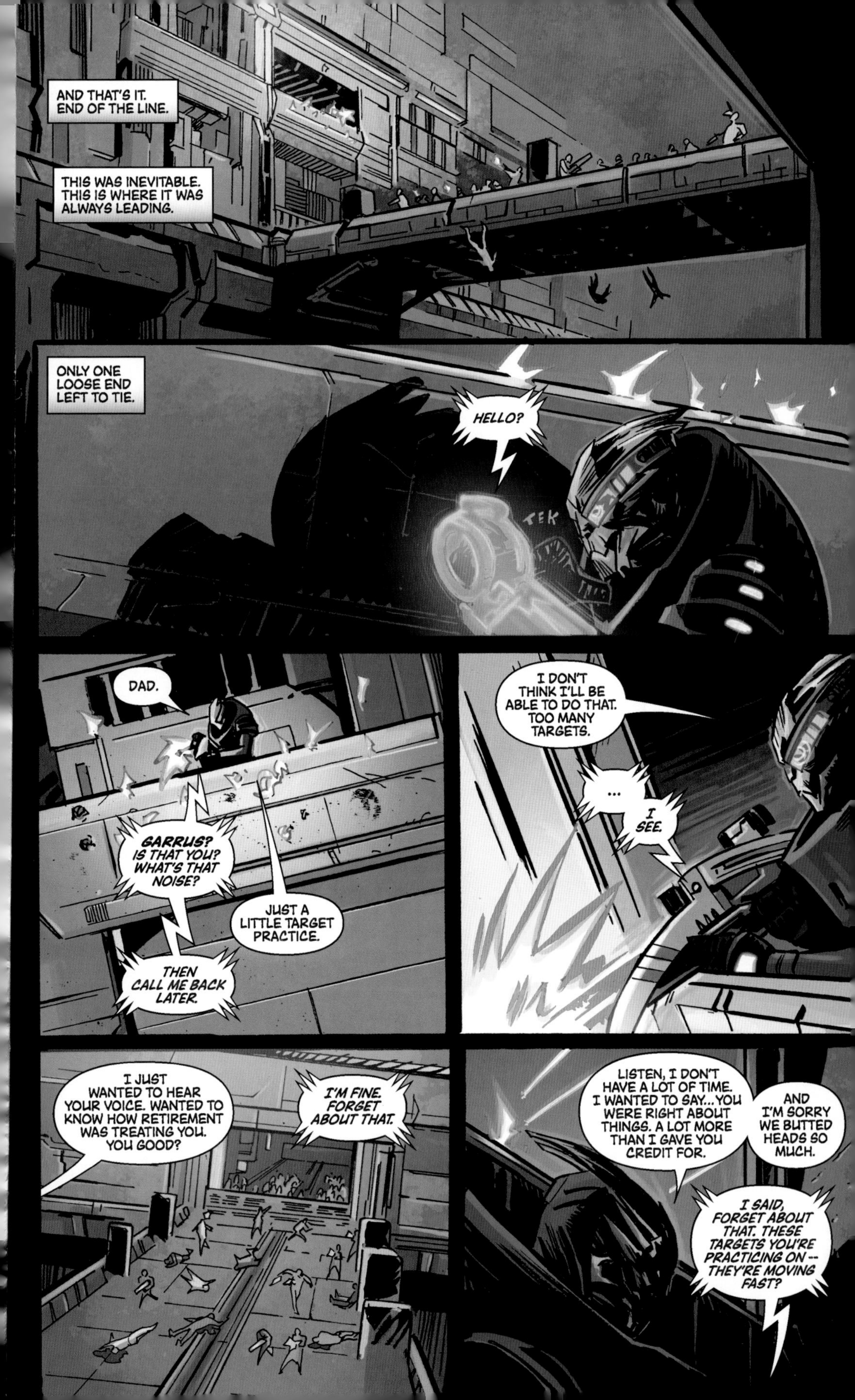
AND THAT'S IT. END OF THE LINE.
THIS WAS INEVITABLE. THIS IS WHERE IT WAS ALWAYS LEADING.
ONLY ONE LOOSE END LEFT TO TIE.
HELLO?
TEK
DAD.
GARRUS? IS THAT YOU? WHAT'S THAT NOISE?
JUST A LITTLE TARGET PRACTICE.
THEN CALL ME BACK LATER.
I DON'T THINK I'LL BE ABLE TO DO THAT. TOO MANY TARGETS.
...
I SEE.
I JUST WANTED TO HEAR YOUR VOICE. WANTED TO KNOW HOW RETIREMENT WAS TREATING YOU. YOU GOOD?
I'M FINE. FORGET ABOUT THAT.
LISTEN, I DON'T HAVE A LOT OF TIME. I WANTED TO SAY... YOU WERE RIGHT ABOUT THINGS. A LOT MORE THAN I GAVE YOU CREDIT FOR.
AND I'M SORRY WE BUTTED HEADS SO MUCH.
I SAID, FORGET ABOUT THAT. THESE TARGETS YOU'RE PRACTICING ON -- THEY'RE MOVING FAST?

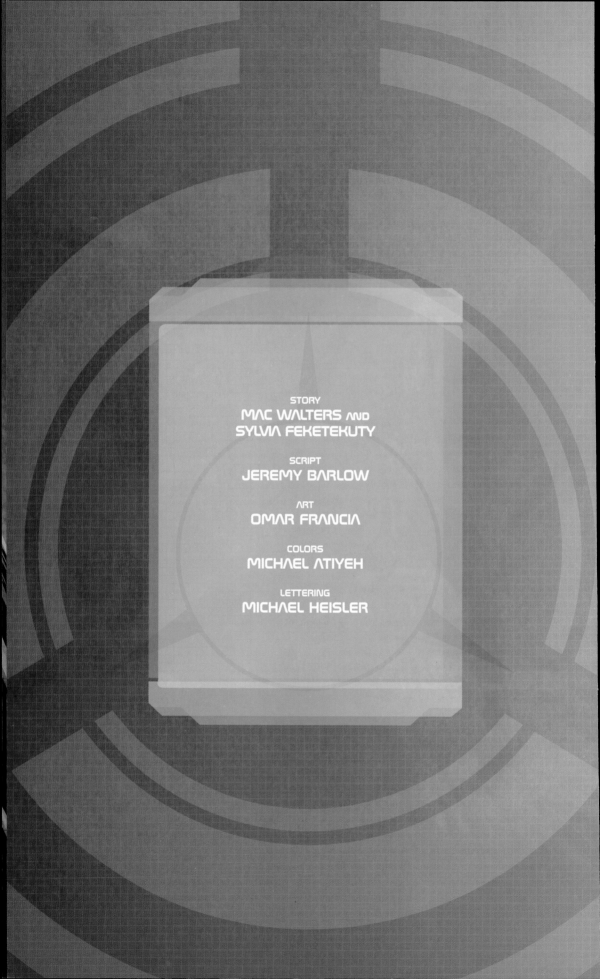

STORY
MAC WALTERS AND
SYLVIA FEKETEKUTY

SCRIPT
JEREMY BARLOW

ART
OMAR FRANCIA

COLORS
MICHAEL ATIYEH

LETTERING
MICHAEL HEISLER

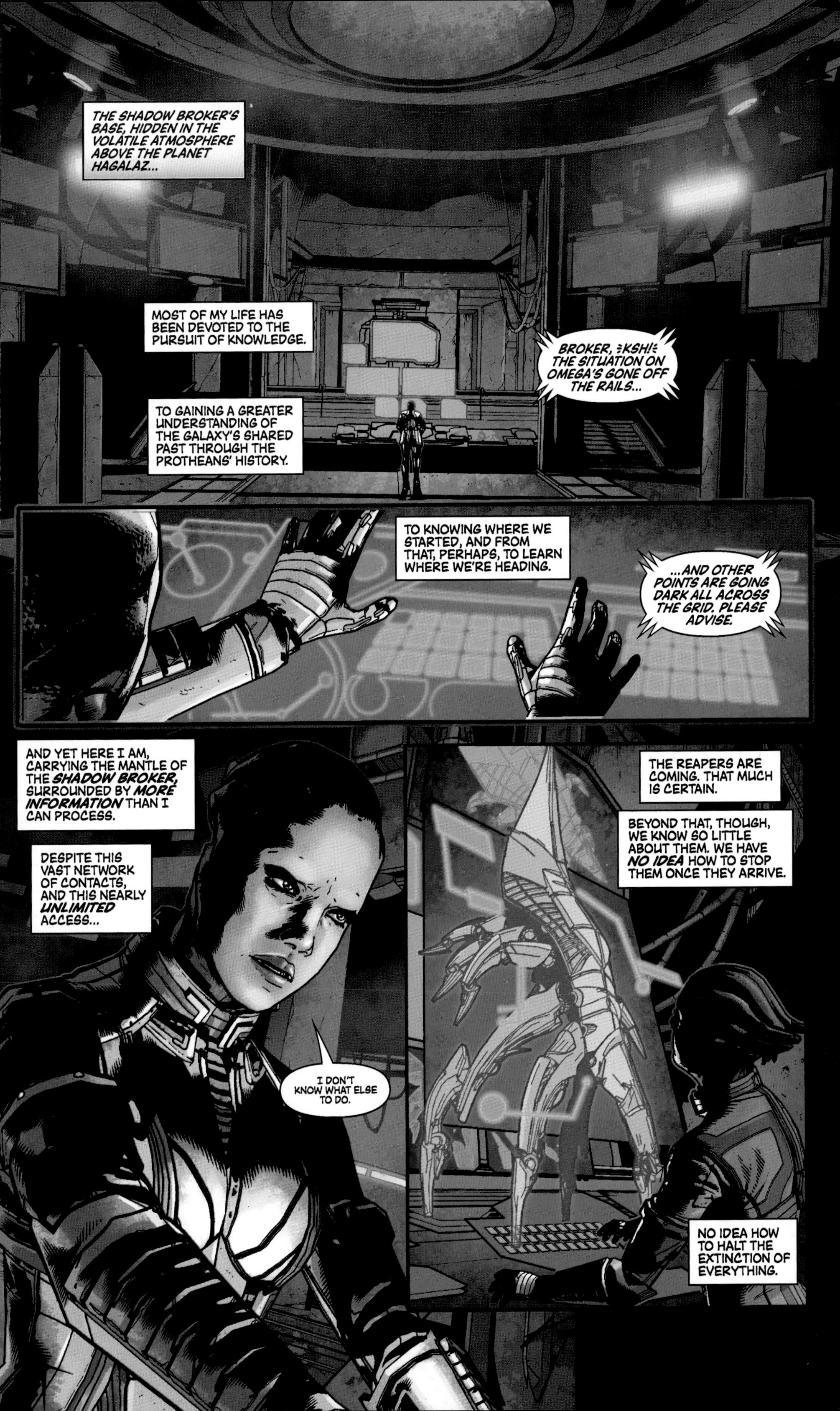
THE SHADOW BROKER'S BASE, HIDDEN IN THE VOLATILE ATMOSPHERE ABOVE THE PLANET HAGALAZ...
MOST OF MY LIFE HAS BEEN DEVOTED TO THE PURSUIT OF KNOWLEDGE.
BROKER, KSH! THE SITUATION ON OMEGA'S GONE OFF THE RAILS...
TO GAINING A GREATER UNDERSTANDING OF THE GALAXY'S SHARED PAST THROUGH THE PROTHEANS' HISTORY.
TO KNOWING WHERE WE STARTED, AND FROM THAT, PERHAPS, TO LEARN WHERE WE'RE HEADING.
...AND OTHER POINTS ARE GOING DARK ALL ACROSS THE GRID. PLEASE ADVISE.
AND YET HERE I AM, CARRYING THE MANTLE OF THE SHADOW BROKER, SURROUNDED BY MORE INFORMATION THAN I CAN PROCESS.
DESPITE THIS VAST NETWORK OF CONTACTS, AND THIS NEARLY UNLIMITED ACCESS...
I DON'T KNOW WHAT ELSE TO DO.
THE REAPERS ARE COMING. THAT MUCH IS CERTAIN.
BEYOND THAT, THOUGH, WE KNOW SO LITTLE ABOUT THEM. WE HAVE NO IDEA HOW TO STOP THEM ONCE THEY ARRIVE.
NO IDEA HOW TO HALT THE EXTINCTION OF EVERYTHING.

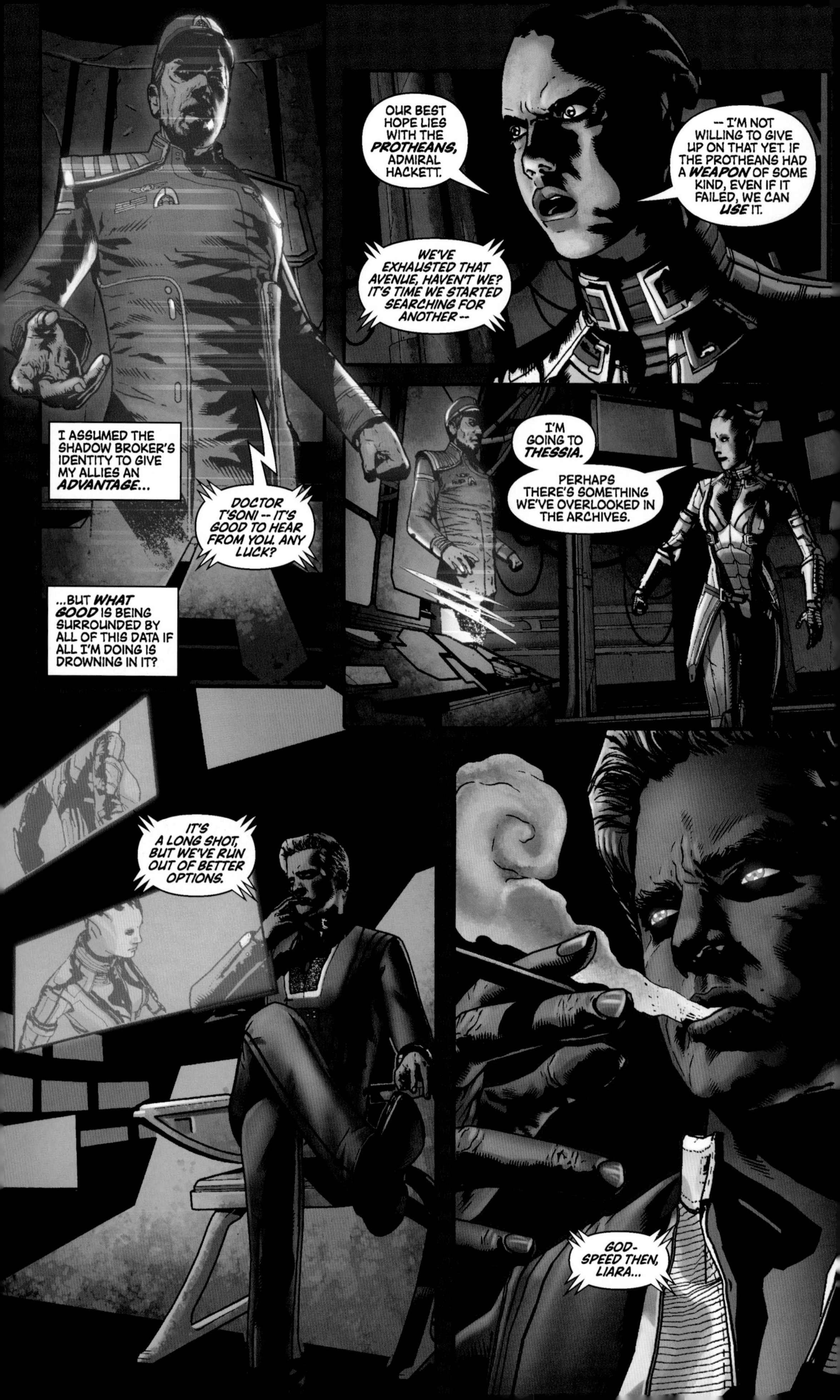
OUR BEST HOPE LIES WITH THE PROTHEANS, ADMIRAL HACKETT.
WE'VE EXHAUSTED THAT AVENUE, HAVEN'T WE? IT'S TIME WE STARTED SEARCHING FOR ANOTHER --
-- I'M NOT WILLING TO GIVE UP ON THAT YET. IF THE PROTHEANS HAD A WEAPON OF SOME KIND, EVEN IF IT FAILED, WE CAN USE IT.
I ASSUMED THE SHADOW BROKER'S IDENTITY TO GIVE MY ALLIES AN ADVANTAGE...
DOCTOR T'SONI -- IT'S GOOD TO HEAR FROM YOU. ANY LUCK?
...BUT WHAT GOOD IS BEING SURROUNDED BY ALL OF THIS DATA IF ALL I'M DOING IS DROWNING IN IT?
I'M GOING TO THESSIA.
PERHAPS THERE'S SOMETHING WE'VE OVERLOOKED IN THE ARCHIVES.
IT'S A LONG SHOT, BUT WE'VE RUN OUT OF BETTER OPTIONS.
GOD-SPEED THEN, LIARA...

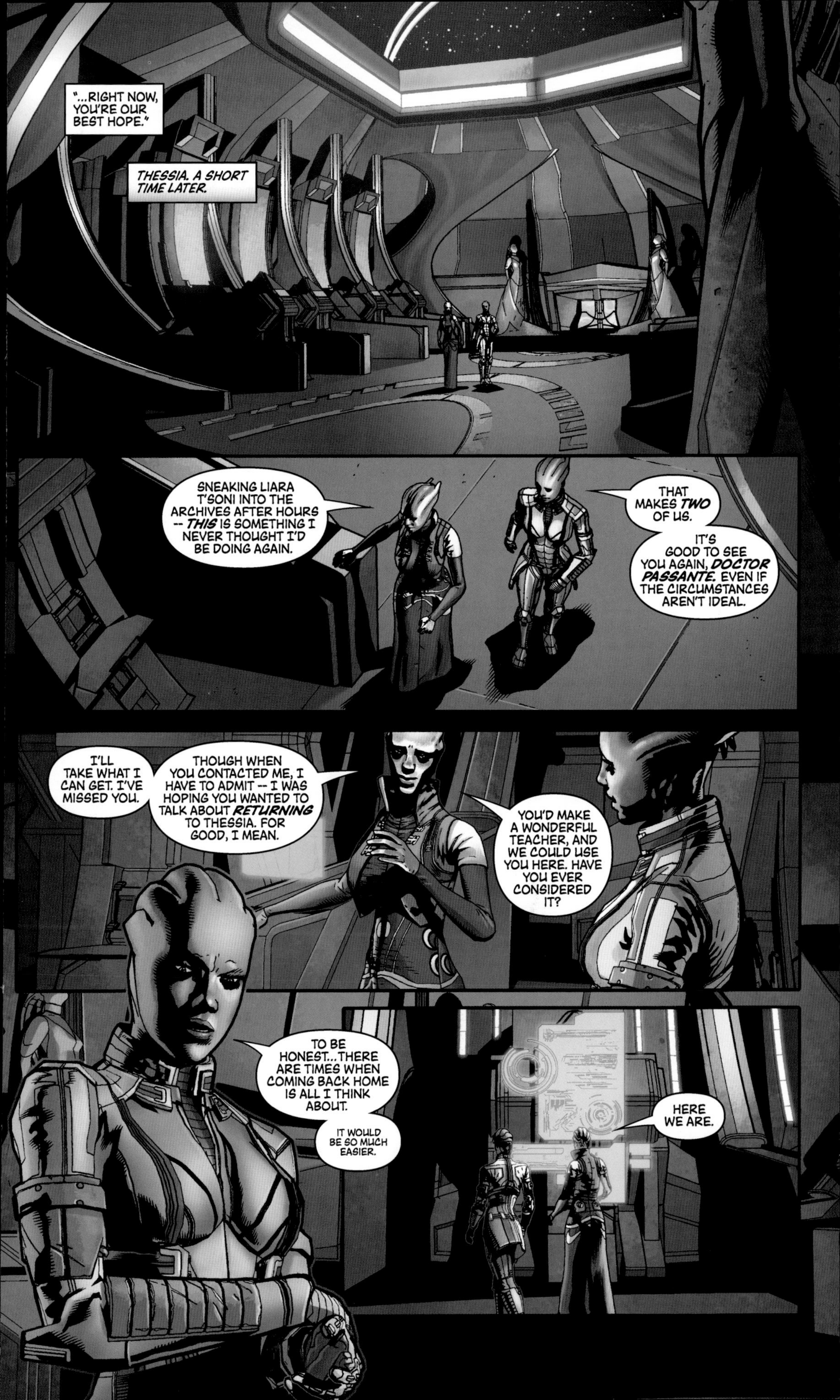

"...RIGHT NOW, YOU'RE OUR BEST HOPE."
THESSIA. A SHORT TIME LATER.
SNEAKING LIARA T'SONI INTO THE ARCHIVES AFTER HOURS -- THIS IS SOMETHING I NEVER THOUGHT I'D BE DOING AGAIN.
THAT MAKES TWO OF US.
IT'S GOOD TO SEE YOU AGAIN, DOCTOR PASSANTE. EVEN IF THE CIRCUMSTANCES AREN'T IDEAL.
I'LL TAKE WHAT I CAN GET. I'VE MISSED YOU.
THOUGH WHEN YOU CONTACTED ME, I HAVE TO ADMIT -- I WAS HOPING YOU WANTED TO TALK ABOUT RETURNING TO THESSIA. FOR GOOD, I MEAN.
YOU'D MAKE A WONDERFUL TEACHER, AND WE COULD USE YOU HERE. HAVE YOU EVER CONSIDERED IT?
TO BE HONEST...THERE ARE TIMES WHEN COMING BACK HOME IS ALL I THINK ABOUT.
IT WOULD BE SO MUCH EASIER.
HERE WE ARE.

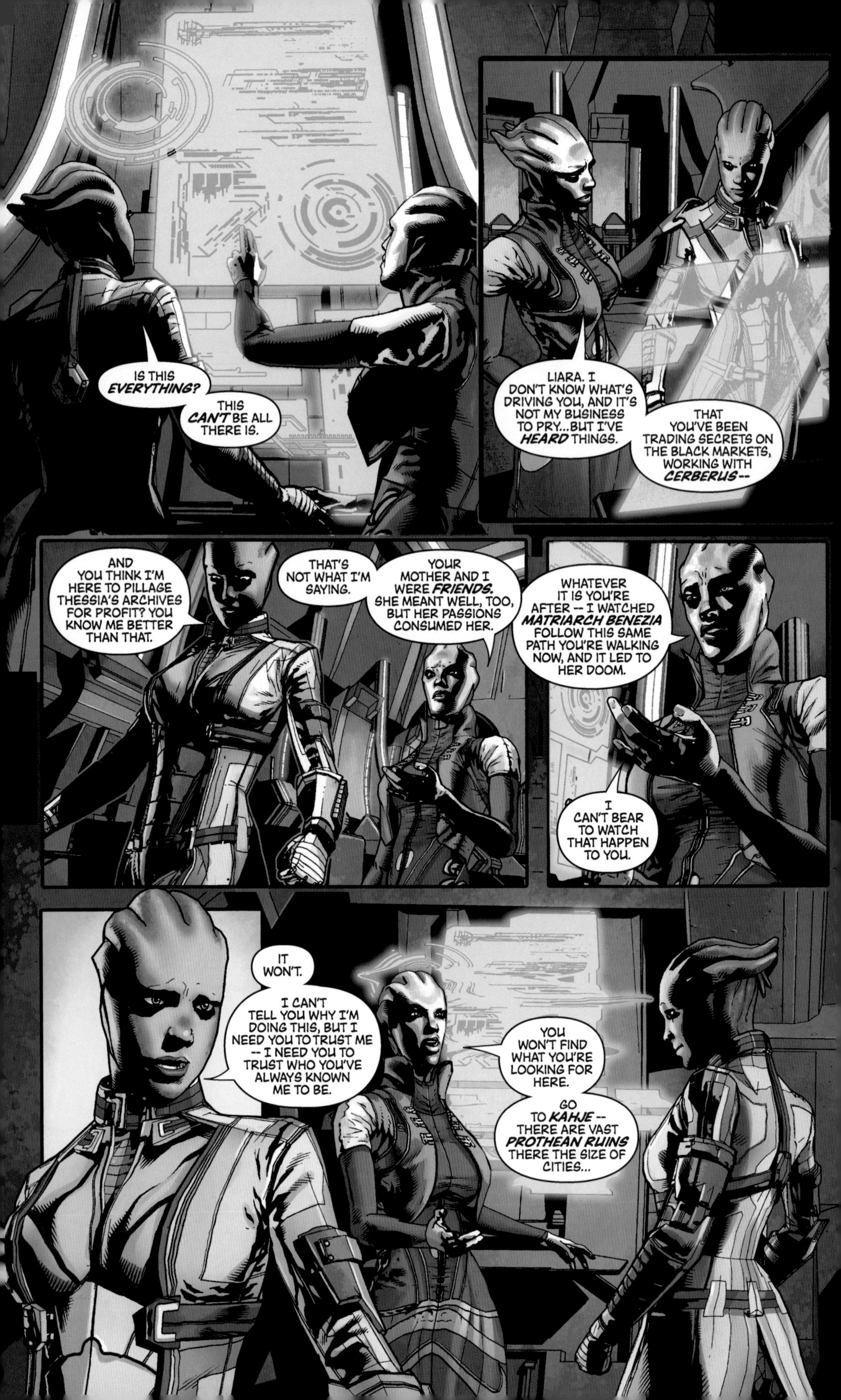

IS THIS EVERYTHING?
THIS CAN'T BE ALL THERE IS.
LIARA. I DON'T KNOW WHAT'S DRIVING YOU, AND IT'S NOT MY BUSINESS TO PRY...BUT I'VE HEARD THINGS.
THAT YOU'VE BEEN TRADING SECRETS ON THE BLACK MARKETS, WORKING WITH CERBERUS--
AND YOU THINK I'M HERE TO PILLAGE THESSIA'S ARCHIVES FOR PROFIT? YOU KNOW ME BETTER THAN THAT.
THAT'S NOT WHAT I'M SAYING.
YOUR MOTHER AND I WERE FRIENDS. SHE MEANT WELL, TOO, BUT HER PASSIONS CONSUMED HER.
WHATEVER IT IS YOU'RE AFTER -- I WATCHED MATRIARCH BENEZIA FOLLOW THIS SAME PATH YOU'RE WALKING NOW, AND IT LED TO HER DOOM.
I CAN'T BEAR TO WATCH THAT HAPPEN TO YOU.
IT WON'T.
I CAN'T TELL YOU WHY I'M DOING THIS, BUT I NEED YOU TO TRUST ME -- I NEED YOU TO TRUST WHO YOU'VE ALWAYS KNOWN ME TO BE.
YOU WON'T FIND WHAT YOU'RE LOOKING FOR HERE.
GO TO KAHJE -- THERE ARE VAST PROTHEAN RUINS THERE THE SIZE OF CITIES...

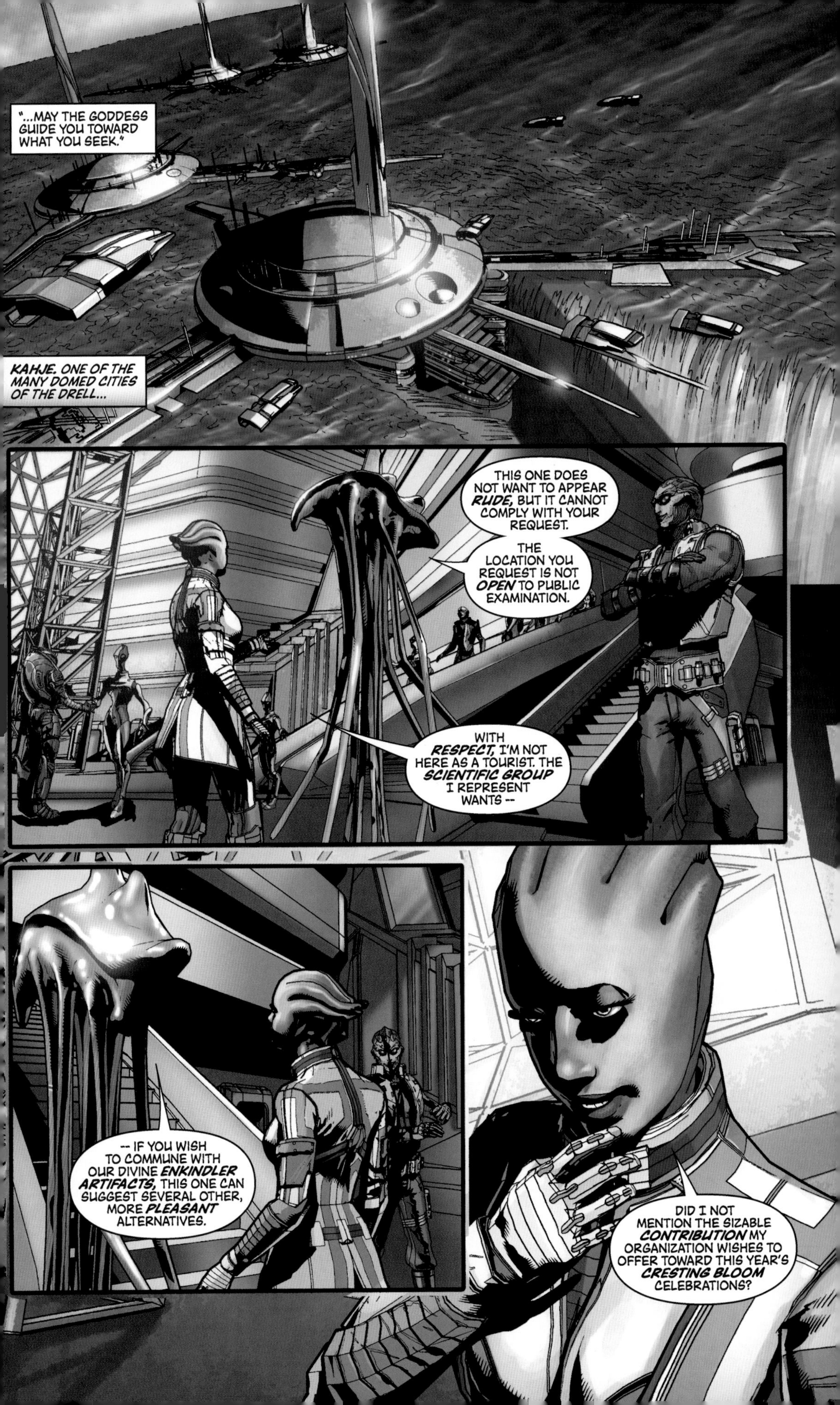
"...MAY THE GODDESS GUIDE YOU TOWARD WHAT YOU SEEK."
KAHJE. ONE OF THE MANY DOMED CITIES OF THE DRELL...
THIS ONE DOES NOT WANT TO APPEAR RUDE, BUT IT CANNOT COMPLY WITH YOUR REQUEST.
THE LOCATION YOU REQUEST IS NOT OPEN TO PUBLIC EXAMINATION.
WITH RESPECT, I'M NOT HERE AS A TOURIST. THE SCIENTIFIC GROUP I REPRESENT WANTS --
-- IF YOU WISH TO COMMUNE WITH OUR DIVINE ENKINDLER ARTIFACTS, THIS ONE CAN SUGGEST SEVERAL OTHER, MORE PLEASANT ALTERNATIVES.
DID I NOT MENTION THE SIZABLE CONTRIBUTION MY ORGANIZATION WISHES TO OFFER TOWARD THIS YEAR'S CRESTING BLOOM CELEBRATIONS?

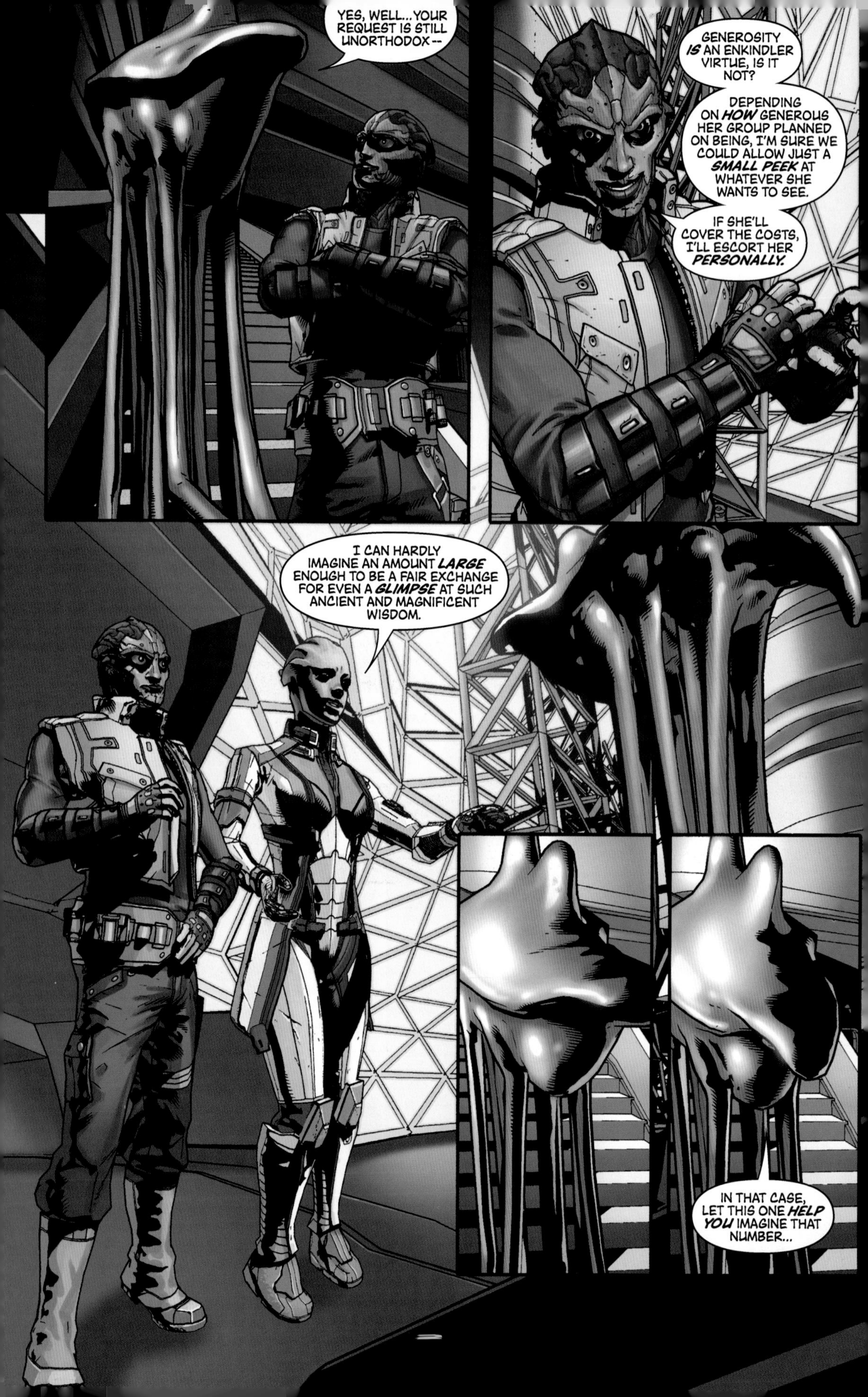
YES, WELL... YOUR REQUEST IS STILL UNORTHODOX --
GENEROSITY *IS* AN ENKINDLER VIRTUE, IS IT NOT?
DEPENDING ON *HOW* GENEROUS HER GROUP PLANNED ON BEING, I'M SURE WE COULD ALLOW JUST A *SMALL PEEK* AT WHATEVER SHE WANTS TO SEE.
IF SHE'LL COVER THE COSTS, I'LL ESCORT HER *PERSONALLY.*
I CAN HARDLY IMAGINE AN AMOUNT *LARGE* ENOUGH TO BE A FAIR EXCHANGE FOR EVEN A *GLIMPSE* AT SUCH ANCIENT AND MAGNIFICENT WISDOM.
IN THAT CASE, LET THIS ONE *HELP YOU* IMAGINE THAT NUMBER...

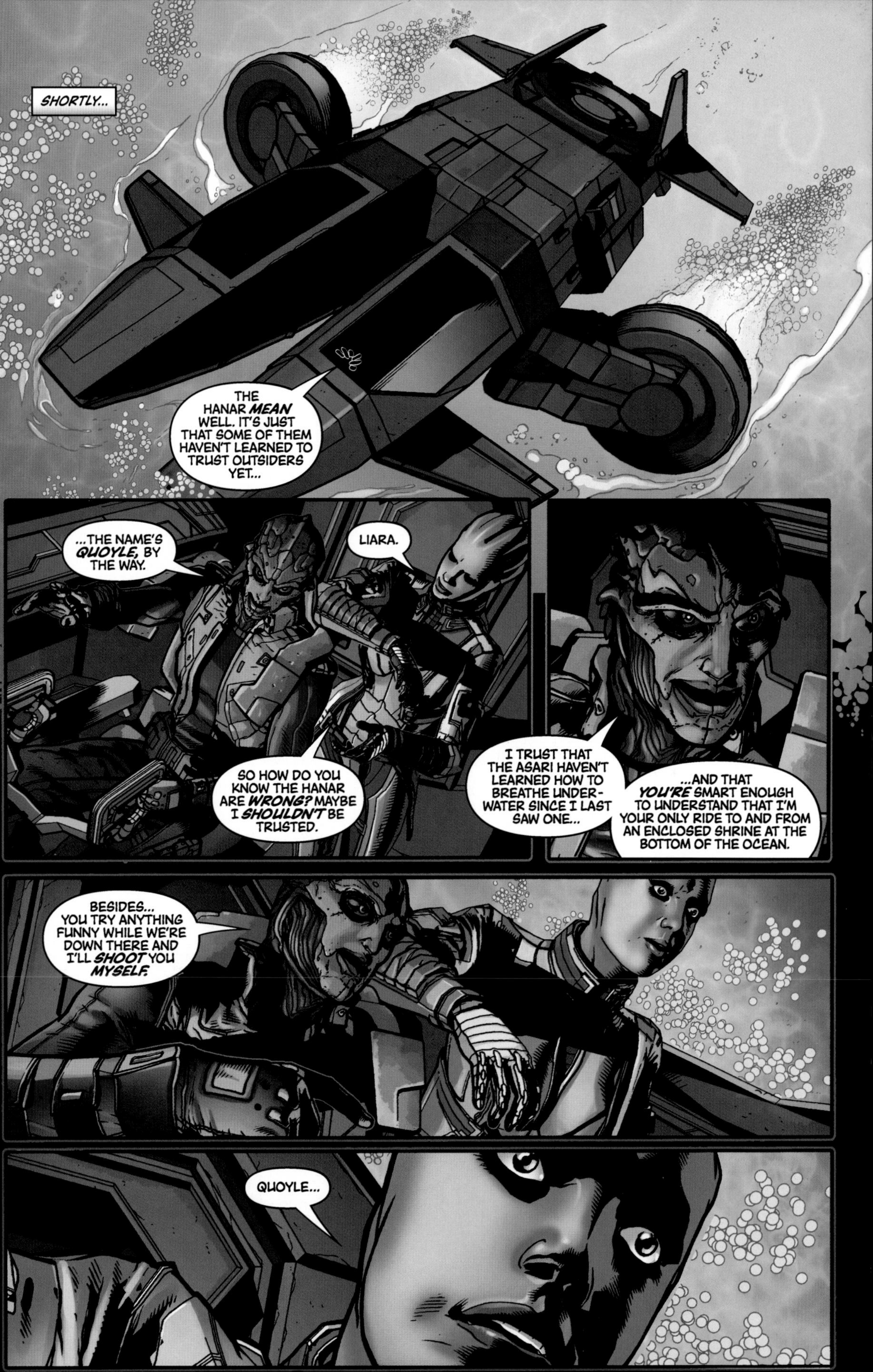
SHORTLY...
THE HANAR MEAN WELL. IT'S JUST THAT SOME OF THEM HAVEN'T LEARNED TO TRUST OUTSIDERS YET...
...THE NAME'S QUOYLE, BY THE WAY.
LIARA.
SO HOW DO YOU KNOW THE HANAR ARE WRONG? MAYBE I SHOULDN'T BE TRUSTED.
I TRUST THAT THE ASARI HAVEN'T LEARNED HOW TO BREATHE UNDER-WATER SINCE I LAST SAW ONE...
...AND THAT YOU'RE SMART ENOUGH TO UNDERSTAND THAT I'M YOUR ONLY RIDE TO AND FROM AN ENCLOSED SHRINE AT THE BOTTOM OF THE OCEAN.
BESIDES... YOU TRY ANYTHING FUNNY WHILE WE'RE DOWN THERE AND I'LL SHOOT YOU MYSELF.
QUOYLE...

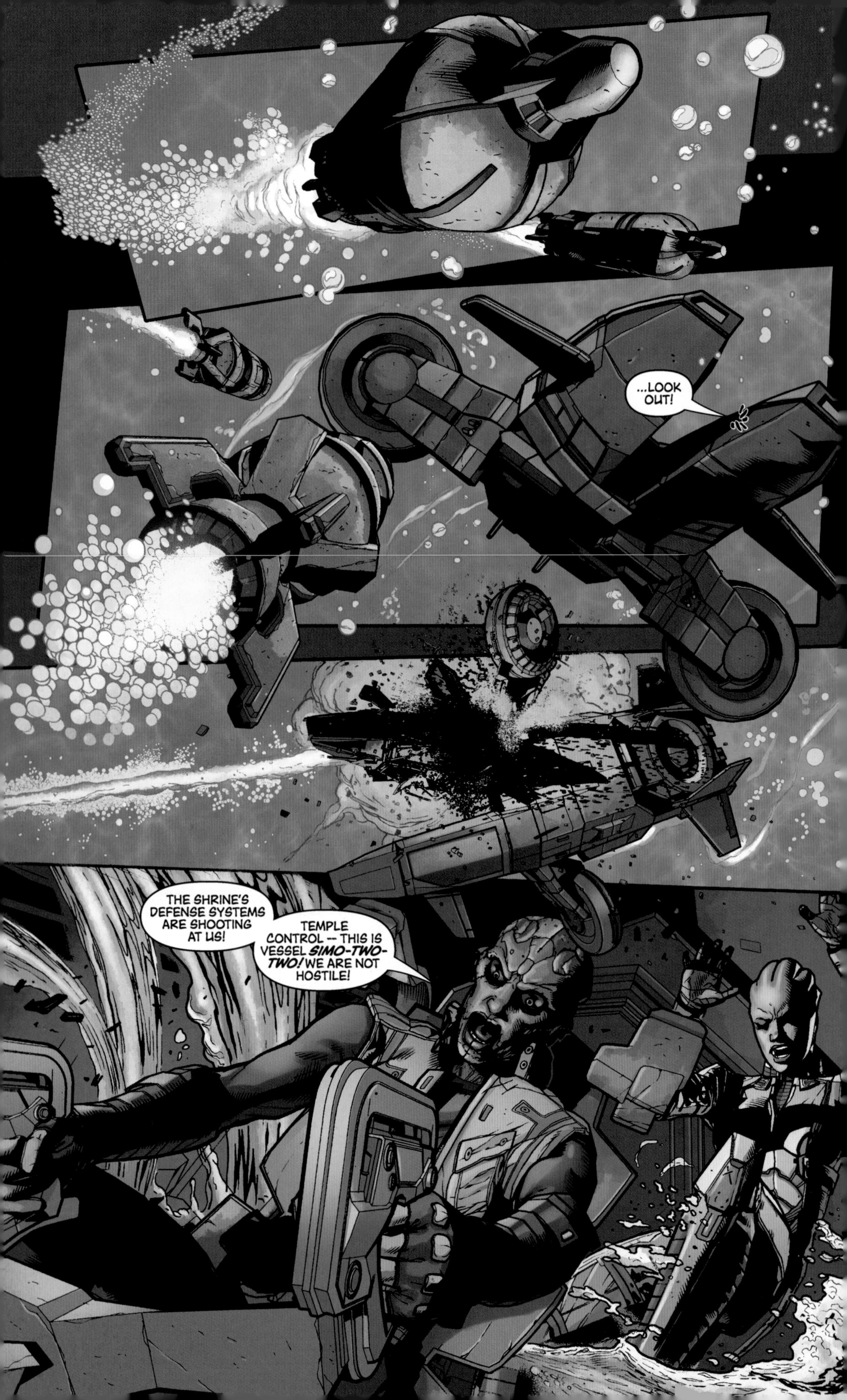
...LOOK OUT!
THE SHRINE'S DEFENSE SYSTEMS ARE SHOOTING AT US!
TEMPLE CONTROL -- THIS IS VESSEL *SIMO-TWO-TWO!* WE ARE NOT HOSTILE!

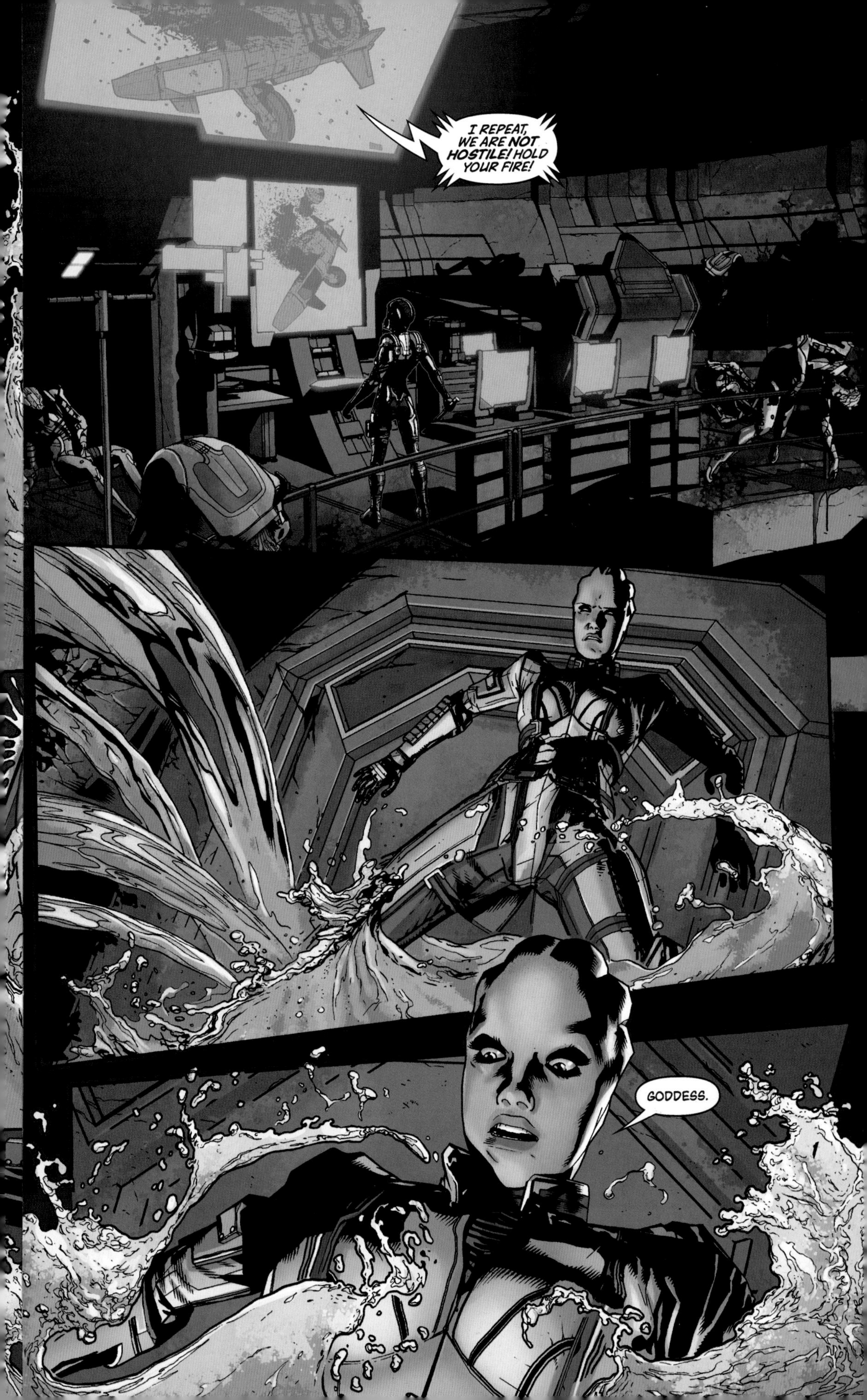
I REPEAT, WE ARE NOT HOSTILE! HOLD YOUR FIRE!
GODDESS.

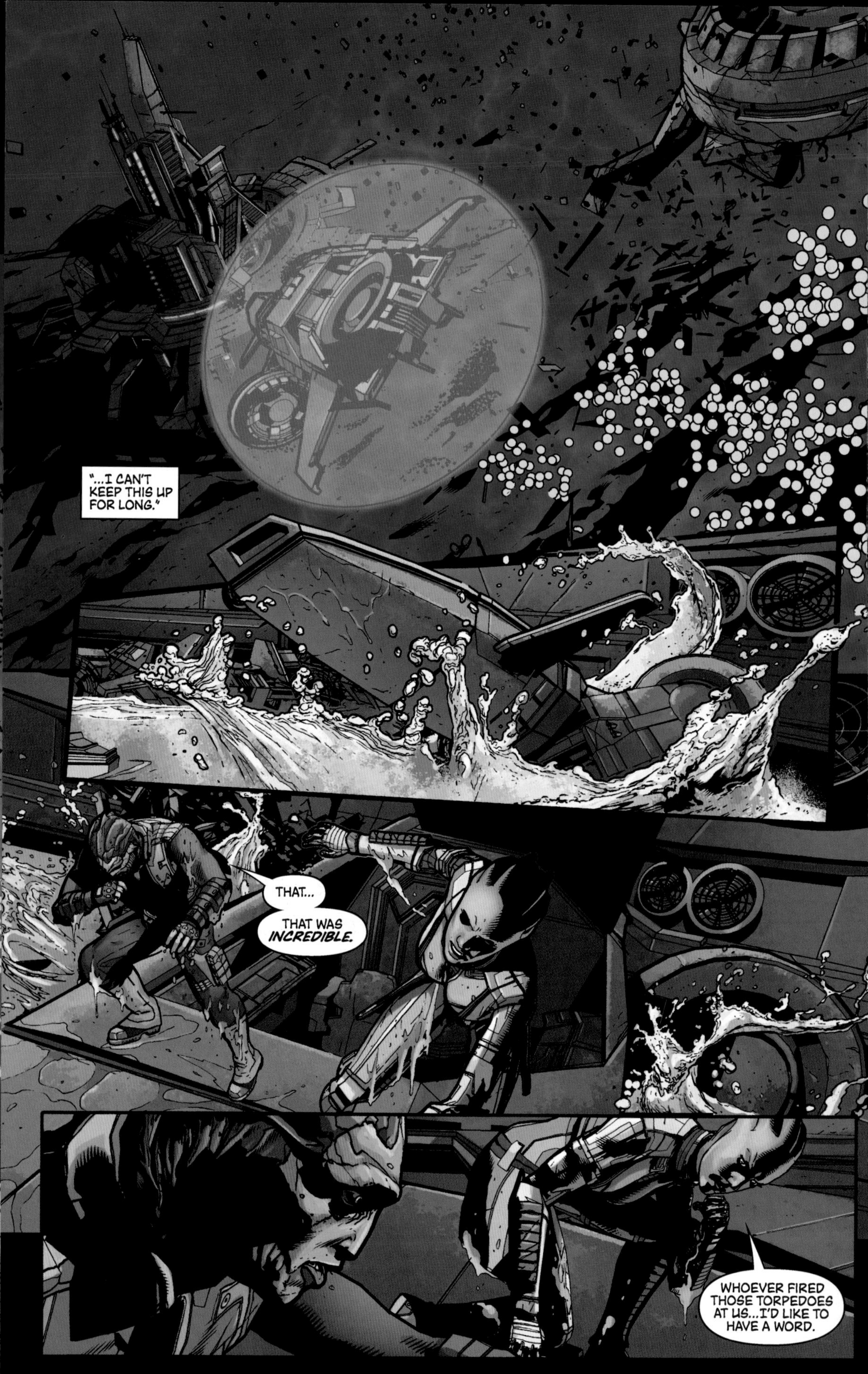
"...I CAN'T KEEP THIS UP FOR LONG."
THAT...
THAT WAS *INCREDIBLE.*
WHOEVER FIRED THOSE TORPEDOES AT US...I'D LIKE TO HAVE A WORD.

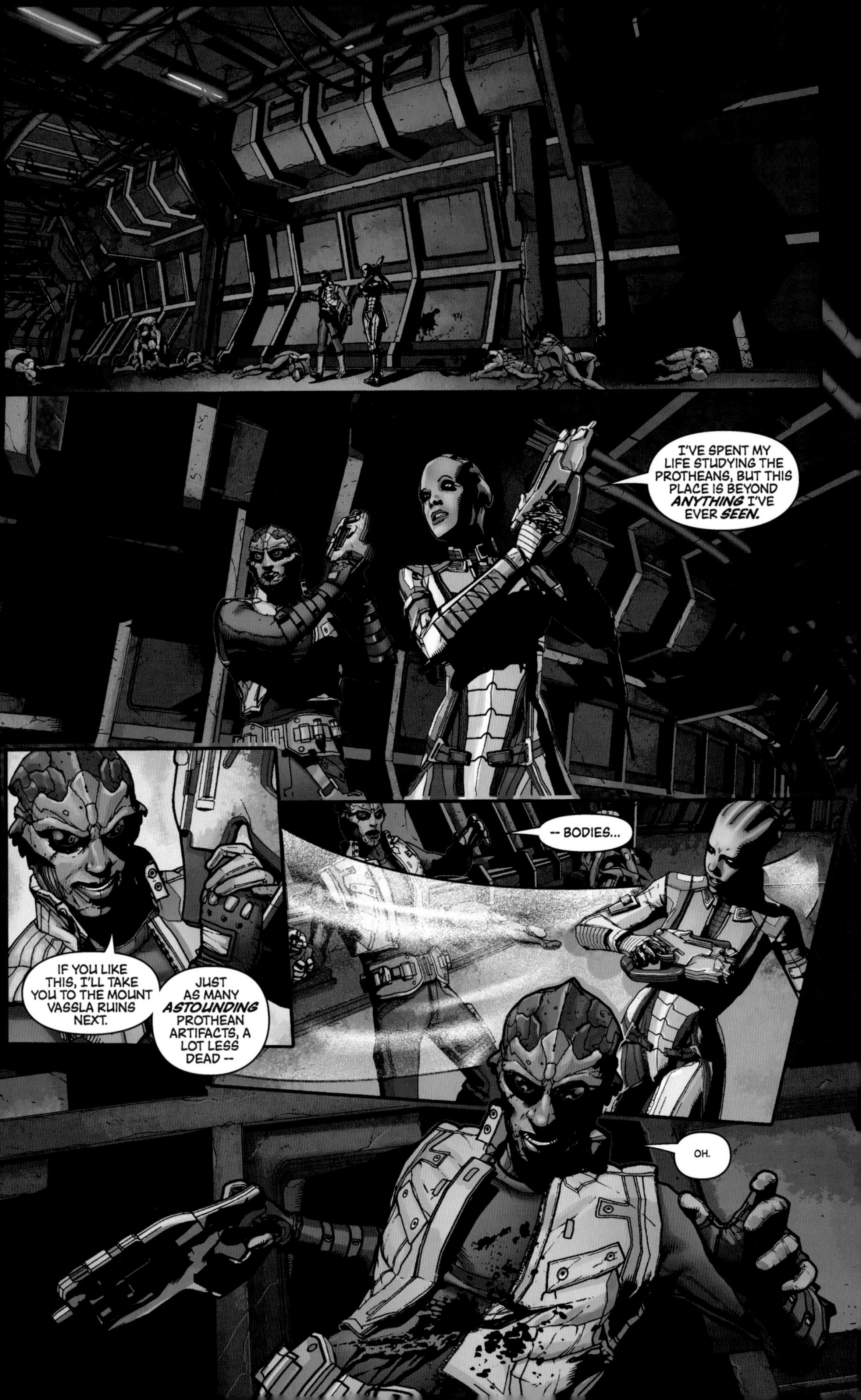
I'VE SPENT MY LIFE STUDYING THE PROTHEANS, BUT THIS PLACE IS BEYOND *ANYTHING* I'VE EVER *SEEN.*
IF YOU LIKE THIS, I'LL TAKE YOU TO THE MOUNT VASSLA RUINS NEXT.
JUST AS MANY *ASTOUNDING* PROTHEAN ARTIFACTS, A LOT LESS DEAD --
-- BODIES...
OH.

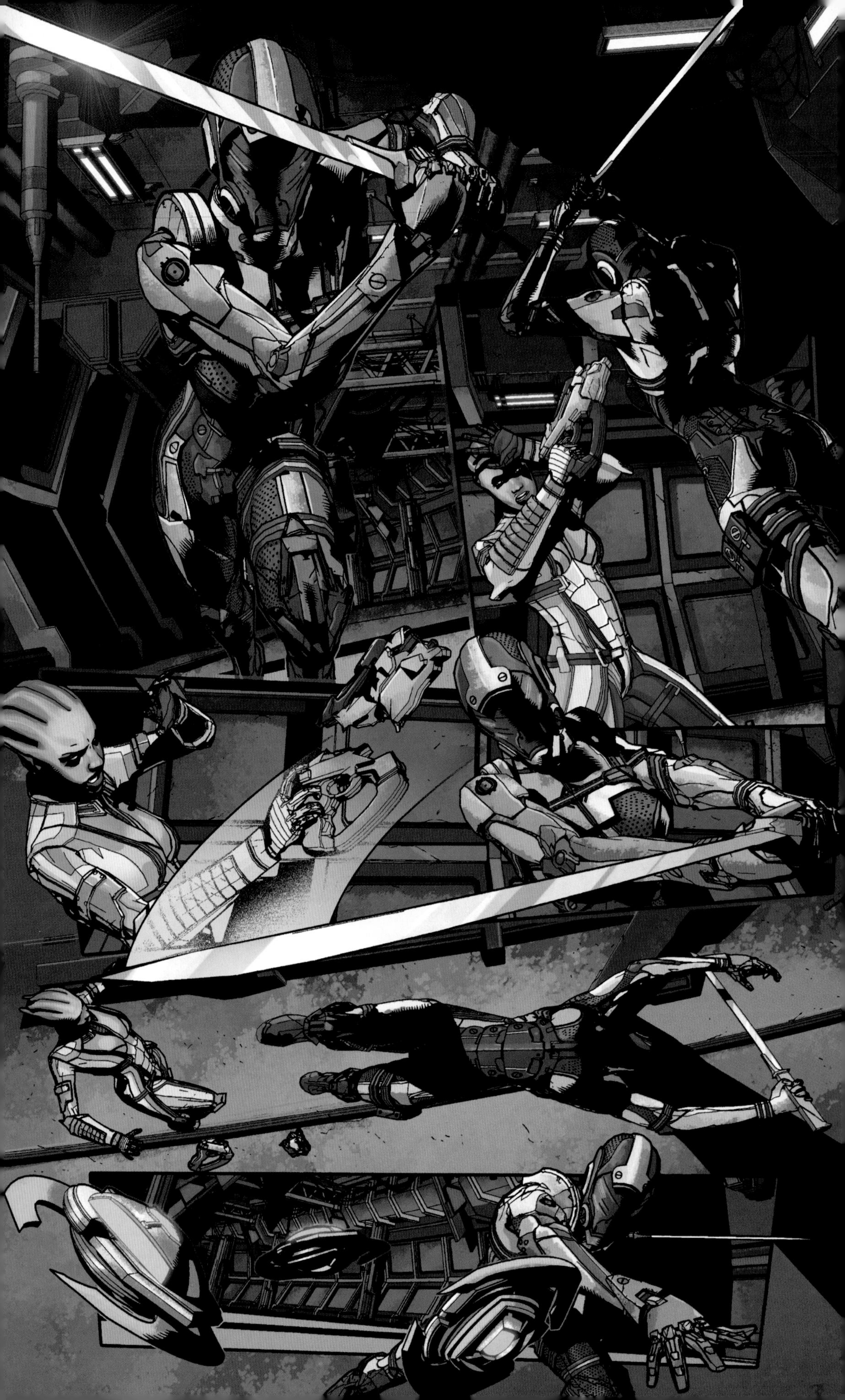

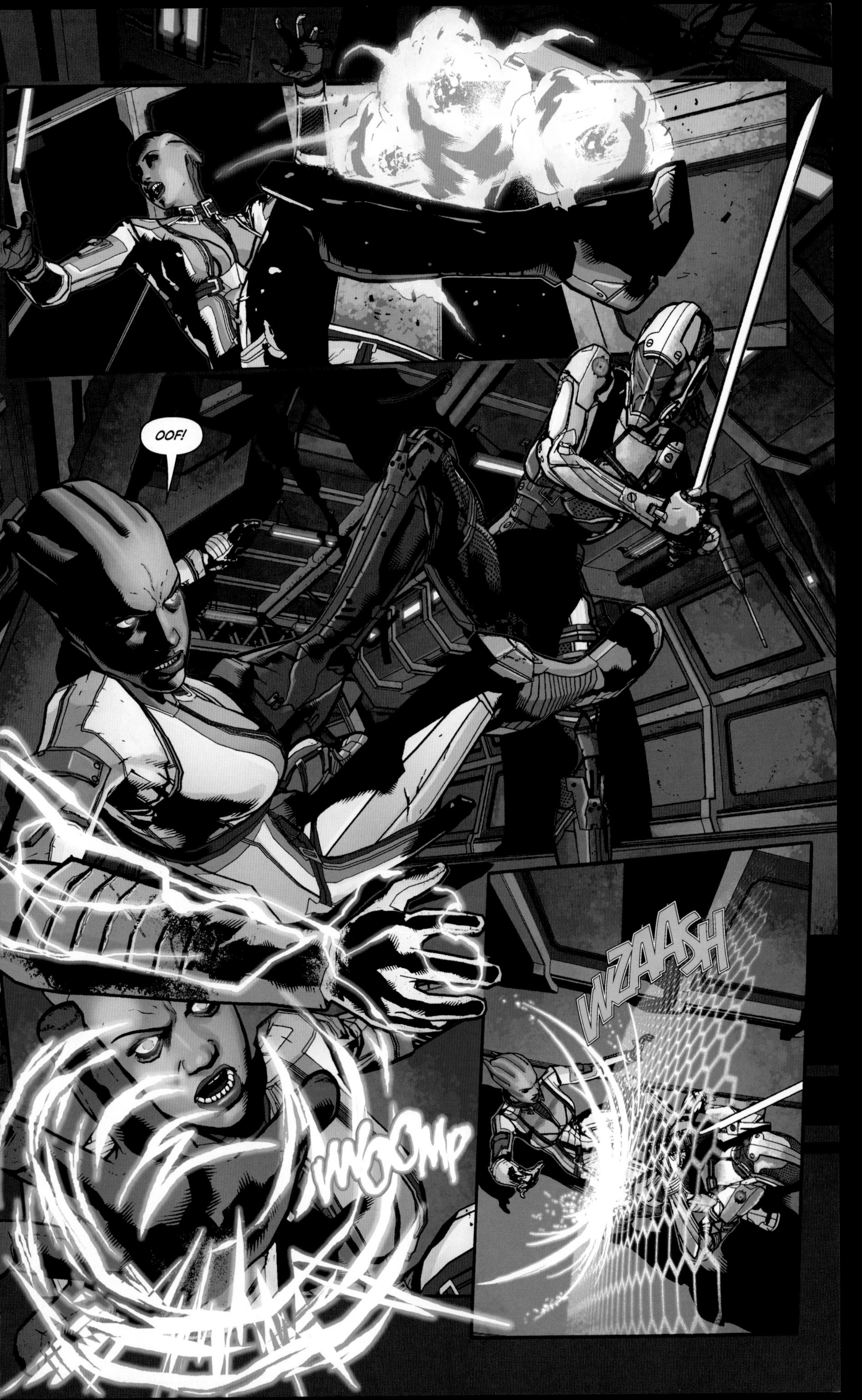

OOF!
WZAASH
WOOMP

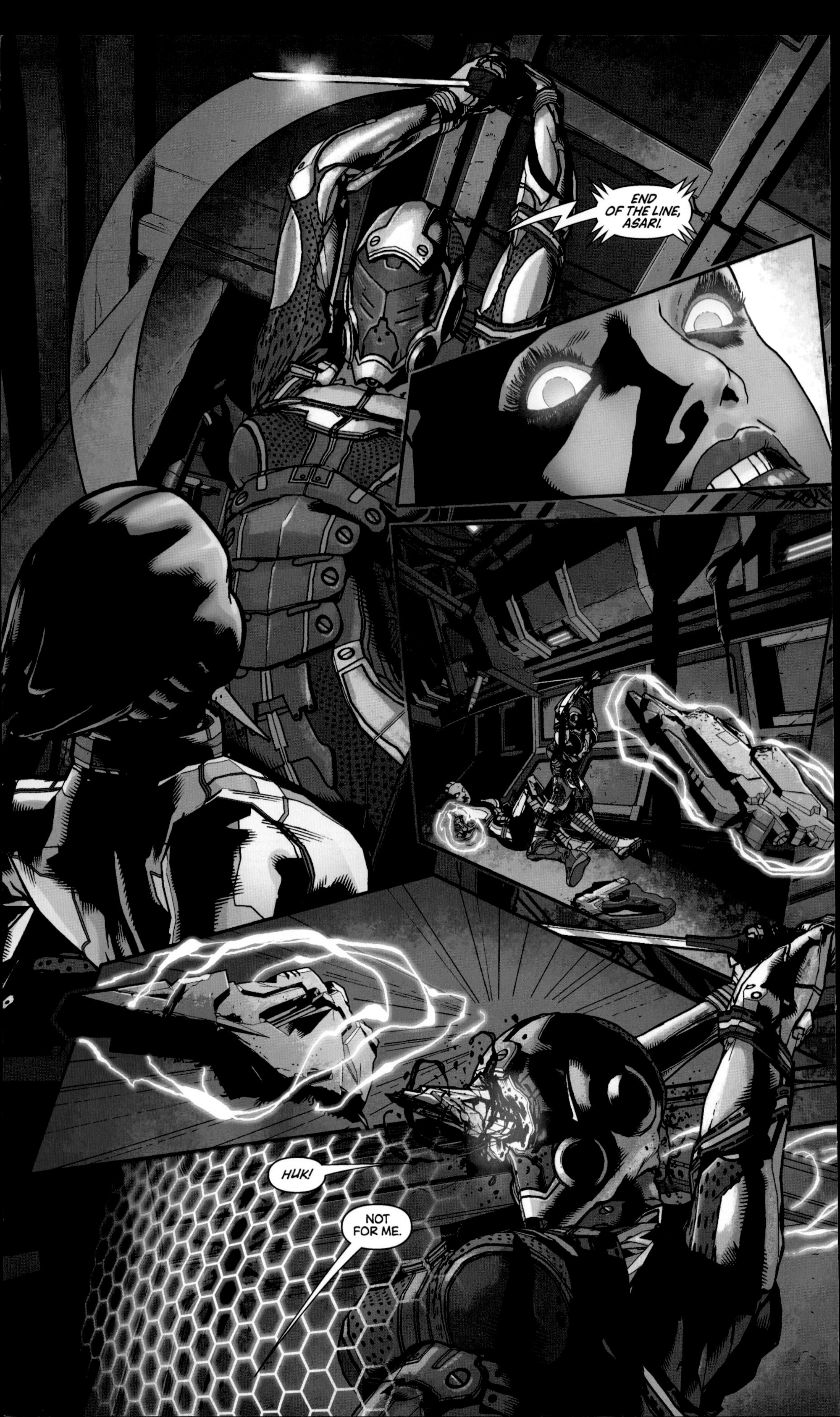
END OF THE LINE, ASARI.
HUK!
NOT FOR ME.

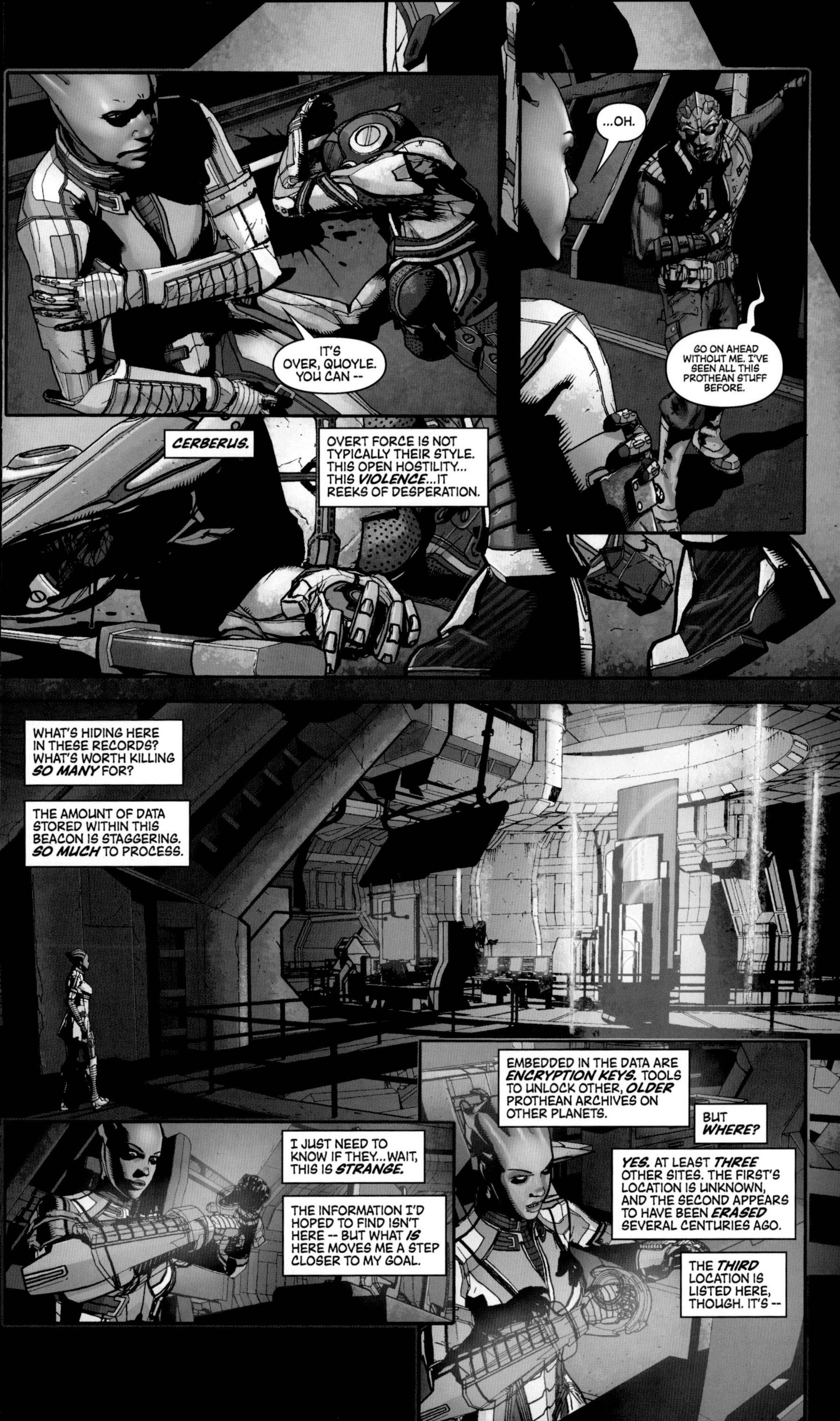
IT'S OVER, QUOYLE. YOU CAN --
...OH.
GO ON AHEAD WITHOUT ME. I'VE SEEN ALL THIS PROTHEAN STUFF BEFORE.
CERBERUS.
OVERT FORCE IS NOT TYPICALLY THEIR STYLE. THIS OPEN HOSTILITY... THIS VIOLENCE...IT REEKS OF DESPERATION.
WHAT'S HIDING HERE IN THESE RECORDS? WHAT'S WORTH KILLING SO MANY FOR?
THE AMOUNT OF DATA STORED WITHIN THIS BEACON IS STAGGERING. SO MUCH TO PROCESS.
I JUST NEED TO KNOW IF THEY...WAIT, THIS IS STRANGE.
THE INFORMATION I'D HOPED TO FIND ISN'T HERE -- BUT WHAT IS HERE MOVES ME A STEP CLOSER TO MY GOAL.
EMBEDDED IN THE DATA ARE ENCRYPTION KEYS. TOOLS TO UNLOCK OTHER, OLDER PROTHEAN ARCHIVES ON OTHER PLANETS.
BUT WHERE?
YES. AT LEAST THREE OTHER SITES. THE FIRST'S LOCATION IS UNKNOWN, AND THE SECOND APPEARS TO HAVE BEEN ERASED SEVERAL CENTURIES AGO.
THE THIRD LOCATION IS LISTED HERE, THOUGH. IT'S --

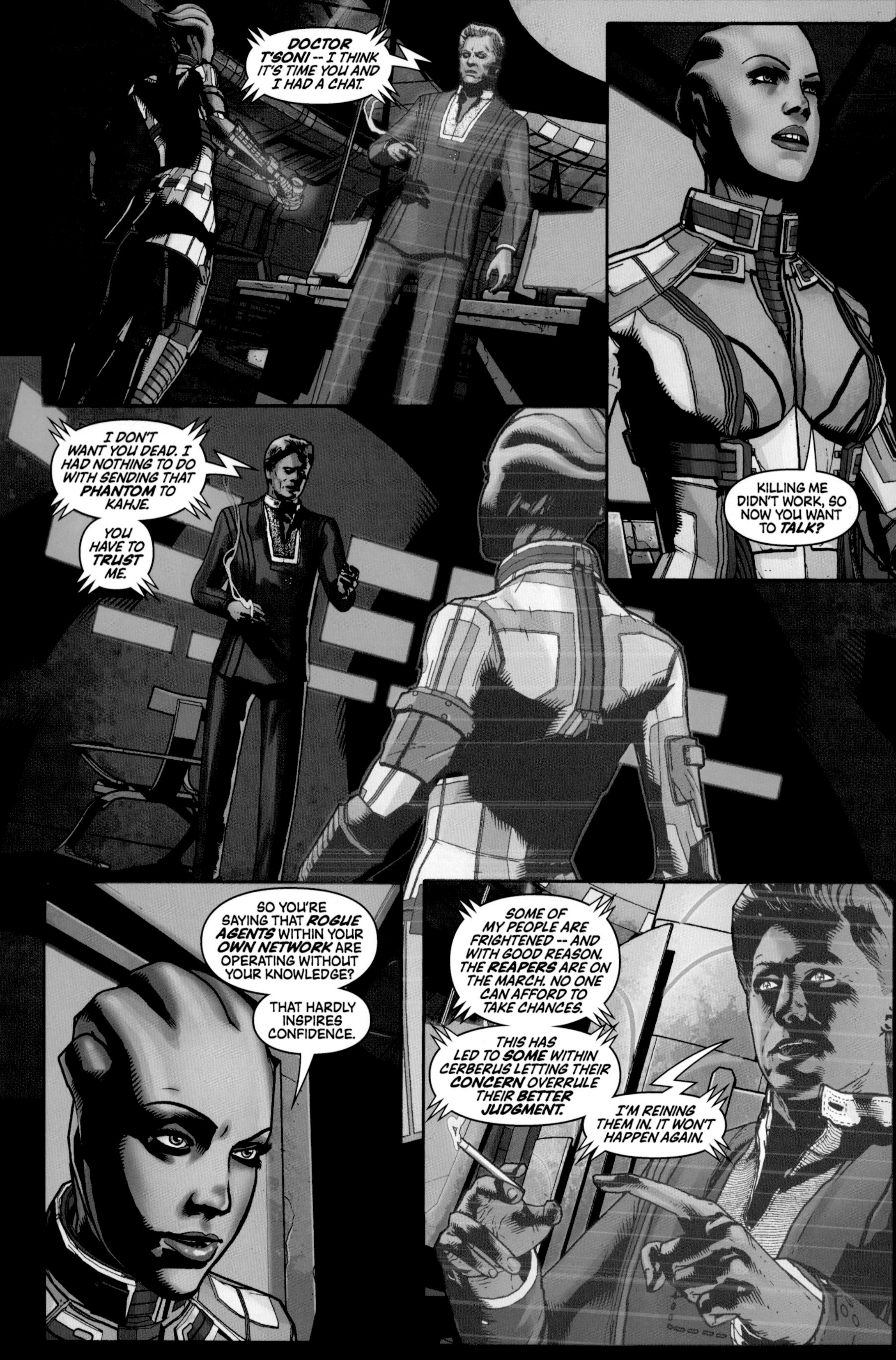
DOCTOR T'SONI -- I THINK IT'S TIME YOU AND I HAD A CHAT.
KILLING ME DIDN'T WORK, SO NOW YOU WANT TO TALK?
I DON'T WANT YOU DEAD. I HAD NOTHING TO DO WITH SENDING THAT PHANTOM TO KAHJE.
YOU HAVE TO TRUST ME.
SO YOU'RE SAYING THAT ROGUE AGENTS WITHIN YOUR OWN NETWORK ARE OPERATING WITHOUT YOUR KNOWLEDGE?
THAT HARDLY INSPIRES CONFIDENCE.
SOME OF MY PEOPLE ARE FRIGHTENED -- AND WITH GOOD REASON. THE REAPERS ARE ON THE MARCH. NO ONE CAN AFFORD TO TAKE CHANCES.
THIS HAS LED TO SOME WITHIN CERBERUS LETTING THEIR CONCERN OVERRULE THEIR BETTER JUDGMENT.
I'M REINING THEM IN. IT WON'T HAPPEN AGAIN.

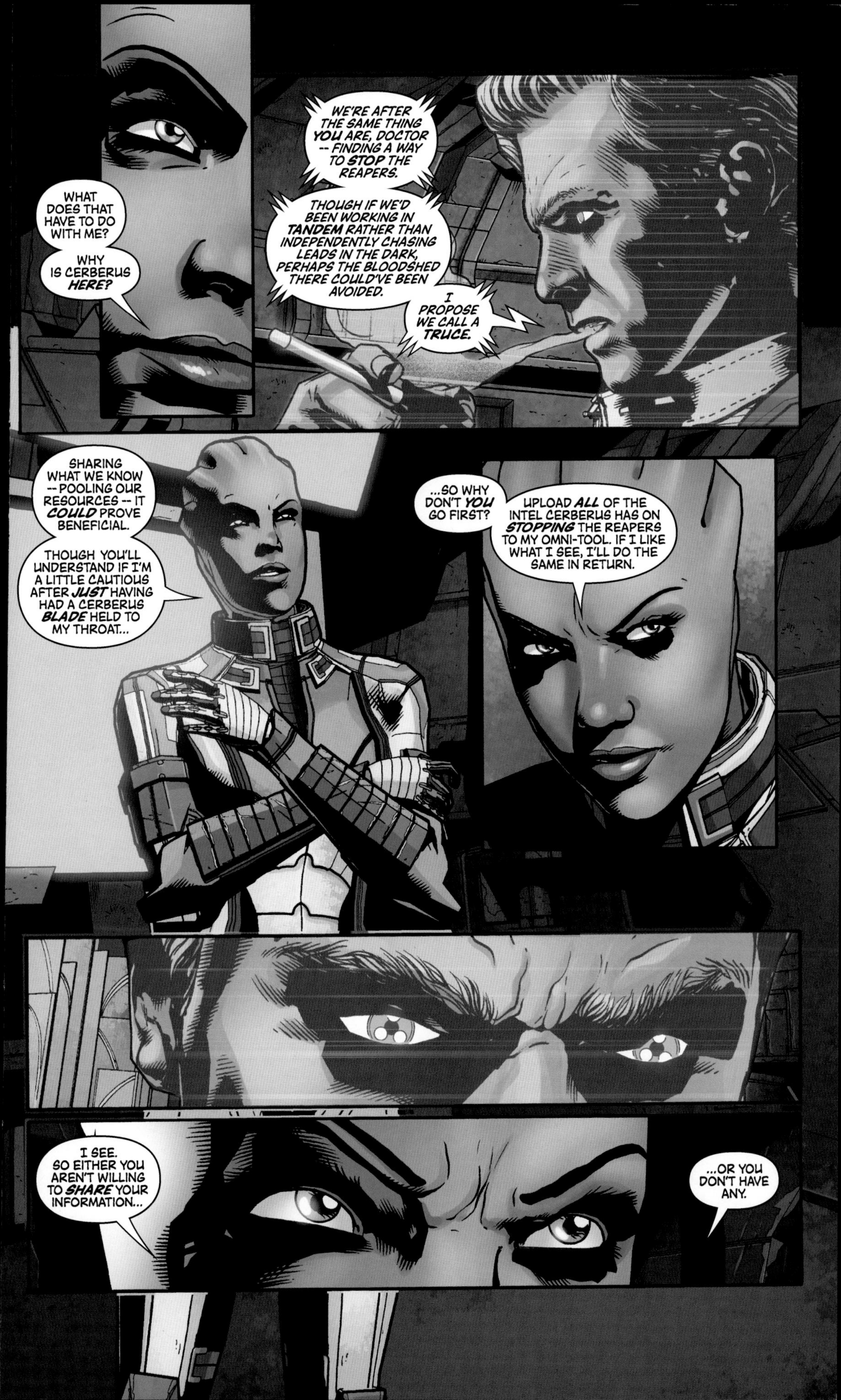
WE'RE AFTER THE SAME THING YOU ARE, DOCTOR -- FINDING A WAY TO STOP THE REAPERS.
THOUGH IF WE'D BEEN WORKING IN TANDEM RATHER THAN INDEPENDENTLY CHASING LEADS IN THE DARK, PERHAPS THE BLOODSHED THERE COULD'VE BEEN AVOIDED.
WHAT DOES THAT HAVE TO DO WITH ME?
WHY IS CERBERUS HERE?
I PROPOSE WE CALL A TRUCE.
SHARING WHAT WE KNOW -- POOLING OUR RESOURCES -- IT COULD PROVE BENEFICIAL.
THOUGH YOU'LL UNDERSTAND IF I'M A LITTLE CAUTIOUS AFTER JUST HAVING HAD A CERBERUS BLADE HELD TO MY THROAT...
...SO WHY DON'T YOU GO FIRST?
UPLOAD ALL OF THE INTEL CERBERUS HAS ON STOPPING THE REAPERS TO MY OMNI-TOOL. IF I LIKE WHAT I SEE, I'LL DO THE SAME IN RETURN.
I SEE. SO EITHER YOU AREN'T WILLING TO SHARE YOUR INFORMATION...
...OR YOU DON'T HAVE ANY.

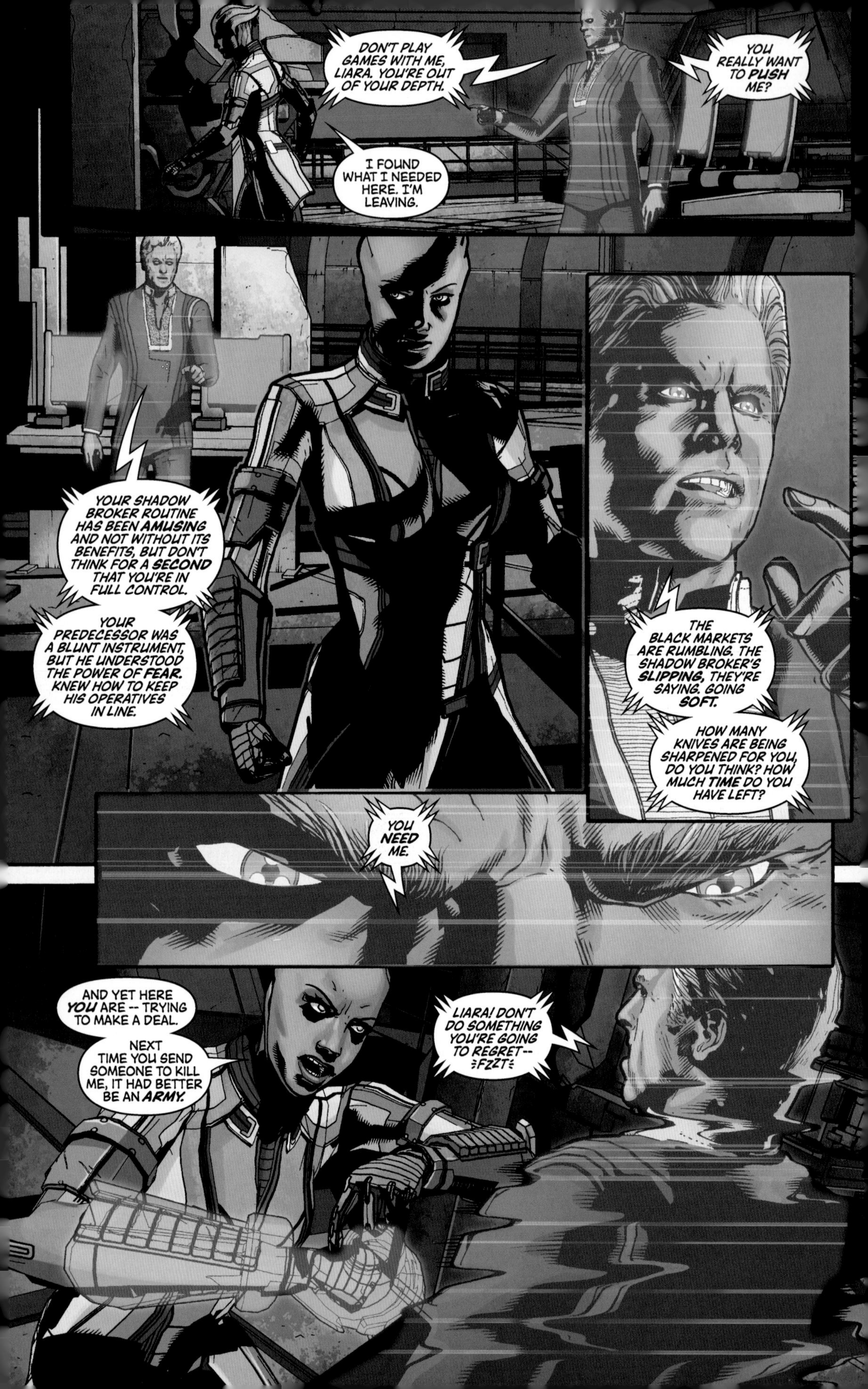
DON'T PLAY GAMES WITH ME, LIARA. YOU'RE OUT OF YOUR DEPTH.
YOU REALLY WANT TO PUSH ME?
I FOUND WHAT I NEEDED HERE. I'M LEAVING.
YOUR SHADOW BROKER ROUTINE HAS BEEN AMUSING AND NOT WITHOUT ITS BENEFITS, BUT DON'T THINK FOR A SECOND THAT YOU'RE IN FULL CONTROL.
YOUR PREDECESSOR WAS A BLUNT INSTRUMENT, BUT HE UNDERSTOOD THE POWER OF FEAR. KNEW HOW TO KEEP HIS OPERATIVES IN LINE.
THE BLACK MARKETS ARE RUMBLING. THE SHADOW BROKER'S SLIPPING, THEY'RE SAYING. GOING SOFT.
HOW MANY KNIVES ARE BEING SHARPENED FOR YOU, DO YOU THINK? HOW MUCH TIME DO YOU HAVE LEFT?
YOU NEED ME.
AND YET HERE YOU ARE -- TRYING TO MAKE A DEAL.
NEXT TIME YOU SEND SOMEONE TO KILL ME, IT HAD BETTER BE AN ARMY.
LIARA! DON'T DO SOMETHING YOU'RE GOING TO REGRET-- FZZT

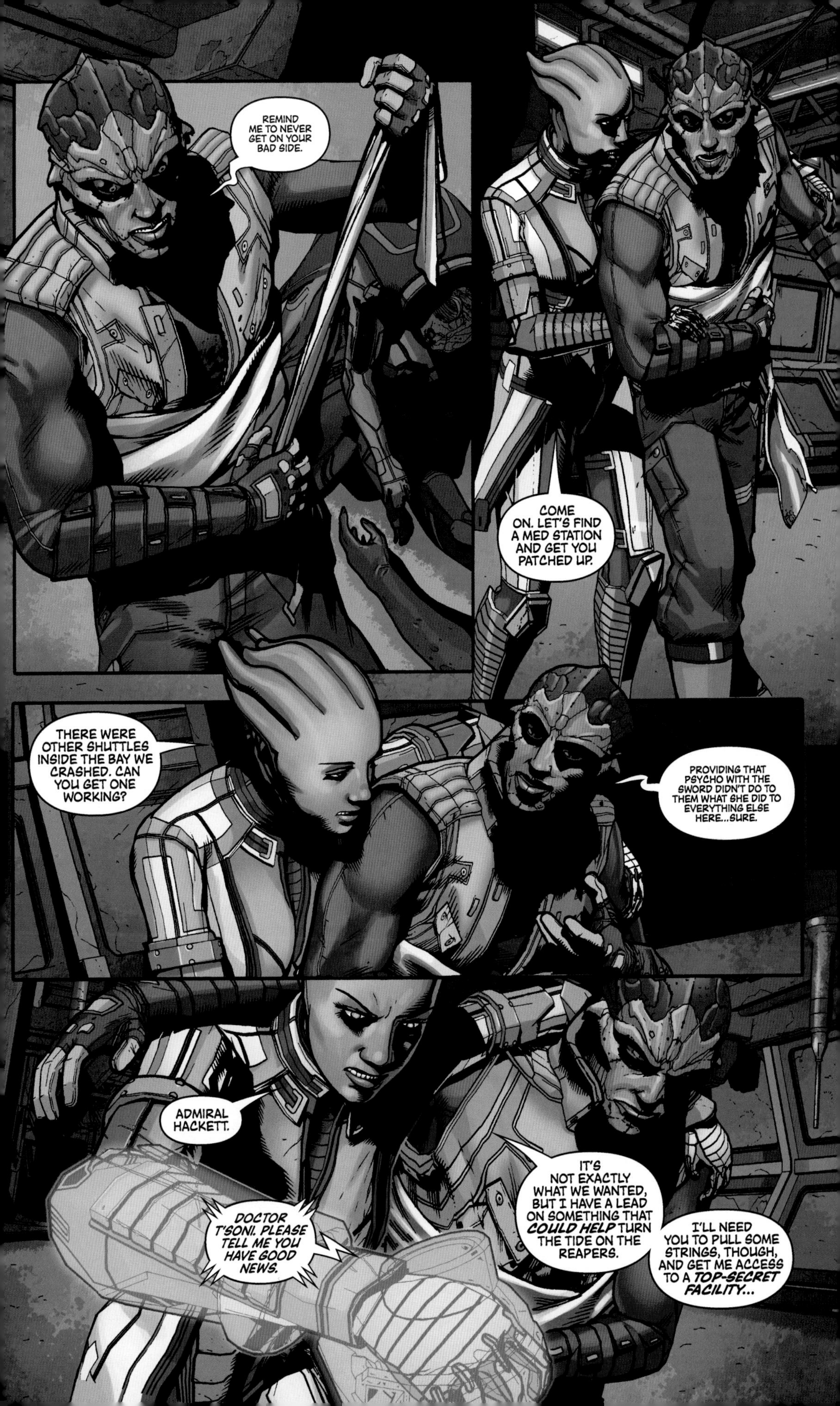
REMIND ME TO NEVER GET ON YOUR BAD SIDE.
COME ON. LET'S FIND A MED STATION AND GET YOU PATCHED UP.
THERE WERE OTHER SHUTTLES INSIDE THE BAY WE CRASHED. CAN YOU GET ONE WORKING?
PROVIDING THAT PSYCHO WITH THE SWORD DIDN'T DO TO THEM WHAT SHE DID TO EVERYTHING ELSE HERE...SURE.
ADMIRAL HACKETT.
DOCTOR T'SONI. PLEASE TELL ME YOU HAVE GOOD NEWS.
IT'S NOT EXACTLY WHAT WE WANTED, BUT I HAVE A LEAD ON SOMETHING THAT COULD HELP TURN THE TIDE ON THE REAPERS.
I'LL NEED YOU TO PULL SOME STRINGS, THOUGH, AND GET ME ACCESS TO A TOP-SECRET FACILITY...

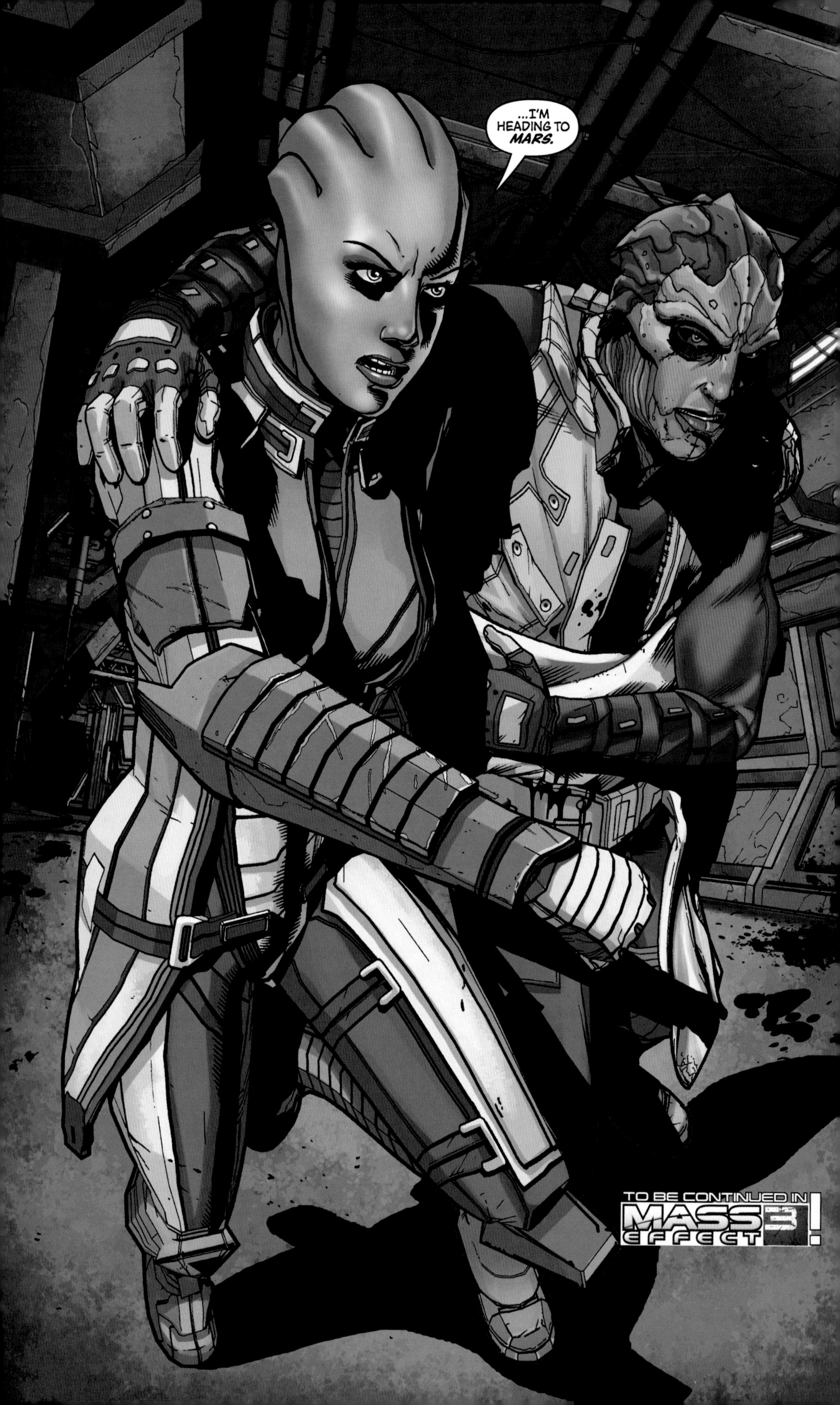
...I'M HEADING TO MARS.
TO BE CONTINUED IN MASS EFFECT 3!

ILLUSTRATION BY
MIKE HAWTHORNE

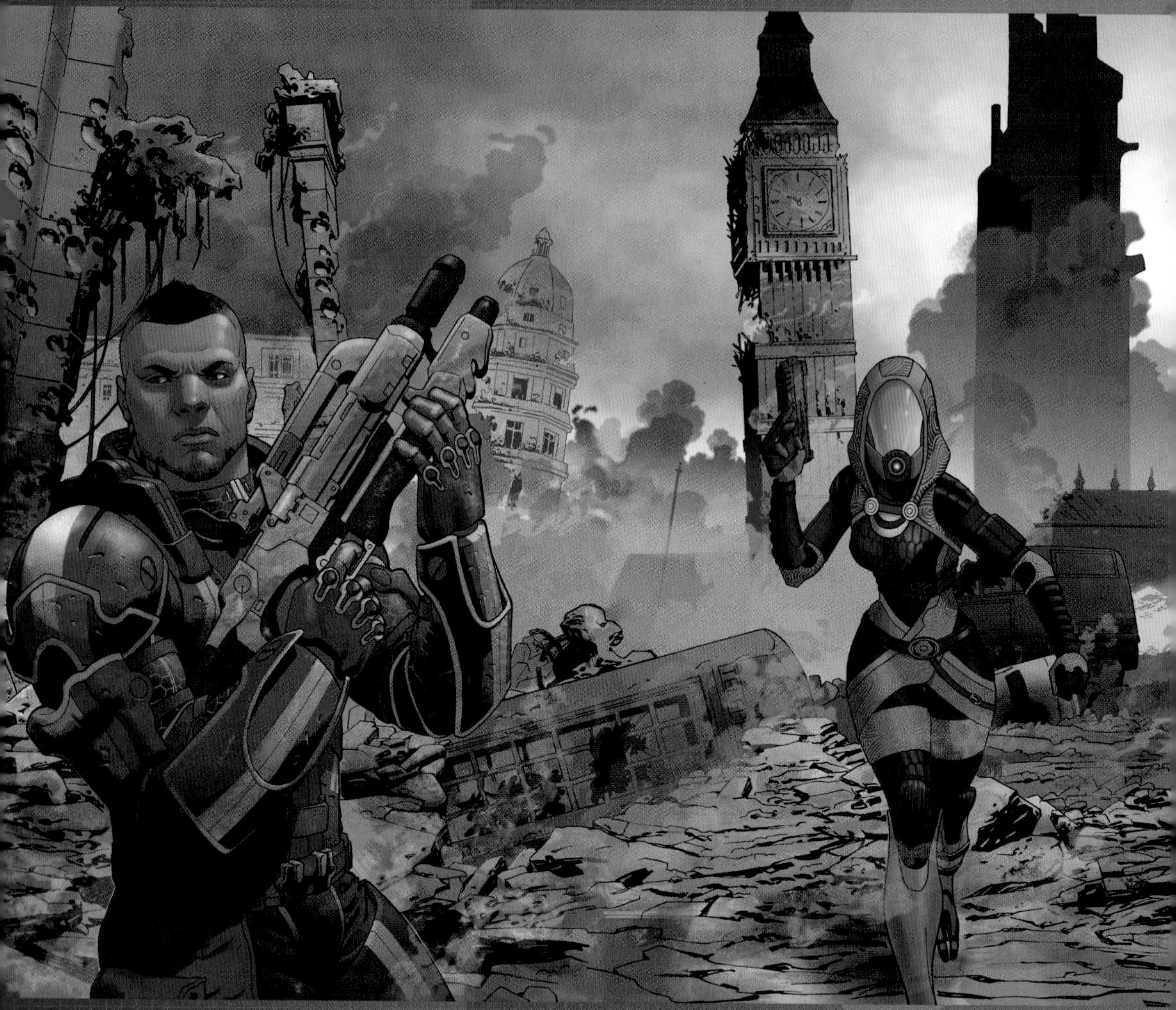

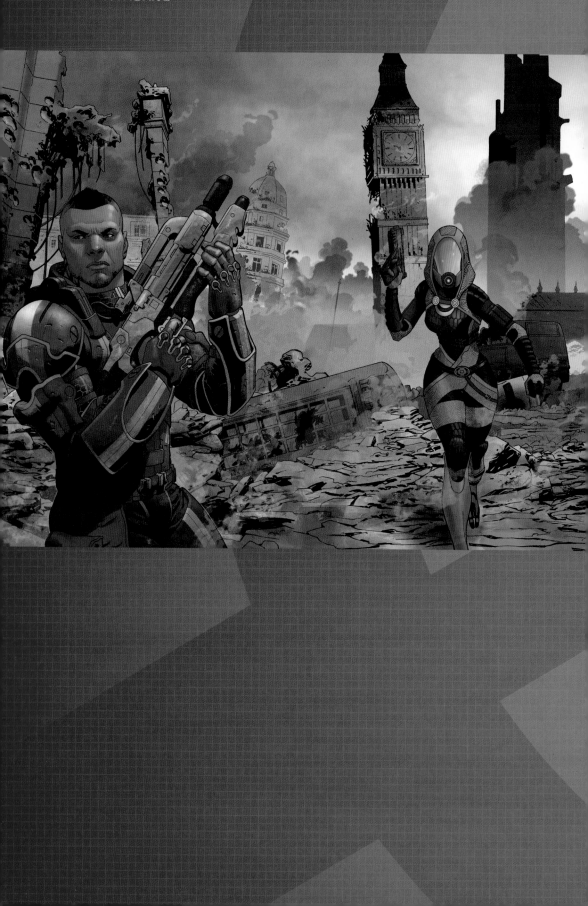

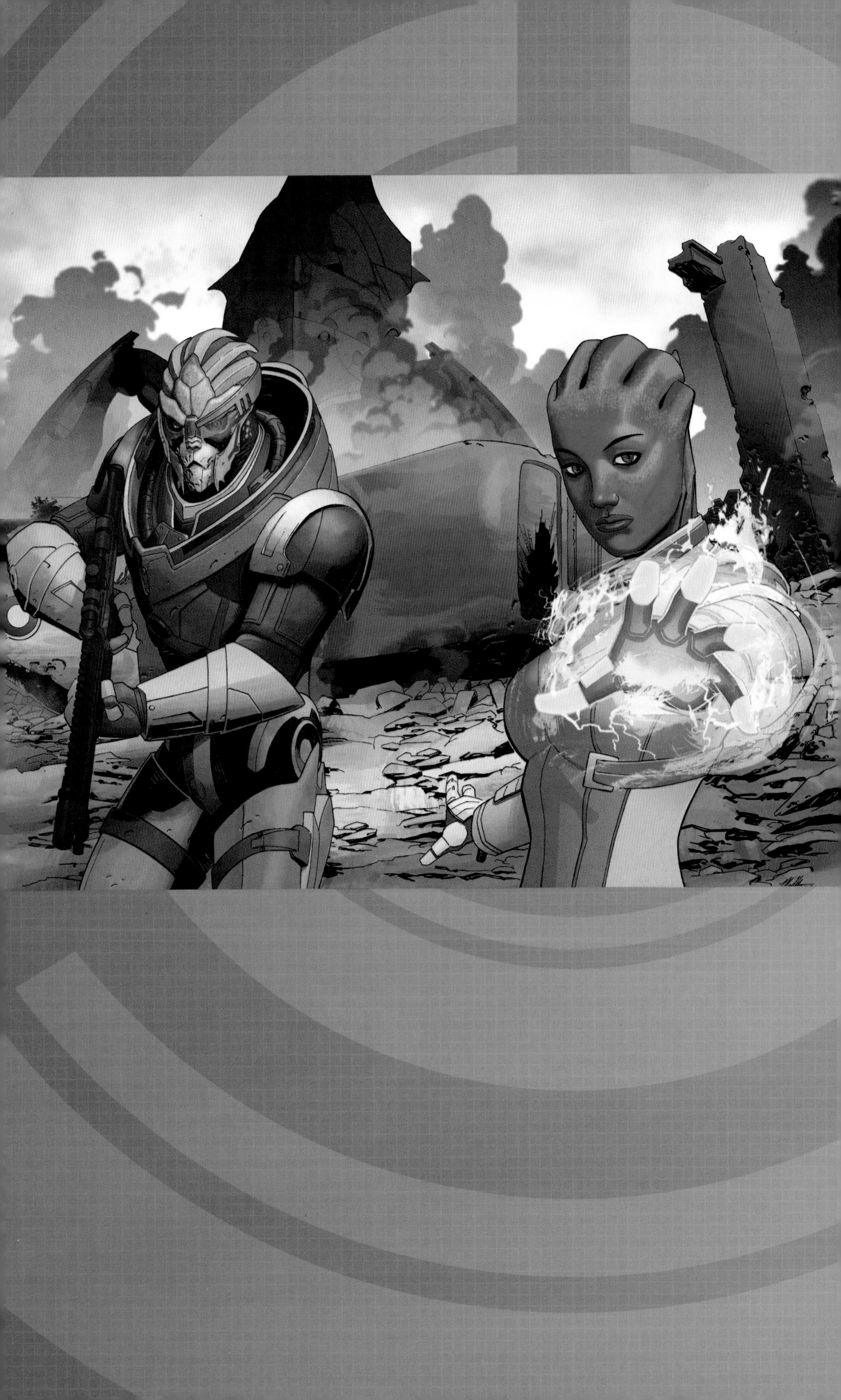

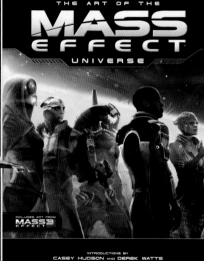